D1546447

ONE-BEER
DAISY

ONE-BEER
DAISY

Facing Death, Life, and
Growing Up Along the Way.

MAIKEL L. WISE

Copyright © 2023 by Maikel L. Wise

All rights reserved. No part of this publication may be reproduced, stored in a retrieval system, or transmitted in any form or by any means, electronic, mechanical, photocopying, recording, scanning, or otherwise, without the prior written permission of the author.

One-Beer Daisy

Facing Death, Life, and Growing Up Along the Way

By Maikel L. Wise

First Edition

Book Cover Design by Olga Vynnychenko

Edited by Debra Kastner and Kris Webb

Library of Congress Control Number:
2023910323

1. BIO026000 2. BIO000000
Paperback Print ISBN: 979-8-9875386-0-9
Hardcover Print ISBN: 979-8-9875386-2-3
EBook ISBN: 979-8-9875386-1-6

Two Wise Ones Publishing
Longmont, Colorado

Dedicated to Mom
For tireless, unwavering,
and unconditional love

For Susan
We are growing old together

Preface

This book is a story about the last two weeks of my mother's life and my memories with her. Facing her death terrified me. During her hospice care, I reflected on my life growing up in a small town on Shiney Rock Road. To truly know her, I'd have to tell the story of what she taught us growing up.

For many years, I tried writing this story but always stopped. The pain ran too deep. It hurt too much to put into words. Then a virus hit the world and I finally found the capacity to write. Writing this story during the pandemic was unexpectedly therapeutic. I began to heal. Those in the pandemic couldn't be with their moms, their wives, or their children as they died of COVID. I was lucky to sit by my mom and hold her hand as she died. She was not alone.

My sister Tash and I felt poor growing up. We didn't realize how rich our lives were until we left home. What we learned as kids prepared us for love as well as the harshness of life.

Mom made great sacrifices to her physical health and emotional well-being to raise Tash and me. She protected us even as she carried her own ghosts, many of which I didn't discover until after her death. I'm sure she did other things I probably don't want to know about. Mom was no saint, but she took care of us. She was there when Pop wasn't. Mom was always there.

It took her death for me to learn how to start living again. Somewhere along the way, I'd lost myself. For that lesson, I'm grateful.

Writing healed and helped me maintain sanity during insane times. Writing allowed me to discover who I've come to be. So much of it is because of Mom. Even today, I'm still a mama's boy.

Clarksville, Virginia

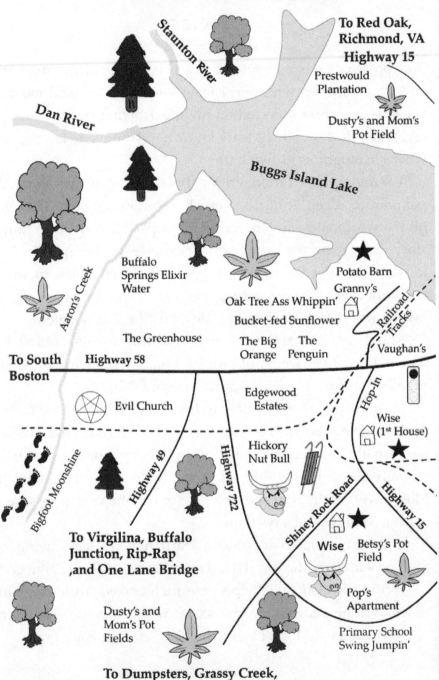

To Red Oak,
Richmond, VA
Highway 15

Prestwould
Plantation

Dusty's and Mom's
Pot Field

Staunton River

Dan River

Buggs Island Lake

Buffalo
Springs Elixir
Water

Aaron's Creek

Potato Barn

Granny's

Oak Tree Ass Whippin'

Bucket-fed Sunflower

The Greenhouse

The Big
Orange

The
Penguin

Railroad Tracks

Vaughan's

**To South
Boston**

Highway 58

Evil Church

Edgewood
Estates

Hop-In

Wise
(1st House)

Bigfoot Moonshine

Highway 49

Highway 722

Hickory
Nut Bull

Shiney Rock Road

Wise

Betsy's Pot
Field

Highway 15

**To Virgilina, Buffalo
Junction, Rip-Rap
,and One Lane Bridge**

Pop's
Apartment

Dusty's and
Mom's Pot
Fields

Primary School
Swing Jumpin'

**To Dumpsters, Grassy Creek,
Aunt Abigail's, Mom and Dusty's
other pot fields, Mr. Cash**

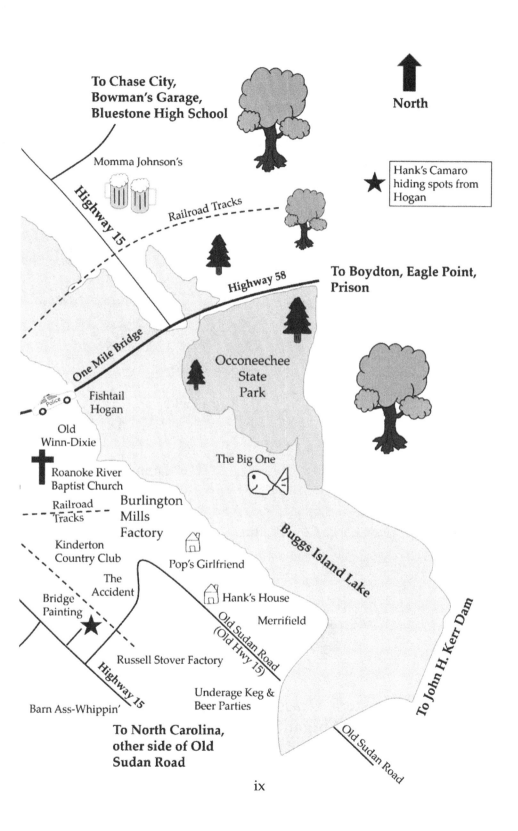

Shiney Rock Road

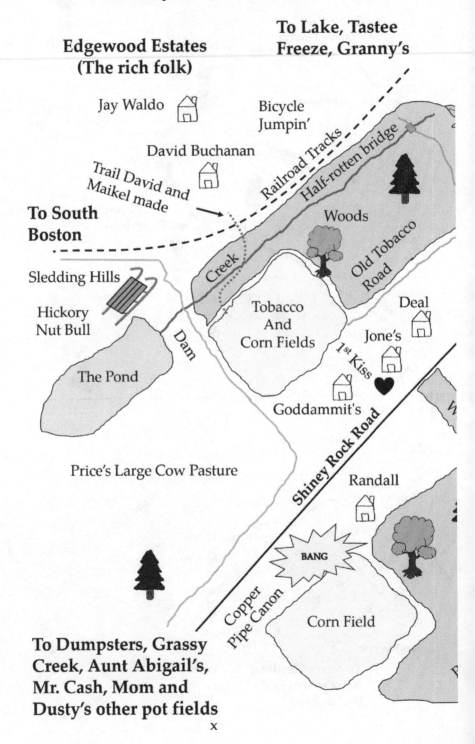

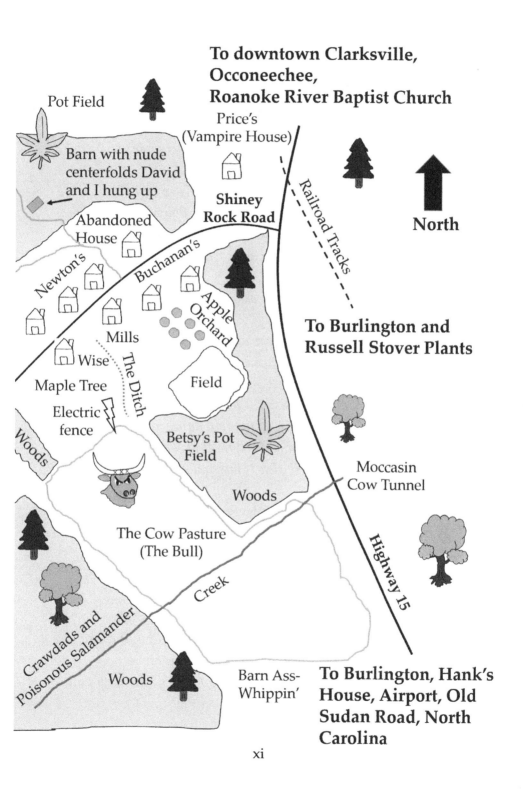

Shiney Rock Road

Silverleaf Maple, Daffodils, and Daisies.
Parents are fighting. Some memories, they're hazy.
I remember the day. We moved to our home.
Work. Play. Always enough. Always some.

Take 15 south. Across the bridge. Turn right.
Pass the Price's place. Over the hill. Slow down. Hold tight.
A modest brick home. Not too big, just 'bout right.
Endless horizons of exploration. I slept well. Well, on some nights.

Playing in corn fields, creeks, and flooded ditches.
Crawdad got my finger. Ouch! That hurt. Son-of-a-bitch!
At Granny's farm with Travis. With Hank some days.
Gathering taters and snaps in the hot summer haze.

Sometimes with my sister. We'd bicker. We'd fight.
Saturday. Hee-Haw is on. Granny will dance for us tonight.
Coffee at Thompson's. Good meat at Vaughan's.
Arrowheads at Bass's Barber. I love one-stoplight towns.

Martha's burgers with slaw. The Penguin for soft ice cream.
Pizza Pub. Laundromat. Our school bus driver, Mrs. Green.
Burlington Mills has a sale. There's one at Peebles, too.
Free popcorn at Rose's. I got new britches. Got new shoes.

Occoneechee has vines, lightning bugs, and snakes.
Cane pole fishing with worms. Love swimming in the lake.
Harvested tobacco. Permeating the air.
Leaves falling and burning. We're going to the Chase City Fair.

Fending for ourselves. Keep it together today.
Mom crying by the window. I don't know what words to say.
Mom works three jobs. One at the prison. Two at the paper.
To help us survive. She keeps going. She doesn't waiver.

Dirt clog fights. Building forts in the woods.
Driving the Suburban. Barely seeing over the hood.
We have butter beans and biscuits. Surely, we're doing okay.
We ain't that deprived. Car broke down. I'm walking today.

Snowing. School is closed. Cow pasture sledding and play.
Bread bags over our socks. We're warm enough all day.
Mrs. Talley. Mrs. Talbott. Mentors away from home.
Mrs. Hester. First grade. Bought my lunch with money of her own.

I remember Mom's tears. I remember the bliss.
I remember my Pop's accident. I remember my first kiss.
The loneliness growing up. Insecurities abound.
Escape to the cow pasture. Big bull. No sounds.

Been away for a while. A few things have changed.
Some things haven't. Like ghosts bound by chains.
Buchanan's, Townsend's, Newton's, Mills', and Kearns'.
Smiley's and Yancey's. These families I knew.

Mom's time's up. She has but one place to go.
With death at her throat. Her eyes speak. I can't say no.
With one place in mind. She's determined to go.
Just over the hill. Home, on Shiney Rock Road.

-Maikel L. Wise

Everything Changes

Monday, February 19, 2007

Courage is when you open Fear's door and drag him out.
Then you inform him he's going down a path
neither of you have traveled before;
And he won't be going back home.

The phone rings. My sister Tash, short for Natasha, is calling me at work. Her voice sounds uneasy. "Maikel, Mom is in the hospital again. Her cancer has spread, and things aren't good."

Year after year, I think Mom may die, but somehow she plows through and fights like she has done every day of her life. I suspect this is another false alarm. Mom will pull through again. She always pulls through.

I move to a more private place to talk, since I'm at work and deep in a project. I try to shut off my engineering brain and focus on what my sister is trying to say. "What's up? What's wrong?"

"The cancer has spread to one of her arteries and she can't leave the hospital. They think she may die." My sister sobs.

"Can I speak to the doctor?"

Over the phone, I hear rhythmic sounds in the background advertising someone's heartbeat. I recognize my sister's footsteps as she moves across the hard hospital floor. I hope Tash has embellished the truth. I have to keep it together.

"Hello Maikel, I'm Doctor Kumar."

"Hello. Thanks for taking care of my mom."

1

"I've heard so much about you, or rather *read* about you from your mom's notes."

My mom can't talk anymore. The tracheal tube took her voice away the previous year due to throat cancer. One tap on the phone means yes, while two taps means no. Sometimes she wants something. It takes me forever to figure out what she's trying to tell me only using taps. I've learned to be patient. I have to. She's my mom. All she really wanted was to hear my voice.

Then I hear words that slice through my heart. "I'm sorry to say, your mom's cancer has metastasized. Some of the cancer surrounds an artery that feeds blood to her brain. We can attempt to operate, but it's extremely risky. If we rupture the artery, it can kill her or cause severe brain damage. It's time to seriously consider your mom's quality of life." Doctor Kumar's chokes up as she strives to maintain professionalism. "She may be okay in the hospital or perhaps a nursing home for six months. We should consider hospice care."

My throat closes around my breath. Several moments pass before I can muster a response. "Thank you, Doctor Kumar." Tears stream from my eyes as I hear Doctor Kumar comfort my weeping sister.

Dr. Kumar continues, "I know your mom. She wouldn't stop smoking even after the tracheal tube. She's so stubborn. I'm so sorry, Maikel."

"It's okay. She's a stubborn mule. Thank you for caring so much. Thank you for taking care of Mama Mule." There're a few moments of silence as I try to find comfort with a bit of humor. "Doctor Kumar, can I speak to my sister again, please?"

"Tash, wh…what does Mom want to do? Do you know?"

Tash sobs again. "Mom wants to go home. She wrote it on a notepad before we called you."

In an *I'm-in-control tone of voice*, I tell my sister, "Susan and I are flying back immediately."

We'd last been there three months earlier to help Mom recover from a hospital visit. I remember how fragile and pale she'd looked. That day, when we picked her up from the hospital, Mom's entire body shook and shivered. Her wavy red hair had been partially replaced with weathered gray strands. Her eyes sagged, though she did her best to hide the pain, both emotional and physical. She was withdrawing from gin. My mom was, and is, an alcoholic.

This time, though, I must face something I have avoided my whole life. I don't know if I am ready or if I have the courage. I've run from death, but I can't run from Mom...no matter what.

Mom with her horn in November 2006.
One toot = yes. Two toots = no.
Lots of toots = I need something or laughing.

Hospice Care (Day One)

Wednesday, February 21, 2007 – Mom's Wishes.

When it's your time, where will you go?
A cold sterile room? Or someplace you know?
Looking out familiar windows and plants by your hands.
Clock ticking, hourglass empty, last grain of sand.

Susan and I land at the Raleigh/Durham airport, and I'm reminded of the smell of home. A combination of stale cigarette smoke and mildew hangs in the air. A layer of sweat breaks out all over my body due to the high humidity. I'm spoiled, living in Colorado where smoking is uncommon and even discouraged. We pick up a smoky "non-smoking" rental car and drive north on Highway 501 toward Halifax Hospital in South Boston, Virginia.

The rolling hills of the Piedmont landscape are relatively lush and green. We drive past dilapidated trailers adjacent to gluttonous colonial plantation mansions. If this were three hundred years earlier, creeks could have been called moats separating the *haves* from the *have-nots*. This place is a place of extremes. There are homes that have rebel flags proudly displaying their hatred just a stone's throw away from a Baptist church.

I find myself disconnecting. I mentally drift off and stop paying attention as we continue driving north. My mind focuses on Mom and what's coming. Susan reaches over and grabs my right forearm. I'm overwhelmed and start crying.

"Pull over," she calmly says to me.

I pull over at one of the many historical markers about some famous Civil War battle.

"Susan, I'm okay. I'm just scared. This is it. I don't think Mom is going to make it this time."

Softly, she says, "Do you remember when we got married and our wedding vows?"

"Yes."

"I've got your back. This next bit is going to be rough, but we'll get through this together." Moments pass and I start to pull myself together. We hug, and Susan comfortingly rubs my back. "Now let's go see Mama Wise."

On a partly cloudy day with a little nip in the air, Susan and I arrive at the hospital. We find Mom's room labeled *Wise* written in grease pen on a whiteboard. Peering through the door, I see Mom is in a room by herself. She doesn't notice us. Her hair is hidden under a translucent blue hair cap. IVs, a blood pressure monitor, an oximeter, and oxygen connect to her making her look less human. I never liked hospitals and especially this hospital. This is the hospital where my Granny died. This is the hospital where Pop was taken after his accident when I was twelve. This is the hospital where Mom may die.

Mom still hasn't seen me, but Tash does and comes out into the hall. We move to a vacant lobby nearby. There's really only one question: *Do we do what we want or what Mom wants?* Susan sits quietly as Tash and I discuss the next step. Thankfully, Tash and I are on the same wavelength. In less than a minute, we agree: *It's Mom's choice. We won't impose our will or our needs on her.*

Mom's eyes brighten up when she sees me walk into the room with Susan and Tash.

"Hey Mom. What did you do this time? Did you fall off the turnip truck again?" I joke. Humor and laughter helps me diffuse tense and emotional situations. For me, it's an effective coping mechanism.

Mom gives several taps on the bed rail, indicating her excitement. She doesn't have her horn to toot. That's a good thing. The hardworking nurses might not appreciate horn-tooting in addition to the call button being frequently pressed.

"Mom, do you know where you are?"

The knot builds up in my throat again. She taps once on the chrome bed rail.

I look at my strong mother's eyes as she lay helpless. "Things aren't good, Mom. You can stay here, and you may be okay for half a year. Or you can go home." My voice is scratchy and high-pitched. "If you go home, you're going to die."

Mom's eyes water. She squeezes my hand for a moment and then lets go. Mom removes the oxygen tube, and it flops to the floor. She tries to talk. She can't. She grabs the pad of paper lying on her belly and writes almost illegibly, "I want to go home."

Mom's watering eyes are contagious, and everyone, including her doctor, who just walked in, tear up. I ask Mom two more times. I want to ensure she understands her choice.

After the final ask, she firmly underlines a single word: *Home*.

"Okay, Mom. We're taking you home."

Her fingernails repeatedly tap on the bed rail, communicating her agreement. Mom can't form a fist with the oximeter attached to her finger. She gives me a thumbs up as best she can.

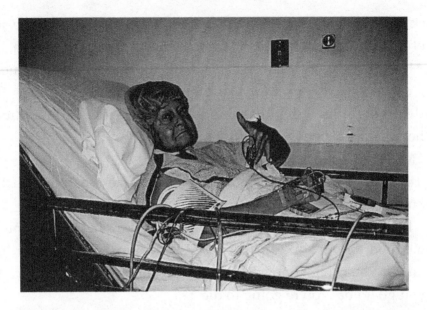

Mom giving us a thumbs up that she wants to go home.

Doctor Kumar pulls Tash and me aside. "Hospice is ready to help you. Please talk to the receptionist at the desk and she'll direct you." She looks at Tash and me with teary eyes and says, "I'll miss her. I'll miss Mama Mule."

The hospice nurse is expecting us. She gives me a checklist on a piece of paper. I'm grateful because I know I won't remember the tasks. I pick up a pint of morphine, liquid Ativan, and orange pill boxes at a nearby pharmacy. We leave South Boston and drive numbly down Highway 58 to my hometown of Clarksville, Virginia to prepare for Mom's homecoming.

"How much was it?" Tash asks. "We're keeping track of how much things cost, and we'll settle up later."

I can't remember. I don't remember giving anyone a credit card, getting my card back, or receiving a receipt. I numbly open my wallet and find my credit card but no receipt.

"I don't know, Tash. We'll figure it out later."

An hour later, a hospice nurse and an ambulance pull up to 119 Shiney Rock Road. The hospice folks move in a hospital bed, medical equipment, and boxes of supplies. Mom is in a gurney outside in the front yard. It is quick. They know what they're doing. Eventually everything is ready, and we roll Mom into the front room, surrounding her bed with chairs for the visitors we hope will come. There's a big front window she can look out and snoop on the neighborhood.

I glance out the window at our neighbor Gladys's house and notice her peering back at me. She's probably already been on the phone with her sister-in-law Betsy, another neighbor on this side of the street. Soon, they'll be over to see what we need. That's what good neighbors do. As a bonus, they'll find material for the gossip mill which seems to work overtime in Clarksville.

There are dried-out potted flowers on the porch. Even watering them now won't bring them back to life. The house doesn't seem as alive and is smaller than I remember. It has lost its zest and spark. Inside, pictures of Tash, Susan, and me clutter most horizontal surfaces. Sentimental items guard their space, surrounded by dust. I walk around the house, reminiscing. I feel so empty. Today was a long day of flying, driving, and arranging for Mom to come home to die. I'm sure Mom doesn't think that. She'll fight as she always has. She's home, and in her mind, she'll live.

I've always avoided death. I remember with sadness my Grandpa Jimmy Lou passing away on a cold and rainy day. I was only four years old, but I still vividly remember it. I never went to anyone's funeral after that. People would ask if I'd attended so-and-so's funeral, and I would make up some excuse about not feeling well, having to work, or having something to fix. It was too much.

I know people say, "It's for them and their family. That's why you should go to the funeral. Pay your respects."

Bullshit! It's for you as much as them. Most folks want to know *How'd they die?*, *Who is going to get their house and land?* or *Did they have life insurance? If so, how much?* This time I can't make up an excuse. I have to face death and it scares me. There's no hiding now.

Hospice Care (Day Two)

Thursday, February 22, 2007 – Vultures and Nicotine.

*Life becomes more precious when Death sits down beside you
and waits for his turn.*

After a sleepless night, we reread all the hospital literature: coping skills, the stages of death, recovering. I can't remember half of it.

We have a nice setup for Mom in the front room. The newly placed birdfeeders bring in many birds outside her window, eating as if they haven't had a home-cooked meal in a week. I clean the dirty front-room windows so Mom can look at the birds, the neighbors, and the daffodils coming up. I remember when she planted those daffodils. Every fall, we'd cover them with pine tags to keep them from freezing in winter. Throughout the day, fresh cut-flowers from visitors begin to accumulate. Some flowers are brought by visitors, but most are delivered from the florist. The living room is looking like a Miracle Grow flower bed with Mom as the centerpiece.

Sitting by Mom, I look out the front room window as a familiar face arrives. My cousin Clarabelle gets out of a car. I immediately get up and warn Susan and Tash.

"Clarabelle is here. Watch her like a hawk and be sure she doesn't steal anything."

Knock. Knock. Knock.

I walk to the door and put on my best superficial face before answering the knock. "Hey, Clarabelle. How are you? Come on in."

"Hey Maikel. I heard about your mama."

Keeping my dialogue as short as possible, I reply, "Thanks." I don't

11

trust Clarabelle and do not want to volunteer any extra information knowing that it would spread like a brushfire in a drought.

I glance over at Mom, the bed-confined raptor, who watches the vulture Clarabelle's every move. She knows. Clarabelle lingers for nearly half an hour offering meaningless conversation and then drops the question.

"Are y'all going to sell the house? I'll buy it for $20,000."

My jaw clenches. The first vulture has smelled death in the air. It's circling and waiting for the carcass. Susan watches me tense up and lays down the law. "Clarabelle, I think you need to go. We're only allowing fifteen minutes per visitor. It's time for Mama Wise to rest."

Clarabelle gets upset and mumbles gibberish.

I reinforce Susan. "You should go. You can come back tomorrow for fifteen minutes."

Clarabelle leaves, and Tash, Susan, and I sit down in the kitchen, relieved.

Tash speaks. "Clarabelle always wanted something for nothing. Granny always said, 'Watch your pocket book when Clarabelle came a knocking.' I'm glad she's gone."

"Me too, Tash. I forgot just how wacky-doodle and clueless she is. This is a reminder of what she did before when other family members died. I don't think she stole anything this time, though."

Susan chimes in, "Well maybe we scared her off. She may not come back."

I glance out the kitchen window toward the back corner of the field. A wake of Black Vultures are perched in a half-dead pine tree.

"Hey, Tash and Susan. Look. More vultures have arrived. They know. I think they should at least wait until she stops breathing, though."

Susan snorts. "That's messed up."

We all laugh at the inappropriate joke and sip our coffee.

I hear ticking on the bed rail, indicating Mom wants something.

I walk into the front room. Apparently Clarabelle's visit stressed Mom out, too, and she hands me her plastic Nicorette cigarette. It was nicotine that got her here. She can't talk because of the tracheal tube inserted in her throat. She's lying in a hospice bed with a plastic breathing hole. The cancerous tumor engulfs an artery that feeds her brain precious oxygen, and on her death bed, she asks for another smoke. I'm determined to impose my will, my control. I resist Mom's desire for a fresh cartridge of her deathly addiction. I am so angry. I pretend to refill her cigarette.

I get the look. She's boldly speaking to me with her eyes. Her motor functions have degraded since the last time I saw her a few months ago, but she manages to open the plastic cigarette and finds it's empty. She knows me. Two taps on the bed rail. I get a second look. This look is her don't-make-me-get-out-of-this-deathbed look. I give in to her wishes. Right in front of her eyes, I install the cartridge and hand it back to her to fulfill her physical dependency and desire. Still wary, she opens it, just to be sure I wasn't trying to trick her. This isn't the first time I've tried resisting her. I fought her alcohol addiction, but eventually gave into her wishes regarding that, too.

I remember telling her, "I'll go buy you gin, and you can drink as much as you want. I have two conditions. First, don't drive after you've been drinking. Second, don't lie to me. There's no need to hide anything or lie to me. Okay?"

At the time, I didn't realize the power of her addiction. I came to the understanding that I couldn't change her, and I couldn't fix things. I was a fixer, and this was a fix-less situation. I have to support her. This is it. I have to love her and give in to her whatever she needs. Truly *accept* her. At this moment with death approaching, acceptance overtakes my desire to control. Just like with the alcohol, a weird thing happens when I gave Mom the nicotine. I become less angry. It's better for Mom and better for me because I stop fighting and trying to impose my will. I'm more at peace with her and myself.

Our hospice instructions state that three times a day Mom can get a dose of morphine and Ativan. The leaflet says once we inject it, she should sleep for a couple of hours.

Tash has been living with Mom while caring for her before this losing cancer battle. Since we know Mom is going to die, we need to clean the house to prepare for selling it. This task would be insurmountable for Tash to do alone. Susan and I have only two weeks to help my sister get rid of all the stuff. It seems wrong doing this before Mom dies, but it needs to be done. We decide it's best to clean things out while she's sleeping.

We give Mom her second dose of morphine for the day and Mom's eyes slowly close minutes later. Last night, we came up with a plan. All items will be placed into the following categories:

1: Items to donate to Goodwill.
2: Items to auction off.
3: Items to return to the appropriate people.
4: Items to keep.
5: Items to throw away.

Mom has held on to all manner of items she deemed *worth some money*. She believed we would inherit it and be wealthy. Susan, Tash, and I are scared. If Mama Wise wakes up and sees us getting rid of things, she will surely come back and haunt us. We don't really believe in ghosts, but if there's a way, Mom will find it. So many memories flood me as we start going through the items in the attic, the basement, and the back porch. It's funny how a broken sled, a bicycle with bent wheels, Uncle Jim's Vietnam boots, a mineral-coated wood stove pot, and a makeshift chicken coop turned into a baby crib look so different now. The last time I visited, they were clutter, junk, and annoying. Now they are memories of our adventures and the life we had here on Shiney Rock Road. Each item has a story, and I remember them all.

Mom in 2006. Sitting in her favorite spot by the kitchen window with the wavy pane of glass. Cases of protein drinks behind her are evidence she was not drinking them.

Moving Day

Friday, March 21, 1975 – Six Years Old. First Grade.

A broken branch. A withered tree.
Holding onto life. Just wait. You'll see.

Mom drives down the hill through the field in her brown Ford Pinto to where her maple tree is. It's raining, and she has the hatchback up. There are two tools hanging out the back, and I know by their shape and weathered-gray handles what they are. I'm hiding in the shadows and dryness of the red cedars on the hilltop. I'm dry here, peering down at Mom and playing with my plastic WWII bomber plane.

Mom is all of five feet tall, but when asked at the doctor's office, she'd say, "I'm five feet and three-quarter inches tall." In her mind, adding the three-quarters made a significant difference. Dwarfism runs in the family on her mama's side but had skipped her. She's just small. Some of the locals in town call her *One-Beer Daisy*, but I don't know what that name means. I suppose it's her naturally curly red hair or her smile. Like Tash and me, Mom is freckled and fair-skinned. She's feisty at times and surely has some Irish blood. If you didn't know her, you'd say she's a hot pistol, ready to fire off if provoked. Her eyes change color depending on what she wears, but usually they're a green hazel with signs of a hard life around them.

She knows where I am and yells, "Maikel, I need your help!"

In my cut-off blue jeans and t-shirt, a size too small, I run barefoot through the cold wet grass. I have no hips or a belt, so I'm always

16

pulling up my shorts, so much so that several of the belt loops are broken.

"Go get your shoes on and help me dig out this tree."

"You just planted this tree," I yell while running to the house for my shoes.

I come back and start to help her dig. A white plastic tag on a branch says it's a silverleaf maple from The Greenhouse up on Highway 58 where Mom works part-time. Two weeks ago, she had to run out and brush the snow off it from a late winter storm. The ground is still soft, but the saturated clay makes a slurping noise as we pry the muddy muck back out of the ground.

The branches sprawl randomly and flex as we lift the five-foot (and three-quarter inches) twig of a tree into a garbage bag. It's already stressed from recently being planted and doesn't seem like it's ready to move again. The garbage bag is extra heavy and stubbornly fights to stay on the ground. We heave the bag into the back of the Pinto, and I throw the muddy pick and shovel into the hatchback, as well. I jump in with Mom and she drives back up the hill and turns south down the road. The open hatchback slams down on the branches. I hear one snap.

Oh shit, I think, not letting the thoughts move to words. I mumble, "Ain't no way this tree is going to make it." I don't care. I just want to know where we are heading.

Mom says, "I have a surprise."

She drives south on College Street, across the bridge over the railroad where trains bring coal to the nearby factories of Burlington Mills and Russell Stover Candies. She slows and takes a right. We pass by the Price mansion that everyone knows is haunted. We heard a man died in there. The mansion had a window above the front door, exactly like the one in a vampire TV show I watch regularly. I

17

figure the vampires could jump out of those windows and get us at night. That's why Tash and I never went there for Halloween. The curtains were closed all the time. We didn't want to take our chances.

Mom continues driving on the road uphill that curves to the left, crests a hill, and then down the backside. She misjudges the car coming the opposite direction and at the last minute decides not to risk it. She abruptly slows down as best as the Pinto can muster. I instantly feel her right arm hit me in the chest and push me back in the seat. I'm amazed her safety arm can hold me back whenever a car or deer pops out in front of us. Who needs seatbelts when I have Mom's arm? We make a left turn.

"We're here, son. This is going to be our new home."

It's a big red brick house that looks to be more than twice the size of our old home. A variety of big pines, oaks, cedars, and a Catalpa tree surround the fancy house. Catalpa trees have heart-shaped leaves and long brown seed pods. We call the seed pods *monkey cigars*. We had a Catalpa at our old house and one of the kids down the street said some folks smoke the seed pods, but I haven't tried it, mostly because my parents say they're poisonous. I think those kids were messin' with me. These trees are the kind with branches low enough that I can climb. The driveway is a semi-circle full of mud puddles where I can test my boatbuilding and dam-building skills. There's a field on the far side with more types of trees on a gentle slope, with lots of places for exploring.

"Mom, does that field go with the house, too?"

"Yes, son. It's about one acre."

"What's an acre?"

She just smiles. "You'll see after everything dries out."

Our home on Shiney Rock Road.

My mind is frettin' about all that grass. Pop isn't going to like cutting it and trimming around the trees. He yanked out most of the trees at the house on College Street because the trimming annoyed him. Seems like he did more damage to the field with tire ruts and leaving holes in the ground where the trees used to be. Eventually, he filled in the holes when Mom nagged him. On the downhill side of the field at this new place, there's a huge cow pasture with big rolling hills. The pasture looks as if it goes on forever. There are no cows on the lower part of the hill. As I am looking about at all the places to explore, I see him. On top of the hill as if bragging stands a big ol' bull. He looks like something I don't want to mess with.

My sister, Pop, Mom, and I move stuff all that day. We don't have much, but it sure takes a while. Most of our possessions were given to us or picked up at yard sales. Luckily, the chinchilla cages stayed at our old home and the poop along with it. Raising chinchillas was

Mom's idea to make some money, but they did nothing but take money instead. And stink.

The chinchillas were a source of some cussin' and yellin' many nights with my parents. "How can we afford to feed them?" "When are you going to find a buyer?" "We need more cages." The pelts weren't worth all that much. All the pee and poop-soaked newspapers made me sick. The smell reminded me of the gooey, rotten slush that builds up on the inside bottom of a garbage can after a rain. When I had to go into their musky pens, I'd hold my breath as long as I could. I'm really happy they're not coming with us. Yay, no chinchillas!

Mom goes to the store while we finish unloading our belongings from Pop's primer-gray 1965 Suburban. A short time later, I hear gravel crunch and mud puddles splash as Mom pulls back into the driveway.

"I have dinner. We're having veal tonight. It was on sale."

A store could mark something up twice as much, but if it had an *On Sale* tag on it, then Mom thought it had to be a good deal. She walks over to the stove and puts in two frozen aluminum-foiled Hungry Man veal meals into the oven.

"Mom, what's veal?" I ask.

"Baby cow. It's really tender."

My stomach turns. I've enjoyed plenty of hamburgers, but my stomach turns at the thought of eating a baby cow. Just doesn't seem right. Thirty minutes later, she pulls them back out. We eat off paper plates on the floor, since we haven't moved the kitchen table in yet.

Pop says, "Our first family dinner in our new home."

I don't hear another word after that. The tomato sauce makes me think of baby cow blood. The breaded veal is gray and still cold in the middle. It's unusual for Mom to undercook things. I like the breaded part. It isn't as crunchy as fried chicken and is a little too mushy, but it still reminds me of Granny's fried chicken.

Mama Wise cooking in the kitchen.

After dinner, Tash and I make a pallet on the floor to sleep. Unlike our last home with orange and brown shag carpet, these floors are oak and hard. If Tash and I run real fast with socks on, we can slide a few feet and clean up the dust at the same time. Normally a pallet was a quilt laid on the floor with another quilt or two on top. This time, I double over two quilts to make the floor a bit cushier under me.

Later that night, I wake up when I hear Pop cussing. The fireplace only has few coals left, and it's not even sunrise yet. There's no more firewood. We forgot to bring more wood from the old house. It's okay for my sister and me, though. We're conditioned to sleep in cold rooms. Seeing our breath in the mornings is a regular event. I doze back to sleep again.

With the temperature dropping, I wake up to add more layers of blankets. We have an abundance of blankets from Granny stacked on top of moving boxes. Some nights in the winters we have so many heavy blankets on top of us that it's hard to turn over onto our sides. Once we've warmed up inside the cocoon of quilts, it's best to hold our pee until morning. If we get up to go, it takes another twenty minutes to warm up again, especially our feet. I'm having a hard time going back to sleep since I have to go pee. I hear my parents' bedroom door open. After a moment, I roll over and notice Pop standing by the front door. He's 6' 3" tall with receding red hair, freckled skin, and a slight beer belly. He's completely naked. This seems strange for this time of night. I can't figure it out. He walks out the front door to the end of the driveway and begins walking down the street with no clothes on. Still bundled in Granny's blankets, I run to my parent's bedroom and let Mom know.

"Mom, wake up. Wake up! Pop is walking down the road naked."

She jumps out of bed. "Stay here. I'll be back."

She puts on her shoes and runs down the road after Pop. Curious about why Pop is behaving this way without the usual influence of alcohol, I shiver and watch out the front window until Mom guides Pop back into the house and back to the bedroom. Once Pop is wrapped in blankets and a stocking cap, she comes into the front room.

"Your father is okay. Moving here and buying this place was a lot of stress for him. His job isn't going well, either. Sometimes he walks in his sleep. He's okay. Now go back to bed."

It's still dark out, so I don't think the neighbors have seen anything. Today certainly was interesting. We moved to a new home, got rid of the stinky chinchillas, and Pop is getting to know the neighborhood with no clothes on. I learned I don't care for veal, but I can't wait to find out what an acre is.

Maikel after moving to Shiney Rock Road.

Meeting the Neighbors

Saturday, March 22, 1975 – Worms and Apple Pie.

What makes a good neighbor? Is it what they do?
Perhaps nothing more than simply being there for you.

Mom opens the creaking Carolina-blue kitchen cabinets and pulls out some of the smaller mix-matched ceramic cereal bowls. After searching in a couple more cabinets, she finds the corn flakes and fills up the bowls. She sets the milk on the counter, and I grab it first. I open the lid and, as always, take a good whiff. The spoiled milk curdles my nose. Mom takes the milk and throws it away after confirming the expression on my face. Spoiled milk is common for us so, it isn't unusual to use water instead. I let the faucet run for a couple minutes until the rusty water clears out. Using water or milk doesn't bother me as long as sugar is a participant. Several heaps of sugar later, I have some seriously thick sugar water.

While Pop drives back and forth unloading more tools, furniture, boxes, and engine blocks from our old home, Mom organizes the kitchen. This house has a newer kitchen stove, but it's still well-used. Mom carefully removes the half-rusted burners and lines them with aluminum foil. When she's done, they look shiny and new. Mom does this to catch the grease splatter. She's a messy cook. With all the Crisco, there will soon be a residue on the stovetop and adjacent counters.

My sugar-filled stomach startles when I hear a *knock, knock, knock.* It's a weird knock and sounds like a mechanical version of knuckles.

24

This house has a fancy lion-faced door knocker made of brass. I've seen well-to-do people's homes with these types of knockers, but on our last home, people just used their knuckles. Only rich people had door knockers, paved driveways, and swimming pools. We're a third of the way there with our door knocker.

Pop yawns. "Somebody's at the front door."

I walk out of the kitchen and barely into the hallway a foot or so. I peer around the corner and see several people on the front porch. Pop calls my sister and me to the door.

I shyly hide behind Mom, expecting the Naked Police.

One of the strangers speaks. "Hi. I'm Gladys and this is my husband Sam. We live across the street. This is Betsy and my brother George. They live beside you just on the other side of the ditch."

Gladys keeps talking and hardly lets Sam or anyone else get a word in. Gladys has a strong Southern accent and she seems like a feisty Southern belle. Sam is older, thinner, and not quite as tall as Pop. He has principal-type eyes behind his glasses. He looks smart and serious at the same time, with a touch of mischievousness. Whew, that's a big word. Like a principal, those eyes could see right through a fella and tell if he was up to no good. Betsy and George are plumper, with more rounded faces, and seem less uptown than Gladys and Sam. Betsy and George could qualify as being one of my aunts and uncles, especially if they had red hair like us.

Gladys motors on. "We made you a pie. The apples are from the Buchanan's up the street. They have a lot of apples in the fall. I'm sure they'll give you some next season. He doesn't like spraying them, so you may have to cut out the worm-eaten parts, but they're still good."

"Oh my God, apple pie," my child brain yells as our new neighbors go back into their manicured homes.

I want it all for myself. My Granny makes pie crusts with lard and butter. There's nothing like a warm slice of apple pie with vanilla ice cream at her house. Ice cream is a rare treat. During the summer or at Thanksgiving time, we sometimes make ice cream on Granny's porch. I know we aren't going to get any ice cream today because money is short. In addition to the first house payment, Mom and Pop had to ask Granny and Grandpa for a couple thousand to make the down payment.

Pop is talking in hushed tones to Mom. "Things are goin' to be tight for a bit. Try to make the food last. Maybe we can get some vegetables from Granny's deep freeze and buy some groceries off the damaged-reduced tables from Winn-Dixie. Got to get there early before somebody buys up everything. I'll go down the road and visit Mr. Cash and see if he can hold the damaged food tables for us."

After eating one of Mom's modest-sized slices of apple pie and finding a black snakeskin in the basement, I hear my dad say, "Com' on son, we are going to see Mr. Cash."

I climb into the truck. "What road is this, Pop?"

"Shiney Rock Road. We're headin' down Shiney Rock Road toward Grassy Creek. There's a dirt road on the left past the dumpsters. I don't know the name of the road, but I'll know when I see it."

Pop drives about a mile or two over the washboard dirt road and pulls up to Mr. Cash's house. Mr. Cash is the manager of the Winn-Dixie grocery store. There are two grocery stores in town: Winn-Dixie and Vaughan's. Winn-Dixie is bigger and is part of a chain in the South. Vaughan's is a local family-owned grocery store. Everyone says the meat is better at Vaughan's, but the other store is cheaper and has more variety. The older people, including Granny and the ones set in their ways, still like shopping at Vaughan's for everything despite the higher prices. I'm more partial to going to Vaughan's, too. I had a run-in with the Winn-Dixie manager, Mr. Cash. I had to apologize to him after sitting on a wine shelf in his store that collapsed and broke a bunch of wine bottles. I thought for sure I was going to get a whippin' for it, and my parents would have to pay for it. After the look Mom gave me, I avoided sitting on any shelf or touching stacked pickle jars in any store.

On Mr. Cash's porch, I hear Pop say, "I appreciate it." Then he shakes Mr. Cash's hand and heads back to the truck. "He said he would hold the damaged groceries for us."

Electric Fence and Mama Johnson's

Sunday, March 23, 1975 – Meeting the Bull.

A golden arc of a stream. Just missin' the wire.
Keep the pressure up. Aim a bit higher.
Lessening flow. Consequences could be dire.
Contact. Zap! My pee-pee's on fire.

The next day we're at Winn-Dixie right at opening time. We reside in the Bible Belt, so the store isn't busy, since most folks are praying away their sins at church services. Sometimes Mom or Granny would drag us to repent, but not today. When we walk inside the freshly-waxed clean store, we quickly walk to the damaged-reduced tables. There are at least three tables of food. Each table has a pile of packaged food as if someone picked up a grocery cart and dumped it upside down. There's Lipton Onion soup mix, six large jars of marshmallow crème, canned shredded beef, Staghorn chili, butter beans, and black-eyed peas. There's even a box with little bags of Fritos. Every can is either dented or missing a label, making it a mystery can. Some of the box packages are about to expire or slightly cut open. We load up four grocery carts of food for all of twenty dollars. Mom doesn't have enough cash and we can't use our S&H Green Stamps. She pays the cashier with some change out of the money jar—quarters, dimes, nickels, and pennies. Mom holds on to a few quarters. She needs the quarters to do laundry soon.

When we get home, Mom puts together one of her best meals yet. "We are havin' *hobo chili*," she says.

I don't know what hobo chili is, but if it's using a can or two of that Staghorn chili, I know it's got to be good. The damaged cans are bent up so bad that the hand-driven can opener can't finish cutting off the top. Pop uses a hammer and knife to finish opening them. I see Mom cringe as Pop misses a couple times, almost slicing one of his sausage-sized fingers. Mom takes a bag of Fritos, turns it sideways, and then cuts it open. She pours the warmed chili right over those Fritos. Then she covers the chili with freshly-diced onions. A hobo himself couldn't have done better. After inhaling our first ever bag of hobo chili, there's a little left over, so Mom lets Tash and me have a second one. That's some gracious living.

After we finished eating as well as hobo royalty, the drizzling rain stops. It's time to figure out what an acre is. I wander around the field next to our new home. Shiney Rock Road is uphill to the north of our property. I've been on Shiney Rock Road many times. If I was to keep going down Shiney Rock Road, I'd pass several tobacco fields and eventually hit Grassy Creek and the North Carolina state line on some twisty backroads. Sometimes these roads and Grassy Creek Bridge flood when the lake is high. When this happens, only the guardrails poke up out of the water. The concrete bridge is still good to walk down even if the water is waist deep. It makes for some good fishing in the middle part. My kind Aunt Abigail and her mean old husband Uncle Henry lived down that way, and we'd go see her sometimes. We'd always leave her place with tomatoes, squash, and okra if she had it.

As I walk along in our field next to Shiney Rock, I eventually run into a small strip of woods to the west. At least it appears to the west from where the sun is at in the sky. There are several game trails going every which way through these woods. I flush a couple of cottontails as I follow one of the more obvious trails. This looks like a good place to put a couple rabbit box traps. The undergrowth is dead but looks as if it could be plentiful when it warms up, and maybe snaky, too. I keep walking west for about a hundred feet or so until I run into an old rusty barbed wire fence marking our border. It's been wet these last few weeks, so moss is growing on the north side of the fence posts and shaded trees. The barbed wire here is old. In some places, trees serve as posts, with some of the tree's bark growing over the wire. I'd seen this before, but not a half a finger length inside a tree. This fence has been here a while and is likely older than me.

I follow another small game trail that runs parallel to an overgrown fence down to the cow pasture fence. In the cow pasture, cedar trees butt up next to the fence that continues south. Those thick cedars would be a good place to stand if it's raining hard or on a hot summer day. Inside the cow pasture, there's a small hill that rises on the right side and less so on the left. The higher part was the last place I saw that mean-looking bull. I keep following the barbed wire fence back towards our back yard. Some of the posts are weathered gray, cracked, and moss covered, too. I have to be careful steppin' on these posts, 'cause moss can be as slick as snot if it's wet. A few of the posts are so bad that the owner has wrapped more wire around the post to keep it from collapsing. Kinda looks like a vertical column of gray splinters forced together in a circle with rusty twisted wire.

About waist level inside the fence, there's a brand-new wire. It has shiny new white plastic round knobs with a groove in the middle. I have a lot to ponder. Kinda looks like one of Granny's thread spools on her pedal-driven Singer sewing machine. I wonder why that wire is so new. Why put new wire on a fence that's almost ready to fall down? Why don't it have sharp rusty barbs on it, either? It makes no sense. I keep walking and hear a snort. It's that ole bull. He looks mean. His eyes are as bloodshot as Pop's after an extended stay at

Mama Johnson's. He's in the corner of the cow pasture closest to our house. I don't think he sees me. Maybe I can sneak up on him.

I move toward him, hiding behind the tall dead grass and a tree or two. I hold still until he drops his head down to eat some grass. Pop always told my sister and me we're one-quarter Cherokee. Our grandfather on our Pop's side is full-blooded Cherokee. We never met him, but Pop told us how he was a tail gunner on a bomber and got shot down over Germany during WWII. He escaped out of Germany by hiding in farmer's manure piles and using his Indian skills to escape. Surely, my Indian background makes me a good hunter and stealth-like. I creep closer.

Then I yell with my arms raised when he comes up to chew. "AHHHHHH!"

He just looks at me, annoyed. He lumbers closer to me and sticks his head on my side of the fence not two feet away. He lets out a nasty wet snort with mucous spewing out of his nostrils. His head and horns are so big that I get scared and back up. Not paying attention, I trip over a wet stump and fall over backward, banging my leg. My leg throbs.

I get a little worked up. "I'll show you."

I jump up to my feet. I zip down my zipper and start to pee over the fence toward him. I'm proud of how far I can pee. Sometimes I can almost shoot up higher than my head. He just keeps looking at me. As my streamflow starts to lessen, my pee hits that brand new shiny wire. Instantly, I'm knocked back, and I scream. I feel as if I just crashed on my bicycle after a jump and feel the intense pain of my pee-pee harshly colliding on the top tube just before crashing. Tears swell up as I fall to the ground. After a couple of minutes, the pain goes away, and the bull keeps staring. I've interrupted his eating. I stumble up and keep exploring.

Just past the corner of the cow pasture is the end of *the ditch*. This part of the ditch is flat with small islands of grass mounds. The stagnant water looks murky and black. It has a decaying smell. The ditch runs downstream from the road, where it flows more freely and marks our border with Betsy and George's yard. Their yard is so clean. All the cinder blocks are stacked next to the shed behind their house. Nothing is left astray, and everything resides neatly in or near their house or shed. Most of the leaves in their yard aren't welcome and are raked up, too. A clean yard, along with the ditch, creates a distinct line between our place and theirs. Our yard is full of pine tags, pine cones, and fallen branches. Some old grass in our yard has grown tall and flopped over after the first frost from last fall. Their grass, cut low to the ground, looks like one of those rich people's golf courses. Water still flows through the part of the ditch that I assume is their ditch. I make it up to the beginning of the ditch, where I find a huge mint patch. I grab a couple of dozen leaves and chew on them until my spit turns green.

Maybe tomorrow, I think, *this will be a good place to set my wood boat and see how far it'll go down.*

Several weeks ago, I constructed my boat out of a piece of two-by-four from some scrap wood Pop had left over from making sawhorses. So far, I have only placed my boat in mud puddles with a couple of green army men. These rapids will test my ship-building skills. I wonder how far down the ditch the green army men will make it before falling off.

I decide that I can't wait until tomorrow. I grab my boat and two army men. I duct tape the army men down to the boat. Since I don't need wind and there may be some snagging with the weeds, I remove the sail and mast. I let it loose just above the first major waterfall by the mint patch. The modified two-by-four pitches and rolls ungracefully through the river of water. The branches, weeds, and grass continuously catch the boat. I have to free it every few feet. After about two Suburban lengths, I stop. There's just too much debris. I'll need to weed-whack and haul debris out of this ditch to make it boat-worthy. I pull out the boat and head back upstream.

The headwaters of the ditch, where it flattens out, is the run-off from Shiney Rock Road. Directly across the road is Sam and Gladys' place. Their manicured yard is superior to anyone else's on the street. It isn't even grass growing season yet, and their grass is as green as a meadow after a long April shower. Sam happens to be out there putting something on the grass. It looks like he's covering the whole yard with small white rocks. After going back and forth a couple times, Gladys yells at him. Annoyed, he goes away for a few minutes and comes back to where he left off. She sure seems bossy. I figured he might be taking care of the yard to get away from her. Maybe that's why Pop putters on the vehicles and lawnmowers all the time. Mom yells for me, and I abandon my boat by the ditch.

Inspired by Sam, Mom says to Tash and me, "I need you two to help me in the back yard."

We walk out the back door in back of the kitchen. There're half-rotten steps that lead down between the house and the well house. Even Mom has to duck her head to keep from hitting the electrical wires. Mom grabs one of these metal green fence posts and starts pounding right in the middle of the back yard. Tash and I hold the post lower than normal since Mom's aim isn't consistent. She misses every three swings or so. The maple tree doesn't look so good.

"Help your sister hold up this tree while I tie it down to this post."

Mom ties an old shoe string from the stake to the tree and to the broken branch. Her knots ain't that fancy but hold. Then she wraps the broken branch with a couple of layers of masking tape to hold it together.

"There're so many trees here, Mom. This tree may not make it. Why do we need another one?"

She tells me, "You'll see. Don't worry about the little things. In the end, it'll all work out."

I don't understand.

Across the road, Sam is still at it. This time he's spreading something I recognize—grass seed. The rest of the neighborhood will have a hard time catching up, and he certainly will win the blue ribbon. Come to find out, all of those small little white rocks he was using was fertilizer. We used fertilizer on Granny's farm, but more of the natural, smelly kind. I ain't never heard of anyone putting fertilizer on their yard. It makes no sense. Why would a person want to make it grow faster? That means he'll have to cut more grass. Pop never liked cutting grass, and Mom had to nag him to do it more often.

Mom casually and encouragingly says to Pop, "The neighbor's yard looks so good and fancy. Looks almost as good as Kinderton Golf Course. I don't think there's a single weed in it. All the weeds decided to hang out in our yard. Why don't you spend thirty minutes in the yard?"

She has a convenient way of saying things like this to him after his second or third beer. Maybe she's trying to get him to slow down his drinking. It seems like most men in town drink beer. Possum, the town drunk, would sometimes go down the sidewalks with a beer in his hand, pushing a lawnmower in the other, with his pack of dogs following him. Some of the men like Pop and my cousin Hank go to Mama Johnson's and drink several beers after work or on weekend afternoons. Usually only men hang out at Mama Johnson's place, but sometimes my sister and I go with him. If we're lucky, we could get pickled eggs or pickled pig's feet. That pink vinegar sure makes things taste good.

Pop slams down his third beer. "Come on, son. We're going to cut some grass."

We don't have a garage. Pop pulls off the tarp exposing the Western Auto push-mower that still has last year's grass caked on it. Pop checks the gas tank. It's bone dry, and he fills it up. He pulls and pulls on the starter. The lawnmower just won't start. He's known for being one of the best mechanics in town. However, this lawnmower is getting the best of him.

"I'm not sure if this thing is getting any spark. Why don't you hold onto this wire and we'll see?" Pop asks.

He pulls. My arm jolts as if someone is ripping it off me. I'm still fully traumatized from my recent cow pasture fence experience, but this time my arm hurts instead of my pee-pee. He begins to laugh and laugh. I start crying and run to Mom.

Mom can tell I'm in pain, "What's wrong? What's wrong?"

"I held this wire and it hurt me," I tell her.

The screen door opens and springs back with a decaying bang. "I'm sorry, son. It didn't hurt that bad," Pop says. "Come here. Give me a hug."

I go over to him and abruptly Mom yells, "You son-of-a-bitch! You knew that would hurt him. Get the hell out of here."

Pop grins and looks at me with bloodshot eyes, "Come on, boy."

We jump in the Suburban and head to Mama Johnson's. When we pull in, my cousin Hank is already there. Seems like every time we come here, Hank is either here or arrives shortly afterward. His Harley is proudly parked, showcasing all the chrome. I'd noticed there were some scratches on the side of that chromed-out chopper.

Pop joins Mama Johnson, Hank, and another older man at an antique oak round table.

Appearing slightly guilty, Pop says, "Go get a pickled pig's foot or an egg."

I walk up to the clutter counter. I don't see anything to pull the pink egg out of the jar. At home, I have no problem pulling things out of jars. At other people's places, I know better.

I used to think, *If they don't see me, how will they know?*

However, adults usually have a way of knowing. I ask Mr. Johnson, "How do I get them out?"

He laughs and fuels my normal bad behavior. "Just reach in. The vinegar will kill any germs."

Even so, I don't think he knows I still have lawnmower grease on my hands, but I do what I'm told. Mr. Johnson is right. There's no shortage of vinegar in the jar, and it feels like my nose is cleared after the first whiff.

I sit down at the table, and the older man looks at me.

"Hello son. I live across the street from you, two houses down from Sam and Gladys. My name is John, and my wife is Maddie. How old are you?"

I'm really nervous. I'm not used to speaking to older people besides family and teachers.

"I'm Maikel. I'm six years old."

John is a small-framed man with gray slick-backed hair and glasses. He has deep lines connecting his nose to the corners of his mouth. It reminds me of a puppet's mouth, but the lines are above the mouth. Even though he is wearing a plaid shirt and blue jeans, he kinda looks gussied up to me, since his clothes are free of holes and stains. Good enough to go to church, if he's the church-going type. He looks over to my cousin Hank.

Maikel standing by Hank's Harley under Granny's carport.

Hank often wore t-shirts with a front pocket where he kept his cigarettes. Like his brother Travis, he's freckled and has thinning hair. For some reason, Travis and Hank always like growing mustaches, even though their hair above their lip is sparse and gone in the middle part. Their mustaches look like two caterpillars who don't quite meet up in the middle. Hank is average-sized, but he can be as mean as a snake. He's hot-tempered and will scrap with anyone if they make him mad.

Hank and his friend, Charles Cole, have a reputation in town for craziness. Clarksville has all types of crazy. There's *that's some crazy shit* crazy. Or *they ain't right in the head* crazy. I guess Hank is the *party-type* crazy. After all, we're all crazy. It's just a matter of what kind and how much, I reckon.

On some Sundays, Hank comes to Granny's house with a hickey on his neck or a bruised eye from the night before. With Hank, it's either lovin' or scrappin' and didn't seem like there's no in between.

He has a nervous twitch in his eyes, nose and mouth. When he talks, he blinks his eyes a bunch and twists his mouth and nose sideways. He sometimes reminds me of that lady on the TV show *Bewitched* when she's doing a spell, except Hank does it all the time. I don't think nothin' of it since he's always nice to me and lets me ride in his Camaro at Granny's. Sometimes he drives fast down the road and then stops right in the middle of the road.

He'll put a dollar bill on the dash and say, "When I say go, try to get that dollar. If you can grab it, you can have it."

The big block Camaro accelerates so fast that I can never grab it in time. Even so, he still lets me have the dollar bill. I like Hank, and he's as good as a cousin can be.

Hank is talking about getting his Harley back from the shop. "So let me tell you. I just got the engine bored out on the Harley and had some longer chopper forks put on. Thought I would see what it could do. I motor down the road doing 'bout seventy and then the engine locks up."

I notice he's a little nervous and starts blinking his eyes faster. His nose and mouth start twitching more rapidly between words, too.

"So the rear tire locks up and starts squealing. I have to lay the bike down. I'm sliding on the pavement and my one leg gets pinned between the pavement and the exhaust. I feel my leg burning like hot grease. Then my ass starts getting really hot, so I shift my weight to the other ass cheek. It's gettin' hot from rubbing on the pavement. I keep switching ass cheeks until I stop sliddin'. I pull my leg out from under the bike. My calf has a giant busted blister on it from the exhaust. I can't push the bike down the road 'cause the wheel is locked up so I start pushing it into the woods. Then guess who shows up? Fishtail Hogan! That's bullshit!"

All of the men start laughing, and Hank's twitching accelerates at an impressive rate.

John looks at him and says, "I guess your hot ass got in trouble."

The old men laugh so hard that they all start crying. The rivalry between Hogan and Hank is legendary. Hank is always racing through town and outrunning Hogan with his car. Hogan is the Chief of Police in Clarksville, but I don't know why Hank calls him *Fishtail Hogan*.

The phone rings. Mama Johnson hands the phone to Pop. Mom knows where Pop and I are. Before leaving, Pop says I can take another pickled egg. I contaminate the pink-filled jar again as I hear Mom yelling over the phone. Pop's ass doesn't have giant blisters or strawberries on it, but he did get an ass-chewin' over the phone. In the end, Mom forgives him, and he's not in trouble no more. It's been a long day of pee-pee and finger zapping, boating, tree planting, ass slidin' and chewin', and contaminating food. I'm pooped.

Hospice Care (Day Two, Afternoon)

Thursday, February 22, 2007 – Tom's visit.
Three Buckets of Chicken. Flowers on Betsy's Porch.

Susan, Tash, and I are slowly sorting through all the items in the house each time Mom gets a dose of morphine. The piles are getting bigger and are not dissipating fast enough. What's important? What should we keep? I struggle to determine.

Knock. Knock. Knock.

I know the sound of the lion door knocker. Susan and Tash stay upstairs in the attic. I climb down the creaky attic steps and softly yell, "Hold on," before walking around Mom's hospital bed to get to the front door.

"Hello. I'm blah-blah-blah. I brought you some food. I hope you and Dolores are doing well. Here you go."

Though he didn't say *blah-blah-blah*, that's all I heard. I step out on the front porch steps and softly reply, "Thank you. Thank you so much. Mom is sleeping." Mr. Blah-blah-blah tells me he has to go.

I'm numb, and my memory is nearly nonexistent. I don't know this guy, but he knows Mom. It appears he's about the same age as she. The House of Wise is now up to three large buckets of Hardee's fried chicken. Each bucket could feed four Clarksville people or six to eight regular people. I love chicken, and I love mashed potatoes, but there is no way we can eat three large buckets. This food is on the opposite end of the healthiness spectrum from the food Susan and I typically eat back home in Colorado.

"Tash and Susan. Want some more chicken?"

Tash responds, "You know who would love it? Tom."

"You know, you're right. He doesn't have much money. We can feed him with all this extra food."

I walk out the front door. As I step down to the bottom of the front porch steps, I don't hear the screen door slam behind me like it used to when I was a kid. Mom installed one of those fancy glass storm doors with hydraulics. I walk across our field, which seems smaller now, and up to the side door of Tom's house. Anyone who knows this house never knocks on the front door. If they do, Tom probably doesn't know them and doesn't want to talk to them anyway.

Tom walks to the door, and I say through the screen, "Tom, we have so much food. Here, you take some. You won't need to buy any food for the next two weeks. We'll bring as much as you want."

"Goddammit. Goddammit. Goddammit." That's all Tom can say. The tears in his eyes say more than his mouth can ever muster.

I think Tom is saying thank you, but I don't speak Goddammit.

I remember a few years ago Tom came to the door when Susan and I were visiting. Mom opened the door, "Goddammit, Goddammit!"

Mom looked at him. "Oh, you want a Hardee's cheeseburger."

Tom stuttered, "GGGGoddammit!"

Mom was interpreting a Baptist's blasphemous word. "Oh, a large iced-tea. I'll be right back."

I looked over at Susan and said, "Mom learned another language. Goddammit." We laughed and never figured out how she understood him.

I walk back to find Tash and Susan sitting at the kitchen table.

"The funeral home called. News travels fast. Mom made some prearrangements with them. We can show up anytime this afternoon. Betsy is gonna stay with Mom," Tash states matter-of-factly. We rarely leave Mom alone even when she is sleeping. We don't ever want her to wake up alone.

We hop in our smoky-smelling non-smoking rental and drive down to the funeral home. Tash and I still haven't decided which funeral home to use. This call may have decided it for us. We walk in and are directed to the funeral director's desk. Before we start talking to the funeral director, he pulls out a paper with Mom's requests. Mom signed it with a green crayon.

"Natasha and Maikel. In some states this would work, but it doesn't meet the legal requirements in Virginia. I'm afraid it's not valid even though I witnessed it," Mr. Michael Lyon states in a professional tone.

"No worries. Tash and I will honor as many of the requests Mom has on that piece of paper as we can."

Since Mom has already discussed some details with this funeral home, we decide to use Watkins-Cooper-Lyon Funeral Home. Prior to meeting Mr. Lyon, I was seriously leaning toward using the Harris Funeral Home since I went to high school with the owner, Ricky Harris. This is one less decision to make. We start going through some details.

I don't feel right planning details of Mom's funeral with her still alive, but I have to soldier on.

The first question is, "Do you want her buried or cremated?"

Tash and I say, "On Mom's note she said cremated, and that's what we'll do."

"Do you want a viewing before the cremation?"

I look over at Tash. Tears roll down her cheeks.

"How do you feel about it, Tash?"

"You decide, Cale." Tash uses this term of endearment, Cale, when she's being extra nice or wants something.

I look back at Mr. Lyon. "I don't like viewings. Viewings prolong the pain and sorrow. We can put up some pictures during the funeral."

Reassuringly, Mr. Lyon says, "That's fine. I understand. A lot of people, especially the younger ones today, do that. Do you want to pick out an urn and a plot in the cemetery?"

I look over at Tash. "I don't care to have Mom sitting on an urn on a shelf or mantle someplace. She'd be just has happy in a Roman Meal bread bag. All she would want is to be close to us. But Tash, if you want to get an urn, we certainly can, and I'm okay with it. I don't know about a plot in the cemetery."

Tash blows her nose. "Can we decide later?"

Mr. Lyon says kindly, "Yes. Tash. You two can decide later."

I remember one of Mom's requests after Loretta's funeral.

"Mr. Lyon, after the funeral, can we all go outside in a circle? We would like friends and family to say a few words and share their memories."

"Yes, we can do that. We've done this for some other families."

I notice Tash is looking at some necklaces that Mom's ashes can be put in.

"Tash, pick one out if you like."

After a few more details, Susan, in her accounting voice, requests an itemized list of all items related to the funeral. Mr. Lyon says he will have it for us tomorrow. We say goodbye for now.

Just before we leave, Susan says, "Maikel. Let's take a picture of Mr. and Mrs. Lyon. Believe me, you'll want pictures later."

I trust her. She's usually right, and especially so when I think I'm overwhelmingly right. Just before I snap a shot, Susan jumps in. She photobombed the shot. I know my wife. Her goal of lightening the mood makes us all laugh.

**Mr. Michael Lyon, Reverend Jane Lyon, and Susan
(photobombing to cheer Tash and me up).**

When we get back home, our neighbor Betsy is sitting by Mom's side.

Betsy asks, "Well, how'd it go?"

"All right. It wasn't as difficult as we'd thought it would be," I say.

"Did they ask you about putting flowers on your porch when your mom dies? It's kind of a tradition 'round here," Betsy says in an *I-don't-think-much-of-that* tone. "When my husband George died, I told them I don't want nothing to do with them flowers. I woke up one morning and the flowers were on my porch. I loaded them in the car and took them back down there. I don't want no flowers on my porch, especially since I didn't ask for them."

Betsy and the rest of us started laughing. She's feisty.

Tash looks at Betsy and says, "Betsy, when they put the flowers on our porch, we are going to move them over to your place before you wake up. You okay with that?"

"Tash, I'd throw the damn things away if you don't want them."

We all laugh harder.

I can't resist and have to say it feed Betsy's feistiness. "Now Betsy. You need to watch that language. Don't make me tell the preacher about your swearing. Sounds like I know why you sit in the back row at church."

We keep laughing. We need to laugh.

Susan joins in. "Betsy, since you're here, want some fried chicken? We have plenty."

"I'll take a leg or two. Throw in some coleslaw and potatoes with gravy, too, if you have it. I won't have to make mac and cheese again."

Betsy leaves with two full plastic bags of food. Susan, Tash, and I conspire.

Susan says, "For the next few days, we should put a couple of flowers on Betsy's porch each day to get her ready for the big bouquet. Just enough to get her riled up."

Mom with flowers on her front porch. November 2006.

David and Goddammit

Saturday, March 29, 1975 – Six Years Old.
New Friend and Cussin' Man.

I glance over and watch Betsy sweeping off her porch again. Seems like she sweeps it every morning. Betsy tidies up her porch like her husband does their yard. I come back inside from playing in the ditch to find Mom sitting at the kitchen table. She's looking out through a window that has a wavy pane of glass. I've seen that type of glass before on some of the old barns where Granny's 'help' used to stay. Mom has a good view of the road. She can see John and Maddie's house and the house for sale right beside it. Just to the left of that and much closer is a big sweetgum tree. Its lowest branch is a bit of a jump, but I can reach it. Sweetgum balls are fun throwing while they're green. Sometimes I try to hit squirrels or Tash. Squirrels are more fun because they don't hit back. Mom sits there staring, smoking a Doral Menthol cigarette, her favorite brand, and holding a glass of tea with the same hand. I ask if I can go exploring. She says, "Yes." Within seconds, I'm through the screen door and hear it slam behind me.

Pop yells behind me, "What'd I tell you about slamming the screen door?!"

I'm too scared to go into the cow pasture with that bull guarding it. Instead, I walk behind the "For Sale" house across the street. I heard tractors behind the "For Sale" house yesterday and want to see what they're doing. I crawl through another barbed wire fence to the edge of a field. This field was cleared from a forest of oaks, poplars, and pines and is just freshly plowed. Some of the dirt rows have big red-clay clumps. Small stalks of corn are broken and partially buried in the dirt clumps. I start walking on the field, but the chunks of red dirt make it tough goin', so I decide to just walk around it. It's a good thing, too. I find a huge patch of blackberry bushes near the remaining forest. I want to eat some, but I remind myself that this summer when they are still ripening. I'll have to remember to come back. I make it over to the other corner and find a crude trail. It looks like a well-used deer trail, the kind that twists and turns between the trees. Somebody else has found and used this trail recently. I notice human footprints near a mud puddle that's devoid of leaves. My Cherokee Indian tracking skills are finely honed. Before leaving the house, I thought about bringing my bow and arrow, but suction-cupped arrows may not provide much protection.

At the bottom of the trail, I try to jump a small creek. My left shoe slips and is pulled into the muddy meandering water. With mud and water gushing out of my shoelace holes, I notice the trail continues slightly uphill to railroad tracks. I thought I heard a train last night. Now I know. There are so many trees. I can't make out where the trail ends, but I follow along. Just across the tracks, I can barely make out a dirt road. On either side of the road are brush, grass, and weed piles discarded by some of the locals. This road appears to enter the Edgewood Estates neighborhood. A lot of rich folks live in this place. Sometimes on weekends our family drives around town and cruises through Edgewood. There are lots of fancy door knockers, paved driveways, and swimming pools there.

As I meander on the other side of the moat I just stepped in, I notice a man and kid cutting grass at the closest house. I assume the kid with him is his son. He looks familiar and about my age. I'm too shy to say anything.

He speaks up first. "Hello, I'm David. I've seen you in school. What's your name?"

"M…Mai…Maikel," respond, stuttering nervously. Then I remember. "I've seen you and the other bigger guy jumping off the swings."

"You must be talking about Jay. He lives a couple blocks over there." David says, pointing. "I ain't never heard of the name Maikel before. Where did you get it?"

"Pop reads a lot. He named my sister Natasha and me after characters in a Russian spy novel."

"David! Git back to work!" His father yells.

I don't want to cause any trouble, so I let them be and head back home.

Instead of going around the recently plowed field again, I decide to go straight through. On the other side, I arrive at a fence where someone has cut the barbed wire and made a poor man's gate. The poles are leaning over since there's no tension in the wires, but that's fine with me. I cautiously push down the wire some more with one foot and step over it. *Made it.* I didn't get barbed.

I stroll straight toward Shiney Rock when I hear a loud voice. "Goddammit! Goddammit! Goddammit!"

The loud man has a twitch in his right arm, which shoots out horizontally to his right and then tucks back into his ribs with a closed fist. It's like he's hidin' his playing cards so no one could see. I quickly switch to the opposite side of the road.

"Goddammit!"

Man, I really pissed off this guy, I think. I run outta there expecting a holy bolt of righteous lightning to strike, and don't want to be anywhere nearby when it does.

I don't think I walked on his property. Frightened, I don't stop until I get home. Mom hasn't moved. She's still sitting at the table staring out the window, drinking her tea and smoking her cigarette.

"Mom, Mom, Mom! This man up there started cussin' at me. I didn't think he'd mind."

She smiles and says, "You mean Tom. Some of us call him 'Goddammit.' He's a nice guy, and he isn't mad at you. He has Tour...Tourite...Tourette Syndrome. It means something ain't firing right in his head and he cusses all the time."

I think about it a bit and say, "Well you and Pop cuss all the time. Is it like that?"

"No. Tom only knows cuss words and can't say anything else. He upsets the church-goin' folk with all that swearing, but he's a nice man."

Mom has a way of explaining things in a way I can understand.

"You'd best get to bed soon. We're getting up early and going to Granny's. It's time to do some planting."

Tractor Man, Rock Potato, and Sugarfoot

Sunday, March 30, 1975 – Six Years Old.
Messin' with Granny and a Big Man.

Potatoes, cut eyes, blankets, and lime.
Tractors, deep rows, and spring planting time.
Tree trunk arms. Excavator hands. Moving bricks in a pile.
Giant, tender Sugarfoot, with a Teddy Bear smile.

In the House of Wise, Sunday morning breakfast is usually a treat. Mom boils some eggs, wraps sausage around them, and bakes them. Like most things, they're overcooked. We're usually never in danger of getting sick from eating undercooked food except maybe that veal that still haunts me. Her fried eggs are always extra crunchy on the edges. Hamburgers are never pink in the middle and have a blackened crust on both sides. Tater tots are always charred and part of them sticks to the bottom of the baking pan as if melting together. Sometimes when Mom cooks sausage-wrapped eggs, the tops burn when she leaves them in the oven too long on broil. I like the charred parts. We eat and then ride over to Granny's in the Suburban.

Granny has a big white house with a porch facing Forrest Hill Road. We often sit outside on the porch swing in a couple of rocking chairs and do the typical Baptist thing and judge others who drive by. The preacher says we aren't supposed to judge anyone, yet all of us do it. We just say we don't, and we especially don't do it on Sundays. That's the Lord's Day to judge.

Sometimes Granny says, "That's so and so. He set fire to that field

50

in the back when Nixon was president." "Lawd, that girl always messes around with somebody else in back of the wood pile." "They found a moonshine still out back of his tobacco barn."

There's no shortage of gossip or judgment in Clarksville. For a while, I thought "Judgment Day" was every day of the week except Sunday. It's on this porch where we'd ask Granny to tell us stories about the Great Depression.

"Granny, how'd you get by then?"

"We didn't have much, but neither did a lot of other folks. Sometimes, we'd go down to the train station. We'd pick up pieces of coal and corn between the rocks. When they'd unload, sometimes a bag had a hole in it. We'd pick up the pieces and have some coal for the stove that night. It was enough. We got by. You had to get there early, though. Other people were doing the same thing. Some of the bigger boys would jump on the coal car and grab bigger pieces of coal before the train got to moving too fast."

Granny's expression was sad when she told these stories, but we wanted to hear them anyway. Like Mom, she just kept going and never complained about much.

Sometimes I'd ask, "Granny, tell us how you met Grandpa."

"Wheeeew honey. It was too much. There were three of them. Three men at once wanted to court me. There was one at the dinner table, one on the porch, and one in the parlor. They all knew each of them were there, too. One would say, 'Come here, Ruby,' and then the other would say, 'Nah, don't mind him, come over here.' They about ran me ragged." Granny would smile when she told this story.

Tash would usually say, "You must have been very pretty."

Granny modestly replies, "I was all right. But I tell you, they 'bout ran me out. I suppose Jimmy Lou was the nicest one and wasn't so bothersome." Her eyes always brightened up. We loved hearing this story on the front porch swing while she gently rocked in her faithful rocking chair. It made her happy.

**Granny Ruby sitting in the rocking chair
on her front porch telling her stories.**

The porch wraps around one side where there's a large chest-type deep freezer. It's nearly always full of vegetables, sausage, and a ham or two. Some of the posts holding up the porch roof aren't quite straight but are still termite-free. Granny's house has a tin roof that makes ping sounds during thunderstorms we'd hear some nights when we slept over. With fatter or faster falling raindrops, the pinging would keep us up until the storm dissipated.

The farm has a lake, a rock quarry, and old barns with cool rusty tools hanging on rusted nails. There are five fields scattered about where Granny grew crops. Large red and white oak trees shade the barns. In between the barns and trees, generations of old cars, and farm equipment are scattered and in various stages of decay. A rusted Model T, Ford Falcon, '57 Chevy and a tractor with an integrated saw blade provide days of entertainment. Nearly everything is slowly rusting away or is being consumed by vegetation. Sometimes we walk down the old tractor road to the lake and go fishing there for bluegill, bass, or catfish.

Granny's house on Forrest Hill Road with the wonky porch and chest freezer.

Granny's farm went all the way to the lake.

With the crisp sausage eggs still rumbling in my belly, we pull up and find my cousin Travis working on the old '49 Ford tractor. He's always working on that thing and somehow manages to get it going every time. Granny meets Mom as she steps out of the truck first. I never noticed before but Granny and Mom are about the same size except for Granny's girth. Granny often wears dresses that look like big floral-patterned gunny sacks with sleeves. She has thick glasses like the bottom of an RC Cola bottle. Those glasses kind of remind me of the old man on the Sanford and Son TV show. Cola bottle glasses or not, Granny's eyes are as sharp as a hawk. She can stand on the end of a vegetable row and see a half a dirt clog throwing distance away if I miss a weed in the tomato plants.

"Wheeeeeww! You missed one," she'd yell. How'd she know?

We aren't there long before Pop asks Granny, "Mrs. Yancey…"

Pop is cut off mid-sentence. "You can call me Ruby, Gary," Granny reminds him.

Granny has an affinity for Pop. A few years ago, when I was really small, Grandpa hit Granny. Pop jumped up, picked Grandpa up by the throat, lifted him off the floor, and slammed him against a wall.

With Grandpa's legs dangling like an opossum stuck in a trap, he said, "Don't you ever hit Mrs. Yancey again! If you do, I'll knock the B'Jesus out of you!"

After that, Pop could do no wrong with Granny. Grandpa would go in the other room when Pop was there. They never spoke much to each other after that.

"Ruby, you mind if I plug in the golf cart? We have a long day, and I wanna make sure it's charged."

Granny counters, "You don't have to. We charged it last night. How 'bout you go down to the potato barn and get the rest of the potatoes? We need to cut the eyes out, so we have something to plant."

After tossing a few empty buckets in the back, Pop and I take off in the golf cart. We head past the red oak where we made Brunswick stew last fall in a large kettle hanging from a ginormous branch. The potato barn is an old tobacco barn that made for a good root cellar. The trees around it have gotten so big that the barn is always in the shade. Inside on the floor are about a dozen of Granny's old quilts. Under them lies our task. In the fall, we gather the potatoes behind the tractor plow and carry them down to the barn in buckets. After spreading them out in a single layer, we cover them with lime and throw the blankets over them to keep them from freezing.

Planting comes a couple weeks before the last frost around the end of March. Pop and I sort through the good potatoes and chuck out the half-rotten ones. The buckets fully loaded, we drive back to Granny's farmhouse. Pop tells me to take the buckets of potatoes to Granny for her to clean and cut while he works with Travis on the tractor. The buckets are so heavy that I have to drag them. On the way to her back porch, I find a smooth, round river rock that looks like a potato, and I set it in the bucket.

"Granny, Granny, I have the potatoes. Can I eat one raw?"

She takes the bucket and quickly skins one for me with her paring knife. I eat the whole thing just like an apple. To me, raw potatoes are just about as good as cooked ones. After cutting out the eyes from some of the potatoes, she finds the rock I placed in there.

"Come here, Sugar." I walk over and look at her. "I know you put that rock in there. You wouldn't want me to dull my knife, would you?"

"No, ma'am."

She smiles and taps me on my butt as I go to witness the tractor-starting saga.

"What's wrong with it, Travis?"

"I don't know. Seems like it won't get no spark. Engine turns over okay."

The whole area smells like gas but nothing has caught fire yet. He moves some wires and uses the hand crank. It kicks back on him a couple of times. After saturating the air intake and our lungs with ether, he gets the grumpy gray beast started.

"Can I sit on the back while you change out the bush-hog for the plow?" I ask.

"Sa...sa...sa...sure, Maikel. Just hold on tight. Don't want you fallin' off."

Travis is younger than his brother Hank. He is kind of like an older version of me with freckles and reddish hair.

A while back, Mom told me, "Travis is all right. Sometimes his words don't come out right, but he's always helping out your Granny."

Travis and I get the plow hooked up, and he drives slowly to the field. The tractor sputters and the brakes don't really work, but we manage to plow the whole field and not kill anyone. By that time, Granny has all the potato eyes cut out and it's time to plant. Travis is afraid to turn off the tractor, since he knows he might not get it going again. By hand, we plant the eyes face up in the freshly plowed rows. When we finish, Travis and I get on the tractor again. We plow the black soil softly back over the freshly cut potatoes. It's fun riding on the tractor, but my six-year-old hands ache from the death grip I have on the fenders. I don't want to fall off and be turned into veal.

Pop drives us back home and right behind us pulls up a rusty red and white Chevy truck heavily drooping on the driver's side. The truck door opens and an enormous black man steps out, causing the driver's side of the truck to raise a couple inches. This man has large coveralls with a white t-shirt stained cement-gray. His arms are well-established tree-trunks, and his hands are like small excavators.

He has a big ole smile and says to Pop, "Come here, my little white boy."

Pop is a big man, too, at about 6'3" and 240 pounds. I have these specifications memorized because he brags about it so often. However, the man getting out of the truck is about a hotdog's length taller and two large sofa pillows bigger around. He gives Pop a big bear hug and lifts him off the ground with ease.

"Maikel and Tash, come here," Pop bellows. "This is Sugarfoot. He's one of the best brick layers around."

We shyly hide behind Pop's leg as we do with all strangers. Pop and Sugarfoot walk around to the back of the house, planning something.

"You two go inside and draw up a bath," Mom calls. "You have school tomorrow."

Before going in, I walk around the corner of the house and scan the closest hill in the cow pasture. The bull is nowhere in sight.

Granny's '49 Ford tractor. Travis's perpetual project.
(Artist Judie Battle)

Cornrows and Swing Jumping

Monday, March 31, 1975 – Six Years Old. First Grade.
Meeting Demetris.

Monday morning comes quick. Right at 8:05 A.M., the school bus pulls up in front of the house. This bus is different than the one that came to our old house. The door opens. Tash and I climb the steps and scan for open seats. The front third of the bus is the safe zone where most of the younger white kids and black kids sit. The middle part are the white kids coming out of their shell and can have a touch of cheekiness. The back part includes white kids with convict potential. They have a mean-spirited look about them. Also back there are the burly farmer boys of all colors who look as if they could calf-rope you, pin you down, and tie all your limbs together with one hand behind their backs. The farmers don't have to fret about the convicts since they can defend themselves. I prefer to sit up front. Most times, I'm able to find a seat all by myself, but not today. I look for someone who won't beat me up and see Demetris. Plus, I'm closer to the bus driver, who is always on the lookout for bullies hitting someone.

"Are you saving this seat?" I ask.

"Naw. You can sit here if you like."

I sit down beside her, but not too close.

I settle in and stare at her hair for a moment. "Demetris, you sure have a lot of braids and rubber bands in your hair. Does it hurt?"

"Not so much now. It hurt like hell when Mom was pulling it, though. I like my hair with cornrows."

I figure I'd like to have rubber bands in my hair, too. It would be handy for quick access to ammunition to shoot things with.

"Maikel, y'all must be rich."

"Why do you say that?"

"'Cause y'all live in a brick house."

I never thought of that. We do have a lion-head door knocker now! But then again, Mr. Cash saved us the discount tables. I heard Mom and Pop whispering about money last night.

"Y'all have two cars, too."

I nod. We don't chat much after that because girls make me nervous. I get all fidgety and red in the face.

At school, I walk straight to Mrs. Hester's classroom.

"Maikel, you forgot your lunch and milk money again. Your Mom called and told me to give this to you."

Out of her brown coin purse, she hands me a quarter for morning milk and two more quarters for lunch. I hide my fingernails as best I can since there is still lawnmower grease in them.

"Thank you, Ma'am."

I don't see how Mom could have called, since the phone is not hooked up yet. Mrs. Hester gives me 75 cents at least a couple times a week. She does this for a couple of other kids, too. Sure seems like I'm not the only one who forgets their lunch money. I have to put the quarters in my left pocket because the right one has a hole.

Mrs. Hester's first grade class.
Bottom (L-R), Maikel Wise (plaid), David Buchanan (#51).

I watch the clock slowly turn until morning recess. I'm thrilled to stop practicing my cursive letters. I walk fast to the doors on the playground side of the school, then run full speed once I'm outside. I head straight for the swings. David and Jay are already there.

Trying to be cool I say, "Hey. What's goin' on, dudes?"

Jay says, "David has the record for jumping distance off the swing. See that leaf? That's the record."

As Jay is telling me this, they both swing higher and higher.

David goes so high that the chains in the swing lose tension. He freefalls vertically, losing a little momentum. Jay is the first to jump. Just before the swing reaches the forward peak, he jumps out of the swing, becoming airborne. His arms and legs flail in the air as he strives to land in a cat-like fashion. Ungracefully landing on all fours, tumbling and rolling to a stop, he comes up short by two feet. A few seconds later, David is swinging toward us and lets go with near perfect timing. His black Converse Chucks stick the landing three feet farther with catlike grace.

"Wow that is so cool. Can I try?" Territorially, David goes back to "his" swing and begins pumping up again. Jay lets me use his swing.

I don't want them to make fun of me, so I swing so high that the chain loosens like David's first attempt. Focusing on the leaf, I let go and make it all of half the distance. My iron-on knee patches now have a green-grass hue.

My feet are smarting like several bee stings all at once. I can't figure out how David and Jay can jump so far. How did they do it? It must be them rich-people shoes. My hand-me-down Hush Puppy shoes just aren't cutting it.

Jay reassures me. "It's okay, Maikel. The first time I tried, it was ugly. The scabs on my face and hands took a long time to heal."

Wanting more adventures, I ask David, "What are you guys doing this weekend?"

"Nothing, really. We might do some bike jumping. Come over Saturday afternoon and we'll make some ramps. I have to help Dad and Grandpa on Saturday morning. We should be done by noon."

We have a plan. David's Pa is mayor and works at John H. Kerr Dam, but he also does TV repair work, too. Like many folks in Clarksville, Mr. Buchanan works multiple jobs.

Jumping and Crawdads

Saturday, April 5, 1975 – Six Years Old. First Grade.

Always a greener pasture. Some bikes are better.
Sometimes I fall over. Sometimes I go higher.
Dirty shoes, crawdads pinching, Mom crying.
Tomorrow's a new day. Don't quit. Keep on trying.

Saturday arrives and there's no watching Roadrunner cartoons today. I can't wait to go bike riding. Usually, I only go bike riding with my sister. We never really jump much except off curbs. I still ride the same bike as when I was three years old. It's a tad small but works. My tires are solid with no tubes, so I never need any air in them. As I ride around the yard, Pop notices how awkward it is for me to pedal. I feel like a clown on a small bike in Ringling Brothers and Barnum and Bailey Circus going around in circles.

"Son, we have to get you a new bike soon. That one is getting too small."

Heartened by the prospect of a new bike, I head toward the old tobacco road. There is a break in the barbed-wire fence behind Sam and Gladys's house. Mom must have talked to them because Sam told me to use it to access the road. It's less scary than going by the openin' near Goddammit's house and getting cursed at. It's only about 10 o'clock and too early to see Jay and David. I ride over to Edgewood anyway. When I arrive, I don't see any cars in the driveway, so I figure they mustn't be back yet.

Edgewood has mostly flat roads with small hills. Traffic in

Edgewood is slower than Shiney Rock and the cars are different, too. There are a few Cadillacs and Mercedes in front of some of the houses. These are fancy folks' cars. Their yards are a bit less weedy and cluttered than what I'm used to. Most of the houses don't have cracked or chipping paint. Many places have paved driveways.

As I'm riding around, I notice a boy about my age playing basketball a couple blocks to the east of David's house. I don't recognize him. Right across from his house is the red dirt open area with real dirt-made jumps of all sizes. It looks as if somebody shoveled out all the dirt from under their house and made big piles. I can tell this place gets a lot of use, too, with all the bicycle and motorcycle tire tracks. There are a few bricks, cinder blocks, and boards lying about that are good ramp construction materials. I follow a well-worn path and start riding the roller coasters of red dirt mounds. The largest hill is nearly as tall as Pop, so I don't know if I can reach the peak. I pedal as fast as I can and almost make it to the top. I come to an abrupt halt. Gravity wins. I have coaster brakes and push hard to keep me from sliding backward. It's too late. I start sliding and tumbling backward with my bike, but I never let go of the handlebars. My whole right side is covered in red dirt from my face to my shoes. I think Mom might be mad at me for getting my shoes dirty. They used to be white but are now a dingy red. And my pants now have two knees shredded.

The boy playing basketball runs over.

"That was some wipe-out. Are you okay?"

"I'm okay. I guess I wasn't going fast enough. Can you climb that hill?"

"Yep, I sure can. But you need a good start to make it. I usually back up on the other facing hill to get my speed up. My name is Raymond. What's yours?"

"Maikel. I'm supposed to meet Jay and David to make some ramps later. Do you know 'em?"

"I sure do. We ride around here a lot after school."

"Thanks, Raymond. I'd best get going."

I humbly ride over to the Buchanan's place, smacking the dirt-stained areas of my clothing along the way. I'm still a little early and sit on the steps of David's house nursing my pride.

Shortly, a lady walks out. "Hello, can I help you?"

"I'm waiting for David. He said we could go biking together when he gets done helping his Pa."

"What's your name, young man?"

"Maikel Wise, ma'am. I live over on Shiney Rock Road."

"Oh, you're Jimmy Lou and Ruby's grandson. Your mom works at The Greenhouse. Well, Maikel, you got all dirty. Would you like to come in and get cleaned up? I'll make you a bologna sandwich and some tea."

"Yes, ma'am."

Mrs. Buchanan points me to the bathroom, and I wash up at the sink. I got to thinking. She knows my grandma and Mom, so she knows who to go to if I do something wrong. That means I have to be extra careful. I quickly wash up and then dry my hands and face. These folks have two sets of towels. There's a plain towel and a fancy, daisy-patterned towel. I accidentally grab the close, fancy, daisy-patterned towel and contaminate it. Uh-oh. Apparently, I didn't wash thoroughly enough. I turn the ruined towel inside out to make sure only the clean part is showing. So much for being extra careful.

Mrs. Buchanan makes one of the cleanest bologna sandwiches I've ever eaten. She doesn't burn it black in the frying pan. She heats it up in something called a Radarange. I ain't never seen nothing like it. It's a shiny, silvery box with a light that makes a buzzy noise. When she pulls the bologna out, the decadent round meat is bubbled up in the middle and has no burnt black edges. She gives me a big glass of iced tea. The glass is so clean and has no dried water spots unlike our mineral-enriched, water-stained glasses. *Ewwww!* I try to hide my face with the bland tea that is missing at least two cups of sugar. With Mr. Buchanan working three jobs, surely they can afford more sugar. About halfway through, I hear the gravel crunching under tires as David and his Pa pull up. Mrs. Buchanan quickly radars more sandwiches. After David washes up, he wolfs down his first sandwich before I can finish mine. With David being the last one to wash his hands, maybe I won't get blamed for the dirty towel.

"Let's go," he shouts, shoving the last bits of his second sandwich into his mouth.

David hops on his fancy BMX bike. His bike has aluminum mag wheels that don't need truing up if you crash or hit a log. It's all scratched up, but it's black and fast lookin'. Embarrassed, I trail behind him, struggling to keep up with my miniature-circus-looking Western Auto bike. My two pedal strokes are equal to his one. Jay is already out there riding in his paved driveway under his own basketball hoop. We cruised to the dirt field over by Raymond's house where I just was earlier. When we get there, I watch David and Jay easily make it up and over the adult-sized hill.

I have to ask, "Wow, how did you do that?"

Reassuringly, Jay says, "Just peddle like you stole penny-candy from the Winn-Dixie, Maikel."

I ride up the facing hill to gain speed, then ride through so hard I even get a little air. With ease, I make it to the top of the hill and coast down the backside. I start to feel a little mo' sure of myself. We keep riding over it for more than an hour, pushing our limits until each one of us crashes at least once and have multiple bloody wounds.

"David, have you been to the cow pasture next to your house?"

"I sure have. There's a creek that comes down from the sleddin' hill. Lots of crawdads in that creek."

I reply, "What's a crawdad? I've heard of a crawdad before but ain't ever seen one."

Eagerly, David says, "Let's go and I'll show you."

Jay heads home to do his chores. David and I go looking for crawdads. We ride back to David's house, turn left, and cross the railroad tracks. We slowly ride down the same trail I took to get to his place. We weave through the wet-leaved forest floor down to the creek that presoaked my shoe earlier.

"Maikel, let's leave our bikes here and head up the creek toward the cow pasture fence. There are more rocks on the other side of the fence. That's where the crawdad's like to hide."

We walk up the side of the creek, flanking the border until we get to the edge of the cow pasture. David is right. There are a lot of rocks here. We squat down next to a pile of rocks and David sees one right away.

He points. "See there? That's a small one. They kinda look like the baby lobsters you see on TV but just ain't as red."

Over the next half hour, David catches about five while I manage to catch one. I don't tell him that the only reason I caught it was because it pinched me on the loose skin on the inside of my thumb.

"David, I'd better get going. My Mom might be wondering where I've gone to."

"Okay. See you at school, Maikel."

I learned a lot today. I climbed a hill, got some air, and caught a crawdad.

I alternate pushing and riding my bike home, but I'm a little scared to go into the house. Mom might see my shoes. I figure if I go squirt them off with the water hose, they might look cleaner. It's okay if they're wet, since it'll be like they were just pulled out of the washer at the laundromat. After getting some of the dirt sprayed off, I quietly walk in the front door. Mom is crying at the kitchen table and is only comforted by her tea and cigarette.

"What's wrong, Mom?" My heart drops.

"Pop lost his job. It's this Iranian Oil Crisis and cars just aren't selling at the dealership. They had to let a few people go," she said, crying. "I still have a job at The Greenhouse. I can try to get a job at The Big Orange on weekends. Pop is upset, and he went to Mama Johnson's for a couple of beers."

I don't like to see Mom crying. The only other time I'd seen her crying this bad was when they were fighting. She is all of five feet nothing, but she would stand up to Pop and sometimes he'd back down. I walk over to Mom and give her a hug before I realize I've just made a mistake. Mom sees my wet shoes, and in an instant her focus changes.

"Go take those shoes off. Rinse them and the bottom of your pants in the sink. Put your shoes in front of the fan and dry them out before tomorrow."

Mom is sad, but not sad enough to not get after me for tracking mud into the house. When bedtime comes, I don't sleep well because I know I'm not getting a new bike anytime soon.

Occoneechee, Oak Tree Ass-Whippin', and Eight Cinder Blocks

Sunday, April 6, 1975 – Six Years Old. Vine Swinging and Travis's Bad Decision.

A spindly twisty rope within a sheath of bark.
Hanging from the canopy to the forest floor.
Oak woods tainted with a history that is dark.
We hold on. Laughing as we swing back and forth.

Robins announce morning outside my window. With all the recent rain, the worms are everywhere on top of the ground. The robins are as happy as Possum Tillerson, the town drunk, on payday at the liquor store. I peer out the window and see the well-fed birds perching on the scraggly-taped and shoestring-tied maple tree Mom planted what seems like forever ago. They're happy to have a place to rest after pulling worms out of the ground.

I hear Mom in the kitchen cooking Sunday morning breakfast. Mom must have borrowed some money for this grand splurge. Mmm, the butter Mom put on the lard-filled biscuits goes down extra smooth. Sausage links, pancakes, and crispy-edged fried eggs round out the feast.

"Get dressed. We're going to Occoneechee," Pop says in his deep voice.

Pop's voice would go deeper depending on the amount of alcohol, which song was on the 8-track, the time of day, or the seriousness of the conversation, but Pop's deepest voice would be singing the song

I Love to Lay You Down. We all get into the Suburban and ride across town to walk the Plantation Trail.

Occoneechee was named after the Indigenous Americans. There's a lot of remains of the more recent plantations. The Plantation Trail has vines, dark woods, and old chimneys in the middle part. In the summer, it's full of lightning bugs, too. Sometimes when there is a drought and the lake is low, I go to the shorelines and find Occoneechee arrowheads. On Sunday morning walks, though, Tash and I have one purpose. We nearly run to the hill with all the dangling vines. We arrive early at the vine spot and can hardly wait for Pop and Mom to catch up. Pop takes his hatchet and cuts loose a small vine from the ground. He pulls on it and it nearly drops on top of his head.

"That one ain't good enough."

He finds another and it holds. Tash and I grab ahold of it as he pulls us uphill over his head.

"Now hold on tight," he says in his less-deep voice.

Tash and I go swinging downhill at ten feet over the ground before swinging back. We go and go until the vine slips and drags too much on the ground to make it fun anymore.

Mom unexpectedly says, "Let's go to the Penguin for some ice cream."

I thought we were broke with Pop being laid off, but I ain't saying no to ice cream. We slowly drive over the one-mile bridge. We continue west on Highway 58, making it past the one stoplight in town while it's still green. Policeman Hogan is parked by Vaughan's waiting for speeders, including my cousin Hank, to race by. It's just before church gets out, so there aren't many cars on the road yet. At the Penguin, Tash and I ask for a soft serve cone.

Mom says, "I'll be right back," as she walks away.

Mom walks into The Big Orange, which is next to the Penguin.

The Big Orange is a convenience store with a couple of gas pumps. Nobody likes getting gas here and often blame their car problems on The Big Orange's "bad gas." Plus, they only have leaded gas and no Hi-test (Premium Higher-Octane Gas). The only good thing about The Big Orange is that they have a decent candy aisle with the Bazooka bubble gum that I like.

Mom comes back with some papers and happily comments, "They said they still need someone to work on the weekends. All I need to do is fill out this form and they'll hire me."

I can tell Pop is embarrassed that Mom has two jobs, and he has none. He doesn't say anything. His eyes become cold, and face turns redder. It doesn't matter, because my ice cream is melting, and I need to sop it up with my tongue. I'm struggling to find the balance between eating as fast as I can and not getting a headache. A bit of ice cream drips down and hits my still red dirt-stained shoe.

Mom looks down at my ratty shoes. They're wet again from our recent Occoneechee hike. A new hole is starting to form in my right shoe by my big toe. When I wiggle my toe, the hole expands.

"When we get home, let's go up to Leggett's in South Boston and get you a new pair of shoes. When I start workin' another job, I won't have time."

Cones finished and Pop dropped off, Tash and I climb into the back seat of the Pinto and ride to South Boston, where we pull into the Leggett's parking lot. Mom takes my shoes off my feet and heads into the store. After a while, she comes back out with a new pair that happen to be another size larger.

"Those shoes were defective, so I got a new pair for free."

Seems like my shoes are always defective when they're worn out or don't fit anymore. Mom has told that "defective" story to a different person in Leggett's each time, too.

With my new shoes a tad too big and tied snug, Mom drives back to Granny's instead of going home. Pop's already there with Travis.

"C'mon on, Booger, we're goin' to cut some wood."

"What for, Pop? We don't need any more this year."

Pop's voice deepens. "It ain't for us. It's for Sugarfoot. If we get him ten loads of wood, he'll trade us for working on the house."

I have no idea what he's talking about, but I never backtalk to Pop. Recently, he's started calling me "Booger" because my nose is always running. It isn't mean or nothing, but just my nickname. He mostly calls me "Booger" when he wants me to do something or needs something brought to him. Travis, Pop, and I drive up a couple of barns over to the west of the potato barn.

"See those trees? We can cu...cu...cu...cut those down," Travis stutters.

Anything with a motor, Travis has challenges. Like the tractor, it takes forever to get the chainsaw started. After the surrounding woods are saturated with gas and oil fumes, he gets the chainsaw going. Travis starts cutting.

"Move over there. Out of the way," Pop demands of me.

As soon as Travis makes a cut about a third of the way in the base of the tree, the chainsaw binds up. Travis and Pop get a wedge and sledgehammer and start pounding. When the gap in the fresh-cut tree widens, Travis starts cutting again. Pop backs up and stands beside me.

"Now pay attention, Booger. The tree should fall away from us, but if it don't, just step over there by that holly bush."

The oak starts to crack as Travis keeps cutting.

Pop yells at Travis, "It's falling!"

Travis looks up to see the tree is not falling the way he's expecting. Confused that the tree isn't conforming to his will, he starts running.

It doesn't make any sense. Travis is running the same way the tree is falling. I've never seen Travis run so fast. He's running like he overslept and missed the train to the Second Coming. That oak is at least twice as high as Granny's house at the top. It's about to give Travis a real ass-whippin'.

The granddaddy of all switches is going to smack Travis on the bottom, back, and head as if he misbehaved something fierce. Travis knows he's going to get hit by the falling tree. Suddenly, he gives one final sprint. I think, *Whew, Travis! Get goin' before the train leaves the station!*

It's too late. The top branches grab him by the shoulders and push him down into the decaying oak leaves. The thud of him hitting the ground is amplified as the main trunk hits the ground behind him at the same time. I've never seen anyone get knocked down by a tree before. I've fallen out of a tree, but it's nothing like this. We run up to Travis, who's tangled in branches and lying on the ground. He is as white as a puffy cotton summer cloud. The main trunk just missed him. The branches are spread around him. He's all cut up, nervous, and sweaty.

"I thought that tree wo...wo...wo...wouldn't fall that way. We... we...we...we'd better get this thing cut up and loaded."

That oak tree had showed him no mercy. Travis got an oak tree ass-whippin'. I think I prefer switches.

We stay at Granny's for a few more hours, cutting and stacking wood. When Mom, Pop, Tash, and I get back home, we find Sugarfoot in our driveway. He's unloading cinder blocks from his trailer and carrying them around the back of the house. With each hand, Sugarfoot has four cinder blocks. Eight cinder blocks total!

"You want to help me out, Little Man?" Sugarfoot asks me.

He has a giant Teddy-bear kindness. I like how he calls me "Little

Man" instead of "Booger." Pop and I help him unload. Even Pop can only carry two at a time in each hand. I manage only one cinder block at a time. When Pop doesn't think anyone is looking, he tries to pick up four with one hand but can't hold on. I remember shaking Sugarfoot's hand. His skin feels like that double-thick cardboard we get from behind Arrington's Appliance Store. That cardboard is good and thick, really tough for making forts or playing tank tread. If Santa Claus wore coveralls and had short black hair, he'd be Sugarfoot. We finish up just before dark and Sugarfoot leaves. Mom yells, "Dinner is ready."

"We are having breakfast," she announces.

Wow. We are living high-on-the-hog for having two breakfasts in one day.

It looks like it snowed in the kitchen. Flour is on the counter, floor, and smudged on her forehead. Every pan in the kitchen is filled with eggs, ham, patty sausage, and lard biscuits with melted butter. While we were over at Granny's, Mom and Tash brought some food from her freezer and back porch where Granny kept the Smithfield hams hanging. Mom's been busy while we were moving the cinder blocks.

"Now don't go and eat all the biscuits. I'm going to take some to Mr. Burnette. He'd said he'd like to try them. If they're good enough, we can sell them at the auction next Saturday. We may make enough to pay the electric bill before they shut it off."

I went to bed that night with a great combination of meat, lard, and butter in my belly. I thought back to when Demetris said, "Y'all must be rich." She may be right.

All week, David, Jay, and I keep breaking records on swing jumping at school. David always beats us in the end, but it's still fun seeing if we can beat him, if only once and temporarily. Friday comes and the bell rings for recess. Jimmy Sydnor walks out the door with me.

"Hey, Maikel, you want to race?"

"No, Jimmy. You're the fastest one in school. I heard you even beat some second and third graders."

"Come on, man, I'll give you a head start. Just to the merry-go-round."

"All right, Jimmy. Just don't beat me too bad."

"Go!" Jimmy yells.

I take off, and Jimmy quickly makes up the distance and passes me. Suddenly, I see his foot disappear into a groundhog hole. He goes down to the ground. No excuses, I'm going to beat him. Amazingly, I see him roll twice on the ground and get right on his feet at full stride. He flies by me again. Even when he falls, I can't beat Jimmy.

"That's okay," I tell myself.

I knew the outcome before I started. No one can beat Jimmy, and that's just the way it is. It works out, though. I make it to the swings before the other kids do. The stick is still on the ground from yesterday's record. On my second attempt, I beat David's mark. A new record which holds until David gets there moments later. David miraculously makes it three feet farther. Unbelievable!

After getting beat again and trying to focus on something else, I ask, "David, what are you doing this weekend?"

"I have to help my dad and grandpa at his TV repair place again, but nothing after that," David responds in a miserable voice.

It sure seems as if David is tortured by working at the TV repair place and dreads it each Saturday.

"Okey dokey. I'll come by Sunday and we'll go exploring in the woods," I say in a more cheerful tone.

Hospice Care (Day Three, Early Morning)

Friday, February 23, 2007 – Telling Betsy about What Happened with Pop.

Betsy walks over early in the morning and brings us some Hardee's breakfast meals. While eating our cholesterol-infused Hardee's biscuits, I say to Susan, "I think Betsy likes all this interaction."

Betsy points at the biscuit crumbs on the front of my t-shirt. "What's that, Maikel?"

"Betsy," I say, "I think you like all this company and interaction."

"Well, I certainly miss seeing y'all. It's fun visiting and laughing with you. I just wish your mama would get better."

Tash interjects though a mouthful of hash rounds, "Me, too."

Mom is soundly sleeping when Betsy blurts out, "I heard your dad passed away a few months ago. I heard he got remarried, but it didn't work out. Your mama said you two had a fallin' out. I don't mean to be so nosy."

I look right at Betsy. "Of course you mean to be nosy. That's another reason you sit in the back pews in the church, ain't it? That's where the sinners sit. You're Betsy, and we love you. I'll tell you what happened."

Leaning forward, Betsy is intent on hearing this story.

I start a summarized version. "I was still living in Utah when Pop moved in with me. It was the fall of '98. You know he wasn't able to live on his own. We got along for the first nine months or so. It was difficult because he was always calling me at work asking for more Coca-Cola, chips, chili, or something. He would call me up to five

75

times a day. Pop was high maintenance and spoiled by his second ex-wife. She served his every want until she couldn't take it anymore.

"While Pop was living with me, I started dating someone. Dates were sparse for me for a while, living as a non-Mormon in Utah. When I started dating this woman, I slowed down going to the store for Pop, and he didn't like it. He was jealous. One night, she came over for dinner. This was BS: Before Susan. My lady friend decided to spend the night. My bedroom was upstairs. Pop's bedroom was on the first floor, so we didn't bother him.

"Pop was still a member of the Mormon Church and with a high priest ranking. He called the Mormon bishop in the Ward where we lived. Just so you know, a Mormon bishop is the equivalent of a Baptist preacher. One Saturday, I came home from a bike ride and found the bishop and other high priests waiting for me in the living room. They asked me to sit down with them to talk. This 'talk' was really an 'intervention.' They said Pop was uncomfortable with another woman sleeping over."

Feistily Betsy says, "I don't see how it was any business of theirs."

"Exactly, Betsy. I was boiling mad with the invasion of my privacy. The bishop started to say something, and I cut him off. I said to him, 'This is your religion, not mine. I'm not Mormon. The only reason Pop is mad is that no one slept with him. I will not tolerate you judging or imposing your will and religion on me!' I was nearly shaking at this point. I looked over at Pop. 'Why don't you tell them, Pop? Tell them how you committed adultery. It's okay if you do it, but no one else can.'

"Betsy, I was super infuriated. At the time, I didn't know that this was the beginning of the end of my relationship with Pop."

Betsy looks at me with the hook of curiosity firmly seated.

"Oh, Betsy, the story doesn't end there."

As I'm telling Betsy this story, I find that I'm getting worked up again. "The next day, I had to drive Pop to a doctor's appointment. Then he told me that he wanted to go to an assisted living facility now that I wasn't serving his every need anymore. For two weeks, I researched and drove him all over the Ogden area. I finally got him into a top-rated facility. I'd visit him once and sometimes twice a week but stopped shopping for him every single day. He didn't like it and told me so every chance he got.

"Then Pop decided he wanted a cell phone. He nagged and nagged. Cricket phone this and Cricket phone that. I finally got him a damn Cricket phone. The first month's bill was extremely high, over $600! That was almost a week's salary for me. He kept exceeding his allotted minutes and leaving his phone on roaming, so I told him, 'I'm cancelling the cell phone. I can't pay for this.' He didn't like it. He was furious.

"He said, 'It's my phone.'

"I promptly responded, 'It's in my name. You can get one and pay for it yourself.'

"Since the assisted living facility took most of his monthly income, he couldn't afford a cell phone with a bill that high. I cancelled the cell phone.

"In about a month, Pop started begging to come back and live with me again. I couldn't do it. He would manipulate me every day. Often he would use his blindness and paralysis to get things from people. On occasion, he used his condition to sue or threaten to sue people. Word got around town, and even some doctors wouldn't see him anymore. Some people felt sorry for him. The 'feel sorry for him people' were the ones he exploited. He made the choice to drink two six packs and drive the day of his fateful accident.

"Anyway, one day he calls me up. 'This is Gary Wise. You are no longer my son. I'm moving in with my stepsister in Oklahoma, and I don't need you anymore.' This was followed by, 'I can't think of any way a son could disappoint a father more than you have.'" The words are seared into my brain.

"Over the next couple of months, Pop would call me in a drunken stupor, numerous times a week. He left spiteful messages saying I'm not his son. I stopped answering the phone.

"Then one day, I got a message. 'Booger. I'm sorry. I didn't mean those things. Can I please come back and live with you?' Torn inside, I cried, and I almost gave in, but then remembered how he'd manipulated me, hurt me, and disowned me.

"I got a call from Utah Social Services. They told me they had Pop and wanted me to pick him up at the airport. I refused. I told them he'd disowned me, so they needed to make another plan. I was not his son. They called back a few times, but I ignored them and deleted their messages.

"Eventually, Pop got one of his cousins to set him up at a halfway house in Ogden on Wall Street. Come to find out, his stepsister in Oklahoma was an opioid addict and was taking all his money and pain medication. Pop's brother Jim and his sister Julie wouldn't take care of him, either. He'd already burnt those bridges to the ground. Pop repeatedly bounced around from halfway house to assisted living. In July of 2006, Pop died of a heart attack in a halfway house. Alone."

Betsy looks astonished. "That's too bad about your pop. He didn't seem all that bad when y'all was young. I didn't think much of him sleepwalking naked down the road, but he couldn't help it. I never seen him much after his car accident. Nobody should die alone."

"Maybe so, Betsy, but he hurt me when he left us as kids and later, when he disowned me. I couldn't set myself up again."

We sit in silence.

Tash interrupts the quiet. "No need to let those biscuits get cold."

Betsy hands each of us another greasy bacon, egg, and cheese biscuit.

Susan smiles and says, "Y'all better eat fast before Mama Wise wakes up. She's gonna want a bite."

Biscuits for Electricity

Sunday, April 13, 1975 – Creative Income.

A mixture of lard, butter, and flour.
Baked Southern delights. To sell. For power.

Mom wakes up at 4:00 A.M. and starts cooking. I can smell the eggs, ham, bacon, and sausage sizzlin'. Tash and I come to the kitchen, hypnotized by the stomach gods of Southern food. An empty can of Staghorn Chili on the stovetop is now overflowing with ham, bacon, and sausage grease. We've never filled up a whole can before.

"Mom, I thought you said that you're cooking food for the auction next weekend?" Tash asks.

"We might do that, too. Mr. Burnette liked the biscuits so much that he asked if we could make them for today's auction, too."

If that kitchen were a giant rabbit trap, we would have walked in willingly and allowed ourselves to be snared.

"Tash and Maikel, go down to the basement and get all the Styrofoam coolers," Mom commands.

In the depths of the basement, we have a collection of Styrofoam coolers in various degrees of functionality. Some have missing lids. Some have cracks down the side from being mishandled. Two of the Styrofoam minnow buckets have a bad smell of fish. I even see a few dead minnows in the bottom, all dried up from our last fishing adventure. We take the coolers outside and spray them off. At least some of the fish smell washes away. Mom lines each container with a towel. She uses duct tape to keep the other damaged Styrofoam containers from completely cracking and falling apart. There must have been over one hundred biscuits of salty, buttery delights. We can't even get the lids on some of the containers. I carried them out to the Suburban, plotting how I can down two of them before anyone notices. We all pile in and head to South Boston to the auction, enveloped in heavy Southern-food fumes.

This particular auction is in a warehouse that has a strong smell of tobacco leaves, but tobacco isn't being sold today. It ain't tobacco season yet. Most of the warehouse's wood siding inside and outside is weathered gray. With all the antique furniture laid out, it looks like an estate sale. Mr. Burnette walks up to us and says we can set up under an oak tree by the sidewalk. He appears to be one of them rich folks who shops at Hite's clothing store in town. Wearing a Polo shirt with khaki-tan pants, I'm bettin' his driveway is paved. Word around town is that he's one of the best auctioneers in these parts and won some awards for it.

In a fast-paced, clear auctioneer's voice, Mr. Burnette asks, "How much for one of your biscuits and what kind do you have?"

Mom smiles. "Fifty cents. We have sausage, ham, and bacon."

He takes one and hands Pop a twenty-dollar bill. Seems like he should've handed the money to Mom, since she did all the work.

"Thanks. Keep the change."

Mr. Burnette takes a bite. He gets ready to say something, but then shovels in a bigger bite. I think he wanted a confirmation bite before complementing Mom. "That's gooddddddd."

I can't tell if Mr. Burnette sounds like *Andy Griffith* or the other way around. Word gets around about Mom's biscuits and we nearly sell out.

"We made over sixty-one dollars. It's just enough to pay the electric bill," Mom says excitedly to Tash and me.

Pop is off in the crowd in a maze of worldly sentimental treasures being sold likely due to someone passing away. I soon see Pop walk up to Mac and another man. This other man is portly, as if he partook of more than one biscuit each day for the last year. I see them shake hands, and Pop walks back over to us with a grin.

Pop proudly announces, "Good news. I just got a mechanic job at Harold Moore's Gas Station. He's short a mechanic, and someone to fix tires. I start Monday."

With a little less cholesterol-tainted luggage, we load up and finish off the remaining biscuits on the drizzly drive back home. It is supposed to rain on and off for the entire week, and I grimly accept that this weather could affect my biking plans.

Mr. Mac Burnette the auctioneer.
(Photo from Deborah Newton,
Mecklenburg Sun Newspaper)

Crawdads, Salamanders, and the Old Sudan Road

Sunday, April 20, 1975 – Six Years Old.
Avoiding Poison and Driving.

Just over the fence towards the creek. It ain't too far.
Crawdad pinches, backing up into the Mason jar.
I can barely see the road. I push hard on the brakes.
It's coming up fast. We call it Buggs Island Lake.

A soaking wet week goes by, and I call David when he gets back from church.

"David, what do you want to do today? It's as muddy as the bottom of a filled-up outhouse."

David hesitates, then says, "Let's go to the cow pasture behind your place and catch critters in the creek. I'll come by in a few."

I'm scared, but don't want David to know how scared I am. "You know there's a bull back there, don't you?"

"We'll be all right, Maikel. I'll show you how to tame, or better yet, rile up the beast."

David shows up thirty minutes later. We slosh down to the fence at the bottom of our field.

"I don't see him nowhere. Where do you reckon' he is?" I ask in a quavering voice as I scan for the bull.

"Let's stay close to the fence line so we can hop over to safety," David says confidently.

We follow the fence line to the right and turn left at the corner.

Underneath the cedar limbs adjacent to the fence, the grass is drier, and we continue uphill. We crest the hill, and there below us, we see him. He looks up annoyed as we try to hide in the shadows of the overhanging cedars. The bull is right next to the creek, exactly where we want to be.

We edge closer. Suddenly, the beast snorts and tosses his head. He stomps one of his hooves.

"David, if he comes chargin', we need to hop this fence fast. Be ready."

We creep slowly toward him. He snorts again. He's off and charging fast.

"Quick! Go," one of us yells.

With his catlike reflexes, David gets over the fence first. Almost pushing him out of my way, I'm right behind him. We didn't plan properly, so we land in a two-yardstick high of pile of honeysuckle vines. Our legs can't even touch the ground. We're stuck. With dangling feet to attract a predator, the bull skids to a halt. The beast turns and is determined to push through the fence. His large, flaring nostrils make contact with the shiny wire. *ZAP!* With his hooves planted in a well-grounded, water-saturated cow patty earth, several thousands of volts burn his nostrils. Even so, notice the wire bending toward us. The bull pulls back and raises his head. He lets out a loud snort. I watch a moist cow booger arch skyward. As it reaches its pinnacle, the large gooey mass drops. Cow goober lands on David's cheek.

I lose it and start laughing. My laugh is contagious, and David starts cracking up, too. We're stuck and can't easily move. The bull loses interest and heads away. David and I squirm our way out of the thicket and continue to our next adventure at the creek.

The creek is surprisingly clear after the rain. We slip along the muddy banks up the creek to a spot where there are a few rocks and sticks at the water's edge.

"David, I haven't caught any crawdads since the last time in the other cow pasture by your place."

David responds, "Remember to watch those claws. Once they grab hold, they don't wanna let go."

"My granny says the same thing about turtles. 'If that turtle gets ahold of you, he won't let go until he hears thunder.'"

We both chuckle and then spend endless hours perfecting the art of catching crawdads. I discover that if I slowly put a hand in the water behind them, I can take a stick and poke them in the face. Once provoked or pro-poked, they back up into my hand nearly every time. David finds a partially broken old Mason jar next to the creek. Seems odd for a Mason jar to be lying around here. Could be a moonshine still nearby. When we use the Mason jar, the crawdads aren't scared as much when we put it behind them. Plus, the claws won't pinch us. That is, until after we pull it out of the jar. I lift a rock and grab some type of yellow-black salamander under it. David comes over to inspect it.

"You know their skin is poisonous, don't you?" David says in a serious tone.

"David, are you messin' with me?"

"Nope. That's what my grandpa says. You better rub some mud and sand on your hands before you die."

I don't know if he's telling the truth or not. I rub the slime off and hope I'm not going to die today. It's time to go, and David walks back with me to our field. We split and he risks going by Goddammit's house. Safer, I walk up the right by the sweetgum tree.

In the background, I hear "Goddammit!"

Concerned for David, I step up on the side rail of Mom's trailer,

Littl' Joe, to get a better view of the flaming arrows of blasphemy being shot. "Goddammit! Goddammit!" is shouted toward David as he runs back home.

I don't see Mom's Pinto in the driveway. Tash is sitting on the front porch.

"Tash, where's Mom?"

"She went to The Big Orange and has to work until they close."

Pop is under the pin oak, finishing work on a second lawnmower. I'm wary of getting close and don't trust him. If he's working on anything with an engine, I keep my distance. I've learned my lesson not to ever grab ahold of spark plug wires.

Soon, he calls, "Come on, you two. We're going down to the Old Sudan Road."

We jump in the Suburban and Pop drives us to The Big Orange. He picks up a six pack of beer and talks to Mom. Tash gets a grape Pixy Stix and I get a raspberry one, pure sour sugar tubes of delightfulness. As we wonder where we're heading, Pop drives south on Highway 15. Near the North Carolina State line, he turns left on a road I've never been down. Suddenly, he stops in the middle of the road and turns off the Marty Robbins eight-track tape.

Ribbon of Darkness still sings in my head.

He slides over to my side, picks me up, and puts me behind the wheel. Pop reaches over and moves the gear from P to D. The car rolls forward slowly. Since I'm not big enough to reach the gas pedal, Pop takes his left foot and pushes on the gas. I'm so small that I can't see over the steering wheel, so I have to look beneath the top of the steering wheel to the top part of the dash.

"Keep the truck in the middle of the road," he says in a serious deep voice.

The Suburban keeps accelerating and going faster and faster.

Before long, we're going nearly 50 mph. In the distance, I see a car coming toward us and I don't know what to do. I'm scared we are going to crash, and then I'll get a whippin'.

Like Pop tells me, I continue driving in the middle of the road. The truck, heading our way fast, is definitely going slower. It looks as if we're going to hit it. Pop lets off the gas and grabs the steering wheel and moves us over, but then there's another problem. There are signs blocking the road ahead. Beyond the signs, the lake covers what was the entire road.

"Pop, there's no road ahead. How do I stop?"

After a gulp of Budweiser, Pop calmly says, "Push on the brake."

I'm so small that I lose complete vision of the road as I use both feet to push on the brake with all my might with the steering wheel as leverage. We stop, get out of the Suburban, and walk to the lake's edge.

Confused why this road is covered and relieved we didn't crash, I ask, "Why is this road covered with water, Pop?"

"Booger, this is old Highway 15. This was here before the Highway 15 we just drove down. This road was here before they made Buggs Island Lake. Over there is Burlington Mills and Merrifield area."

We still aren't far from the North Carolina border. On the Virginia side, we call this reservoir Buggs Island. On the Carolina side, they call it Kerr Lake. I don't know who is right, but we call it Buggs Island after the Buggs Family, whose land was taken away to make the lake.

Pop finishes his second beer and says, "Come on. Tash, it's your turn."

Barn Ass Whippin'

Sunday, April 27, 1975 – Chainsaw Mistake.

Dusty. Smoke. Chainsaw.
Collapsing debris. Pop trapped.
Silence. Dead. Don't know.

"Come on, Booger. We have a barn to cut down," Pop says.

We have another weekend of woodcutting.

I've grown accustomed to loading up for woodcutting. We heat the house mostly with wood. It's free. It's cheaper than using the oil furnace, in which the pilot light always went out. However, this wood is intended for Sugarfoot. We're trading wood for his concrete and cinder block work for the back porch. I put the axe, wedges, and splitting maul into the back of the Suburban. Pop handles the chainsaw and gas. I don't like handling the chainsaw with the oily sharp teeth. Seems like something bad always happens when the chainsaw is involved.

Pop drives down Highway 15 and turns right just before Clarksville's Airport. Sitting right beside the house is school bus number seven. This must be where our school bus driver Mrs. Green lives. Pop pulls in the dusty driveway and shuts off the engine. Not a minute later, Cousin Hank pulls in behind us. Pop and Hank hop out of their trucks as Mr. Green comes out to meet them.

"Well, hello, Mr. Wise. How yew?"

"Good…good."

"Now, look-e-here. We'll take care of the tin on the roof. We just need y'all to take down der barn and take most of the wood with you. That sound good?" Mr. Green asks.

"Yes sir, Mr. Green," Pop responds.

Hank clumsily unloads the ladders from his truck. The first extension ladder starts self-extending and bangs Hank's knuckles after pulling it out the wrong way. With a few cuss words and blood drippin', this ain't starting out to be a good day. His white t-shirt might need some bleachin' after this chore. Before starting the demolition, we use hammers and screwdrivers to remove the cement chinking material between the logs, so it don't dull the chainsaw. The cement comes out easy, since most of it is already cracked and loose with age.

Pop picks one side of the barn and starts cutting the barn with the chainsaw. He cuts upward through the logs, leaving the corner and top log intact. Then he moves to the other end and repeats. Each time a log breaks free, he waits for Hank to move it out of the way. It looks like they are planning to remove all the logs from one side of the barn. As he gets about five logs up, I notice the barn is starting to bow outward on both sides where the logs were removed. It looks as if the barn is getting unstable, but that doesn't scare Pop. He keeps going up, relying more and more on the ladder to gain height. About twelve logs up, the barn is beginning to bow away significantly on both sides. Pop is about through the next log and *BAM!* The log on which the top of his ladder is resting slips inward and pulls him into the barn. He drops the chainsaw. I see him get pulled in and the aluminum ladder crumbles flat like a beer can. The whole barn collapses on top of him. A huge cloud of dust mixes with the smell of the still-idling chainsaw as exhaust fills the air. A barn that was nearly as tall as our house is now maybe as tall as Pop. He's underneath it. I don't know if Pop is dead.

I start yelling for Pop uncontrollably. "Pop, Pop, Pop!"

I don't know what to do. Hank is now on the ground and yells, "I can see him!"

Maybe he's not dead.

"Come on, Gary, take my hand!" Hank yells at Pop.

I hear Pop groan and slide against the dirt and logs. Pop crawls out from underneath. He's only bleeding a little on his head, arms, face, and hands. He's caked with dust and splinters. I can't believe it. He didn't die! I run up and hug him.

"I'm okay, Booger. Just give me a few minutes." He sits down on a nearby stump to assess his wounds.

"Well, it's already on the ground and ain't going to fall a second time. Might as well finish up." Cousin Hank starts cutting again.

I carry the cut logs and throw them into the back of the Littl' Joe trailer. We named the trailer Littl' Joe after Granny's old mule Joe. Since it was a small trailer, Littl' Joe seemed appropriate. We get a good three more loads of wood for Sugarfoot. Best yet, no one died. But I have to say, cutting wood with a chainsaw sure seems like dangerous business. Trees falling. Barns collapsing. Ladders crumbling. I'm not looking forward to our next chainsaw activity.

Hospice Care (Day Three, Early Afternoon)

**Friday, February 23, 2007 – Occoneechee Walking and Fishing.
Five Buckets of Chicken.**

Two lines tuggin'. Take one. I'll take the other.
My fish is small, but you have his big brother.
Halfway in, the fish rolls and she yells, SHARK!
Cast iron pan ready. Keep fightin' with all your heart.

Just after noon, Susan, Tash, and I need a break, some form of movement outside, away from death. When Gladys comes over, we ask her to watch Mom. I grab the fishing poles and tackle box from the donate pile in the basement. We drive across town to Occoneechee State Park to walk on the trails. Wet, decaying oak leaves litter the forest floor. Vines hanging from trees tempt me to swing. Spring is in the air. Remnants of past plantation houses stand on the tops of hills in the woods and are slowly being consumed by the forest. I remember this place. I remember how we would catch lightning bugs and put them into Mason jars. We'd swing on the vines after Sunday morning breakfast. We'd go fishing in the coves, trying for bass, but would often catch catfish or bluegill.

As a kid, I never thought too much about plantations and slavery and the hard times people had to go through here never knowing freedom to walk wherever they liked as we are doing now. The white settlers and plantations pushed the original inhabitants, the Occoneechee Indians, out. The Buggs family, who probably weren't too keen on losing their land for the reservoir, got a taste of what it

92

was like for the Occoneechee Indians. We stop and read a sign beside the road. Their name is spelled differently from the park's name. I ponder why that is. I now see Occoneechee Park as a memorial rather than a proud historic site of plantations. I've changed in the last two decades. I didn't know how much until I came back to this place. After two miles of sauntering, we get as much of the red mud off our shoes as we can before getting into the still smoky non-smoking rental car. We drive over to a picnic parking lot near an old childhood fishing hole.

We carry our fishing poles to one of the old coves where I used to fish as a kid. This particular cove is where the Big One got away from Tash, Pop, and me years ago. Today, we only have two poles for the three of us. With the lines cast, we sit there and wait. After several minutes, my pole dips. I slowly reach down and take up the slack.

Then Susan yells, "This pole has something, too."

But I'm focused on my pole, where I'm starting my tugging battle with a slippery underwater adversary. I reel it in and it's a small crappie. "They sure fight a lot for their size."

Her pole doubles over. She has a beast on the other end.

"Careful, honey. Check the drag! You only have four-pound line!" I adjust the reel's drag for her. The fish approaches the shore and smooth skin rolls just out of the top of the water.

Susan yells, "SHAARRK!"

Tash and I start laughing. It's not a shark but a large catfish. She finally gets it in to the shore and I pick it up out of the water. After removing the hook, I hand it to her so she can pose for a picture.

"What do you want to do with it?"

In Susan's best imitation of Southern accent, she says, "I'm cookin' it! Tonight, we's gonna eat some fried catfish."

Then the catfish lets out a large croak. "This fish just farted on me." Susan doesn't know much about catfish croaking. Tash and I laugh harder.

I get to thinking, *I wonder if she knows about snipe hunting.*

Susan catches "The Big One" on her first try.

We drive back home with the catfish. There's a little light left even though the sun has dipped beneath the horizon. Only Gladys was with Mom when we left. Now Betsy is there, too. Like two peas in a pod, seems like they're always around each other.

"Your mama was asleep the whole time. We just sat here and talked. We watched all the birds coming to the feeder until it got dark."

We're refreshed from our break, but still emotionally tired. Susan,

Tash, and I sit down at the kitchen table and do nothing for a few minutes. Looks like we've had two more buckets of Hardee's chicken meals delivered. That makes five, but Susan is frying up catfish. I leave the table and head down to the basement to return the fishing poles to the donate pile. I look at the lines of mortar in the walls. The cinder blocks have remained straight and true over the years. I remember Sugarfoot's work on this basement was just in time for my first summer here.

Gladys and Betsy on the couch taking care of Mama Wise.

Summertime and the Streak

Friday, June 6, 1975 – Picking on Mom.

School is out for the year. I have a whole summer to bike, catch crawdads, or do whatever I can dream up. Sugarfoot finishes the basement in record time. His boys helping him don't mess around, either. When done, every seam and cinder block is as straight as an arrow. The basement is longer than the back of the house. Sugarfoot's reputation for workmanship in these parts speaks for itself. I'm sure Sugarfoot's boys are working all summer on other projects, and there isn't going to be much time for them to play.

"Mom, why do we need a bigger basement?"

"I'm going to open a daycare business."

"What's a daycare business?"

After exhaling from the last of her cigarette, she explains, "I'm going to watch kids for people while they work. We're going to call it Jack-n-Jill's Daycare. You'll get to have more kids to play with. We're getting some playground equipment, too. You'll have your own swing, seesaw, sliding board, and merry-go-round. But first, we need to paint the basement."

The basement walls absorb about three coats of white paint before the concrete stops soaking it up. Outside, Pop and Hank add the roof to the basement using Sugarfoot's scaffolding. Hours later, after the roof is covered and nailed down, they coat the top with thick tar while Tash, Mom, and I continue painting inside. Midday, I get on top of the scaffolding and see the tar bubbling in the hot June sun, just like on roads during summer days. We work on the basement every day for two weeks. Windows, doors, and electrical plugs are installed. I begin to think Sugarfoot's kids have it easier.

Mom disappears to the bathroom, and I see my chance to escape. I sneak over to the ditch and start catching frogs on the Betsy side of our yard. I look back toward the house and notice a large pile of two-by-fours and two-by-sixes. The wood is older and weathered but still looks to be carpenter bee and termite free. With the basement almost finished, I can't figure out what this additional wood is going to be used to build. I walk over to Pop.

"Pop, what are you going to do with all these boards?"

"Our next project, Booger, is to build a garage and shop area. Granny gave us this wood that was being stored in one of her barns. How about you move that small pile of two-by-fours over to the front of the house?"

I know the barn he's talking about. The first floor of the barn was full of oak, cedar, and pine planks stacked eight feet high. On the second floor, I found three cases of dynamite that Grandpa used to blow up tree stumps for clearing land. One day, I asked Hank if we could blow up some tree stumps. We went to grab a couple sticks of dynamite when he noticed the glycerin was seeping out of the cases of dynamite. We backed away slowly and stayed away from the barn until the fire department removed them the following week. It's a good thing a chainsaw wasn't involved because someone could've been hurt.

Moving all this wood is a big job, since I can only carry two at a time. Even though this is old wood, some of the boards are heavy. The heavy ones are likely from oak trees on Grandpa's land. He had a small sawmill set up to make these rough-cut boards. The unfinished wood leaves a couple of splinters in my hands, and I'm glad when the task is done.

I feel something poking me in the leg in my pocket. I remember I have a homemade bobby-pin popper there. David showed me how to make it the other day in school. Sometimes on the playground we'd pop the other kids and take off running.

It's starting to warm up, and Mom comes out with some iced tea. Real Southern iced tea is one part water, a handful of tea bags, and two parts sugar. After swigging half my glass, I reach down in my pocket and grab my popper. I set the trigger. Mom starts talking with Pop and I hit her on the butt.

Snap!

"Ouch! That hurt! If you hit me with that thing again, I'll pull your pants down."

I don't believe her. The temptation of provoking Mom is too great. I reset the trigger.

Snap!

Like a black snake catching a rat, Mom's hand shoots out before I can escape. She grabs my arm and pulls me down quick like slipping on an icy porch.

"I warned you!"

I'm only wearing shoes and shorts. My shorts come off and are yanked to my ankles. Mom holds on to my shorts as I fall down on the ground, wiggling and squirming to get away until my shorts completely leave my body. Embarrassed, I cover my pee-pee and run off. Mom and Pop laugh as my bony butt rounds the corner. I crossed a line and Mom gets the better of me. After putting on another set of shorts, I sit in my bedroom and sulk. I'm embarrassed that I was naked outside for all to see.

Pop yells a few minutes later, "Booger, get out here."

I walk sullenly back out to the garage in shame. Mom and Pop smile at me and Pop starts up with a Ray Stevens song *The Streak.*

"I'm sorry, Mom. I shouldn't have popped you."

"It doesn't feel good. Come here."

Mom sets the popper and gets me a couple of times. She's right. It downright hurts. I stop popping her but have a new nickname—*The Streak.*

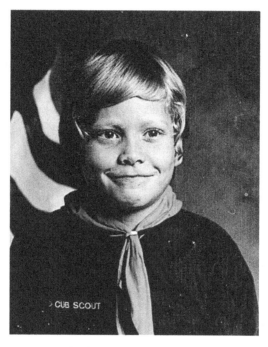

Maikel about six years old.

Grocery Store Dentist and Cardboard Pizza

Saturday, June 21, 1975 – Discount Dental Work.

Real food like meat and cheese is getting scarce at our house. Mom wakes up early and we ride with her to the Winn-Dixie grocery store. Like a pet wanting to come back inside, Mom is at the door as soon as they open. With Tash and me in tow, Mom goes straight to the reduced table. There isn't much on it. She takes the Roman Meal bread which is about ready to expire. I want the package of Hostess white powdery sugar donuts, but she passes that over. She scours every sale item. Her best score are the Jeno's frozen pizzas, marked down to nineteen cents each. Mom takes all of them, thirty boxes total. She can spruce up a thin Jeno's cardboard pizza by adding mushrooms, tomatoes, and extra cheese. Determined to find another deal, she heads to the meat counter for another bargain bin. While Mom digs through the packages of meat, Tash starts crying. Her face turns beet red.

Mom goes to her. "Lord, child, what's buggin' you? What happened?"

Tash says, "My tooth hurts."

Our family dentist, Dr. Fitzgerald, is sorting through the high-end non-sale meat counter. Smoke surrounds him with a smoldering, half-smoked cigarette hanging from the corner of his mouth. "Let's see what we have." A few ashes drop to the floor. Barehanded, he reaches into Tash's mouth and pulls out the tooth. He gives it a look over and hands the bloody tooth to her. "There you go. Feel better?" he asks.

Tash starts screaming, crying even harder.

"Why are you frettin'?" Mom asks again. "It's only a little blood."

Tash sobs. "It ain't that. I...I...I...won't get a Rose's coupon for free ice cream now. We ain't at the dentist's office."

Dr. Fitzgerald chuckles. "You come by, and I'll make sure you get your free ice cream coupon." Tash instantly stops crying.

While Tash rubs her cheek, Mr. Cash, the Winn-Dixie manager, comes to check out the commotion. "How're you doing, Mrs. Wise?" He looks at the pizza extravaganza in our cart. "That's a lot of pizzas."

Mom proudly tells him, "They're on sale. Marked down to nineteen cents."

Mr. Cash answers, concerned, "I think somebody made a mistake with the label gun." He reaches in and looks at one. "Yep, they made a mistake. I tell you what, Mrs. Wise. You can have ten of them at that price, but no more. You'll be putting me out of business."

We're grateful to Mr. Cash for all he has done for us, so Mom puts twenty of the pizzas back. Another customer eyeballs the good deal on the items Mom returns. We take our basketful of sale items to the checkout. Using refunds from Granny's empty cola bottles and the coins out of the change jar, we pay the cashier and drive back home with a measly ten pizzas in the hatchback.

Tash with missing teeth.

Hickory Nuts and the Bull

Sunday, June 22, 1975 – Picking on a Four-legged Critter.

"Bap!" in the head. "Bap!" in the butt.
He's none too happy. He didn't appreciate that nut.
Chargin'. He's goin' to squash us to a pulp.
Best get goin'. Run! Save yourself! Hurry up!

We are still working on completing the basement. While Pop cuts and hangs sheetrock, I pick up the pieces and screw the sheetrock into place. I'm hoping this isn't going to be my whole summer, and I'm tired of being inside all day.

About an hour before noon, Mom brings down some peanut butter and jelly sandwiches for us. She made herself a banana and mayonnaise sandwich, which really grosses me out due to its sliminess.

"David called again. Why don't you take the rest of the day off?" Mom suggests as she watches Pop's reaction out of the corner of her eye.

Pop huffs.

I quickly gulp my sandwich down then race upstairs to call David to let him know I'm heading over. I run down the old Tobacco Road to the now partially grown cornfield. A man on a tractor at the end of the field notices me and waves me over.

"Hey. You Gary's boy aren't ya?"

"Yessir," I timidly respond.

"Now look here. I don't mind you crossing my field but don't

103

make a trail diagonally across it. Either walk around or step over my plants. I saw some boys riding their dirt bikes tearing up my field. Those boys are going to get it. We understand each other?"

Grateful I wasn't gonna be in trouble, I say in the same timid voice, "Yessir."

I leave the farmer, overexaggerating my steps between the rows so he knows I understand. Once I'm on the other side of the field, I run full speed to David's house.

Trying to catch my breath, I say to David. "David, I ran into that farmer on the field behind Goddammit's house. He gave me a warning not to damage his field. Those other boys up the street with their dirt bikes are gonna get it. He ain't messin' around."

"Yeah, I've seen him there sometimes and hide in the trees, so he doesn't see me. Ain't got caught yet."

Just catching my breath again, I say to David, "So what do you want to do today?"

"Let's go check out the barns down the tracks on the other end of the pasture. You know, the ones in the woods toward the South Boston direction."

We climb the large gravel slanty side of the tracks and walk down the middle. The tracks slowly curve to the right. Of course, David and I see who can make it farther walking on the rails. He wins again. I look at the rusty spikes holding the rails down. About every fifteen or so are loose and ain't touching the rails or are out of the railroad ties all together. I'm amazed that the heavy trains ride on what appears to be unmaintained tracks. We follow them until we get to a dirt bike trail that takes us near the barns. Just outside another cow fence, we notice three motorcycles parked with no one around.

I wonder whose they can be. *Can't be the Matherly's. They don't have no money for dirt bikes.*

We look over at one of the barns and see one of the owners of the dirt bikes, Chris Newton. Beside him are the Cragley Kid and someone else we don't recognize. The Cragley Kid can be recognized a half a mile away—bright blond hair and snaky eyes. We cautiously keep our distance from the Cragley Kid because sometimes he can turn on a fella. It doesn't take much of a spark to get him heated up and mad. Chris is all right, though, and never starts any trouble with us. One time, he even offered to let David ride his motorcycle.

"What y'all doing?" David asks in a cool tone.

I know David. He's scared, too, but he always maintains a coolness in every situation. David is "The Fonz" in my circle of friends.

One of them says, "We are throwing hickory nuts at the bull over there."

I didn't even notice that bull was there. I know this bull. It's the same one I've seen behind our house in the other cow pasture. He looks as mean in this pasture as he does in the pasture behind our place, and here we are inside the fence with him.

I look at the nuts the older kids are picking up off the ground. The hickory nuts are still green and hard. Trying to fit in and be cool, David and I join in and start throwing hickory nuts, too. About every half dozen throws, we hit the mark. *Bap!* On the butt. *Miss. Bap!* On the shoulder. *Miss. Miss. Bap!* On the head. He didn't like getting hit on the head, so of course, we completely focus on his head. After a half a dozen hits, the bull shakes his head and turns left, facing us. He's pissed off and starts charging.

All I hear is a loud, "Ruuuunnnnnn!"

We run to the closest barn, an old tobacco barn. I'm the slowest. The bull is charging full speed and is catching up fast. My heart pumps hard. I feel as if it's going to jump out of my chest. Pee may exit below. All at once, like human-size grains of sand, we fight, we push, and we all try to get through the tiny barn door opening.

"Close the fucking door," The Cragley Kid yells.

I flinch. I use swear words, but never use the F-word.

Chris yells, "There ain't no door. It must've fell off."

The bull isn't stopping. He's just outside the door opening pawing and snorting. He's determined to gore and stomp us all. We move to the opposite corner inside the barn. We're trapped.

Someone yells, "Y'all jump up. He can't get us up there." Above our heads runs eight horizontal tobacco poles the entire width of the barn. Everybody grabs one and pulls himself up except for me. I just can't reach it. I jump and I jump, but I can't reach it. The bull's front half squeezes through the small door. The entire barn shakes. I hear him snort as he looks right at me.

Diabolically, the Cragley Kid yells, "He's gonna kill you! You're gonna die!"

Panicked, I back up and run full speed at the wall. Using one of the logs as a step, I push myself upward. I grab David's sweaty hand. He yanks me up. Somehow, I manage to grab hold of a lower pole. I'm so scared. It's not enough to be out of reach of the bull. I want to be as far away as I can be. With a death grip on each horizontal pole, I climb higher. I'm shaking like a leaf, but I'm also glad I can disappoint the Cragley Kid. He's such an asshole. The older kids keep pulling hickory nuts out of their pockets and hitting the bull in the noggin. *Bap!* He's super mad. The bull bucks his head upward and nearly knocks the kid we don't know off the pole he's standing on. The barn shakes again. Scared to death, with sweaty hands and face, I climb till I can't go any higher.

Crunched down at the top, I watch the commotion. I hear buzzing. Then I see the nest. With all this movement and shaking of the dilapidated barn, we've just upset one of my top fears in life—Japanese Hornets. They're swarming all over. I'm already traumatized by this particular breed of hornet from the apple tree in our front yard. When I walk barefoot in the yard, sometimes I'll step on them and they'll sting me on the bottom of my feet, so much pain in the arches of my feet that I remind myself to wear shoes next time but keep forgetting. These hornets can bite, too, making it doubly painful. The quandary ensues: What do I do? Do I get stung to death by hornets, or do I jump down and get gored by the bull?

The bull jumps up again and hits one of the poles, nearly knocking David off. He barely hangs on and avoids falling and being trampled to death and turned into pounded cube steak. The hornet nest is now hanging by a thread. The hornets are super agitated now. A hornet lands on my nose. I swat it away with my free hand. Whew. It didn't have time to sting me.

The Cragley Kid is howling. "They're stinging! They're stinging!"

Chris is swatting at least a thousand or more of them. "Dammit. Dammit. Dammit," he yelps. I wonder if he's related to Goddammit.

David is getting stung on his knee. I get lucky. Everyone except for me is getting jabbed by buzzing needles of death. Even the bull runs out after getting jabbed and penetrated, too. He isn't having nothing to do with them hornets. He's thinking, *To hell with them kids.* I immediately drop to the ground and run out the door, heading in the opposite direction of the bull. I make it. Not a single sting. I can't believe my luck.

A few moments go by, and the other kids shoot out of the barn.

"David, over here," I holler. He's limping as the swelling starts. The Cragley Kid and the others run over underneath the hickory tree picking up a few nuts.

Unbelievable, I think. That's plenty enough for today. "Come on

David, let's go. I hear baking soda on the sting will help ease the pain. We got to make sure that stinger is out, too."

We hurry back to David's place, where his mom removes the stinger and tells me I should go home. She says David needs to rest and let the swelling go down. I wander home, mulling the results of my adventure. I have nothing but paranoia for the next two hours, thinking something is buzzing around me. Hypersensitive to my traumatizing event, I keep looking all around me, raising my t-shirt high around my neck. I freak out when a fly lands on my arm, thinking the worst. The bull won that day. So did the hornets.

The Big One

Saturday, June 28, 1975 – Six Years Old. Learning to Fish.

Caricature of Pop Fishing.

Pop and Mom were making a ruckus in their room last night. Sounded like they were wrastling and praying to God at the same time. 'Oh, God!' they blurted out more than once.

"Come on, Booger. I'm taking you and your sister fishing today." Pop is in a good mood.

Pop fancies himself a professional fisherman. His tackle boxes are filled to the brim with really cool lures. There are hooks with fancy sparkly spoons, hooks with rubbery bug-looking things, and hooks with plastic crawfish. Some of the rubber dangly worms are melted together from the summer's heat.

When Tash and I go fishing, we usually use the cheaper *Zebco's*, or preferably cane poles. I don't have to think when I use a cane pole. Simply swing the wormed-hook out, wait for the nibble, and pull the fish in. Worms seem to work better for us than minnows, and they're cheaper, too. Granny's ditches have humongous worms, but it's best not to get too close to the water, though. Granny's ditch water is a combination of her sink runoff and the poop bucket.

We mostly go fishing in ponds or behind Granny's place in the cove. Today, we are going someplace different. We didn't dig up any worms, so we visit Fred's Bass Pro Shop to pick up some nightcrawlers and minnows. After a bumpy ride on the potholed roads, we arrive at Occoneechee. Pop parks the Suburban near one of the picnic areas and jumps out. He grabs the rods, reels, and tackle box. Tash and I handle the worms and minnows. Tash and I can't keep up as Pop runs as if he wants to get on the first rollercoaster ride at *Kings Dominion*. He appears more excited to catch the "Big One" than I am. When I reach the shoreline, Pop's flyfishing line is already cast into the water. I watch his large arms manipulate the delicate rod, skillfully sending the fly to the perfect spot.

Pop says, "Watch this," as he makes a small circle with the tip of his rod, causing the line to move in a spiral. The fly hops over a couple of feet to the right. He's a master fisherman.

He hands me the rod, but I only disrupt the stillness of the muddy water. Pop allows both Tash and me to try, even though his frustration is taking over. I attempt to give back his toy, but he refuses it and begins to show us the proper way to flyfish. He puts his hand over ours and shows us how to flick our wrists to get the results. Tash and

I tried using flies on our cane poles, but we still prefer worms and a cork bobber.

He says, "Try to get the fly underneath the buck bushes that overhang the water because that's where the big ones lie."

As the morning haze begins to burn off, Pop becomes restless. We have nothing to show for our efforts of the past couple of hours except a few small bluegills, a crappie, and a mud catfish.

We're ready to give up after an unsuccessful morning, but Pop says, "One more time," as he meticulously places the fly underneath a buck bush whose arms of limbs spread out trying to protect the water below. He wants to show Tash and me that if we persist, we can catch the "Granddaddy of all fish." I lose count of Pop saying, "One more time."

The fly twitches as if mortally wounded. Something huge swells beneath the surface. The water boils and swirls. Suddenly, the fly is sucked down into the murkiness and takes off. The line pulls and the fly rod reel screams in alarm.

Beads of sweat form on Pop's forehead as he struggles with the "Big One." Pop's movements exaggerate as the rod bends over double. Tash and I stand back so we don't get smacked by the rod or ruin his moment of glory. Pop's sunburned forehead begins to show lines of focus and concentration. It seems like an eternity. Pop pulls in a six-pound Largemouth. Inch by inch, the hawg of a fish makes it two feet from the shoreline. Suddenly, the line breaks. This sends Pop into an outrage.

"Git it! Git it! Jump on it!" Pop yells.

We're too late. With a flick of its tail, the Big One swims away hungry and scared. As quickly as a popped circuit breaker, Pop throws down his rod and begins to stomp up and down. He's just like us kids who don't get what they want at the toy store. I wonder what we look like, two kids and an adult trading places of maturity. Disappointed and an adult temper-tantrum later, we gather all our fishing gear and make our way back to the Suburban.

Pop looks at Tash and me and says, "I told you we'd catch the 'Big One.' Let's tell everyone that we threw it back."

That day, Tash and I learned a lot about the right way to flyfish.

Hospice Care (Day Four, Early)

Saturday, February 24, 2007 – Remembering Earl, Jaw-clenching, and Finding Sled.

Mom's first morning dose of morphine works like magic. She's asleep within ten minutes. Tash, Susan, and I go to the kitchen to ingest cream with coffee and eggs.

Susan asks, "Didn't you say your mom had a brother? Should we let him know about your mom?"

Tash responds first. "Yes, she did. Earl Yancey. I think he was quite a bit older than Mom. Granny didn't have Mom until she was about forty years old. Earl passed away a few years ago. Even if he was alive, Mom wouldn't care to see him."

New facts about Mom and Granny are popping up every day. I anxiously wait to hear if there is something new coming.

I recall my first memory of Earl. "Tash. Remember when we had Granny's 75th birthday party?"

Tash laughs. "Lord, child, do I ever! Let me tell you! There was some serious jaw-clenching that day."

Susan blurts out, "Huh. Maikel's jaw clenches, too, when he gets mad. I guess it runs in the family."

After breakfast, Susan and I walk down to the basement, down the steep stairs Pop and Uncle Jim put in years ago. These stairs give us easy access and mean we don't have to go outside to get into the basement. I look over by the woodstove and see a sled hanging on a rusty nail like a memorial.

"Hey, Susan, check it out. I remember this sled. The night before it would snow, I'd find an old candle in the house. I'd wire-brush the rust off the runners and coat them with several layers of candle wax. Sometimes screws would fall out of the slats of wood, so I'd go to the garage to force something else in the holes to keep it together. The best place to go sledding back then was the cow pasture."

Carton of Eggs Wrapped in a Mink Coat

Saturday, October 4, 1975 – Respect your Mama.

A carton of eggs, cash, and a mink coat.
The gall of Granny's son. A sorry ole goat.
Mom will set him straight. Jaws tighten and twitch.
She'll make her own brother pick out his own switch.

It's Granny's 75th birthday. Mom, Tash, and I arrive early to prepare for the hordes of people coming. The house is full of sons, daughters, nephews, nieces, and cousins. Even Aunt Loretta came up from Nashville with her two boys Gavin and Dale. It's a big 'to-do.'

Just before dinner is ready, Uncle Earl walks in. This is Mom's brother. He usually arrives just in time to eat. Occasionally, he arrives late, making us all starve. Then after every dinner, he plops himself on Granny's only sofa and sprawls out gluttonously. He takes up the whole damn sofa so no one else can sit. Usually, after his belly processes his fourth helping, the rest of us have to clean up in the kitchen.

His wife follows behind him flaunting a new mink coat. For October, it's as hot as all get out and the rest of us are in short sleeves. Earl's wife is intent on flashing her new mink coat by doing a couple of spins like that Southern belle in *Gone with the Wind*. Once removed and handed to me for safekeeping, I placed it on Granny's bed. I catch a whiff of mink fur saturated in stinky perfume. *Ick!*

Earl moseys up to Granny. "I got you a great present." He hands her a carton of eggs and a ten-dollar bill.

115

I hear a gasp from Mom. Mom's jaw clenches. Her face turns hot-coal red to match her hair. She shoots up out of the chair and glares at Earl. Mom, the red-headed Tasmanian Devil, fires the first round. "What the hell is wrong with you? Get your ass outside."

Granny isn't the type to stir things up. "It's okay, Dolores. Earl means well."

But there's no stopping Mom. He's corralled and bulldozed to the door. He has no choice but to exit. Like a dog who shit on the carpet, he knows he's going to get it.

Tash and I have a prime front row seats looking out the slightly open window. The other cousins have second-rate views by the screen door and the other window. Our Nashville cousins are behind me, quiet so they can hear every word. Some popcorn would be nice for this show.

Outside, Mom and Earl face each other by the switch bush. Tash and I know the switch bush well. We have to pick out our own switches from this bush every time we misbehave at Granny's.

Mom starts cussing. "You piece of shit. It's your mother's 75th birthday and you bring eggs and cash? Your wife comes in here flaunting her new shiny mink coat. You're livin' high on the hog. It probably cost a few thousand dollars. Is her pussy that good that you can't get something decent for your mama? After all our mother has done for you, and this is the best gift you can give her? Get the fuck out of here."

Rarely does Mom use the 'F word'. She won't even let Pop use it. This whole time, Earl's wife is cowering by their car door, ready to escape. She knows enough to keep her mouth shut. All Mom has to do now is to start spinning and snarling and the Tasmanian Devil transformation is complete.

Tash and I are grateful we're not in the crosshairs of Mom's fury.

It's funny, though, when it happens to Uncle Earl. Earl tries to get back into the house, but Mom ain't having none of it and blocks the door. He doesn't have enough horsepower to push back against five foot, three-quarters inches of Mom.

Mom yells, "Maikel!"

I know instantly what she wants. I run to retrieve the perfumed-stench mink coat. After handing the ball of fur to Mom so she can give it to Earl, Loretta yells, "Dinner is ready." Poor Loretta missed the show.

With all that feuding, I forgot all about dinner. This dinner is like Thanksgiving with a different kind of turkey. Best yet, we might get a second helping and leftovers of dessert with Uncle Earl gone. After which, there'll be room for me to lay on the couch.

Frozen Pipes, Mutilated Candles, and Uncle Jim

Wrapped in quilts, Tash and I are plopped down in front of the TV. Channel Five, WRAL, is the news channel many folks in town watch. It isn't because it's the best channel. It's because it's the only news channel our TV antennas can pick up.

"A really cold Artic front will hit the east coast from the north going across the Appalachian Mountains. Mixed with the moist air coming up from the Gulf of Mexico, we'll likely have several inches of snowfall. This area on the south part of the state could see freezing rain," the weatherman says confidently.

We're a good half a Suburban tank of gas from the area getting the freezing rain, so that means we are definitely getting snow here. We know any form of snow is going to close school down. Mecklenburg County doesn't mess around with snow. One time we had blue skies in Clarksville, but nearby South Boston was getting snow flurries. School closed because it was heading our way. I check our front yard after the news report even though I know it's a day early. I open the front door and feel the Artic-chilled wind.

Mom yells, "Close that door! Now brush your teeth and go to bed."

I get into bed and try to sleep, but I'm too eager that it may snow. About thirty minutes later, there's a knock on the front door. It's never good to get a knock on the door this late. It usually means someone did something wrong or needs help. I crack open my bedroom door as quietly as I can. I have to push down on the doorknob on my door, since the top of the door rubs due to the house settling. I hear Tash's door creak and open, too.

It's Uncle Jim. It's Uncle Jim! Uncle Jim visited our last place, but this is his first time here on Shiney Rock Road. Tash and I run out of our bedrooms, and we hug each one of his legs. He's a bit smelly, haggard, and his face is all scraggly.

"Uncle Jim, are you staying with us for a while again?" Tash asks, still hanging onto his leg.

"Why, yes, little munchkin. I'm not sure how long. We'll see. Well look at you. You've grown."

Tash and I are so excited, but Mom firmly tells us to go back to bed. We do as we we're told but keep peeking out our doors throughout the night as Mom, Pop, and Uncle Jim sit around the kitchen table talking, smoking, and drinking beer.

I wake up early Thursday morning and look out by the apple tree in the front yard and disappointedly think, *No snow yet.* Uncle Jim is parked on the other side of the apple tree and is apparently still sleeping. My mind is focused on the upcoming snowstorm and seeing Uncle Jim after school.

The last time I saw Uncle Jim, we had a snowstorm, too. Uncle Jim and I weren't on the best terms last time I saw him. I remember in our old house he was relaxing on the living room chair. Both of his feet were propped up on the coffee table. I ran full speed, jumped in the air, and landed on his shins. I saw the pain in his eyes, and I knew I'd crossed a line. He forgave me, but I still felt guilty for hurting him. He seemed impossible to hurt, though. He's as tall as Pop but has a smaller belly. The Cherokee part of him is more obvious, too, with his high-cheekbone face and jet-black hair color. Uncle Jim has one of the few tattoos I've ever seen close up. It's a chicken saying, "Who me?" He got it in the Marines when he was over in Vietnam. After he went back home last time, I remember playing with his war medals and sharpshooter pin he left behind. I'd attach them to an old Army pack I'd found in one of Granny's old barns.

The weatherman is right about the Artic front coming through. It's getting even colder. Late Friday afternoon just after school the wind starts blowing hard. The excess leaves and pinecones in our yard start to contaminate George and Betsy's yard. A couple of small branches drop off the pin oak onto Pop's Suburban but doesn't do any damage. The temperature drops further from almost long-sleeve weather to I-need-a-stocking-cap weather. As the wind howls, I help Mom remove the toys in the yard before the brunt of storm hits and covers them up. Her Jack-n-Jill Daycare is doing okay. She has about ten kids she watches while their parents work at Burlington Mills or Russell Stover Candy Factory. She makes enough money that she stopped working at The Greenhouse.

"Come on, kids. Y'all gonna get blown away," Mom yells at us as the wind relocates our leaves two houses over.

She doesn't have to repeat it, either. It's getting so cold that I can now see my breath. I might need a couple more of Granny's Singer-sewed blankets tonight. Even the dusty, mice-chewed quilts from Granny's potato barn will do.

When Pop gets home from Harold Moore's Gas Station shift, he, Uncle Jim, and I bring in more wood. We don't have to worry about spiders popping out of the wood this time of year. We brought in enough wood to keep the fire burning all weekend in both the upstairs and downstairs fireplaces. We also have a temperamental oil furnace. Pop uses a broom handle to check the oil level in the tank for the furnace. It's a quarter full and good enough to get us through this cold spell. Mom tosses a couple of extra quilts on our beds and encourages us to go to bed early. Often, Tash and I have to go to bed early when our parents want to drink beer and talk about grown-up things.

I have to pee something fierce. I don't want to get cold feet, but I'm about to burst. I jump out of bed and run to the bathroom. It's freezing in the house. When I flush the toilet, no water refills. My main floater made it through the toilet, but there are a couple of pebble-sized pieces stuck at the bottom. I try to flush again. No luck. I grab the bar of soap and start to wash my hands, but no water comes out of the sink, either. I know we don't have no water bill since we have our own well, so no one could have shut it off. I dry my unrinsed soaped-up hands on our unembroidered bath towel. Leaving a distinct soapy residue, I contaminate a second bath towel, but it's already stained. We don't have any fancy hand towels like the Buchanan's. Our towels are one step above shop rags, but they work just fine. I don't say a word about the water, and everyone is asleep, anyway. I'm scared I broke it and will get into trouble. Mouselike, I quickly but silently tiptoe back to my bedroom to warm up again under Granny's blankets.

Almost dozing, I hear Pop get up and go to the bathroom. The toilet doesn't flush for him, either.

"Dammit all to hell! The pipes froze!"

I remember Mom got after him just around last October, too. "You need to wrap the pipes with insulation in the well house so the pipes don't freeze." I don't know if he did it or not. Most likely not.

"Booger, get up. Come on son, get up. I'm going to show you how to unfreeze pipes."

I don't want to get up. Pop's stern, deep voice is incentive enough to get up anyway because the repercussions are certainly worse. Still in my pajamas, I shove on my socks, shoes, coat, and stocking cap. To keep the bottom of my pajamas drier, I tuck them into my socks.

Once this task is done, it'll probably take an hour for my feet to warm up again. I follow Pop to the well house. The snow is falling steadily and is covering the ground. I should've put a sweater on, too. Since he called me Booger, he's going to want me to do something like get a tool. We walk up to the well house and Pop has a hard time opening the door. Looks like the well house has done some settling like my bedroom door. He forces the door open, and the bare uninsulated pipes stare at Pop saying, "Now I'll bet you wish you didn't go to Mama Johnson's and drink beer."

Pop quickly dismisses using a hairdryer I brought with me. He had me run and get him a blowtorch instead, saying, "It'll be faster." After he gently blowtorches the pipes for about ten minutes, they unfreeze.

"Booger, (here it comes) go get the lamp in the basement by the stove."

Five minutes later, Pop has duct-taped the lamp next to the pipes. The theory is the light bulb right next to the pipes will keep them from freezing. It works. Now I have another responsibility. I have to be the one to turn on the lightbulb whenever it gets cold and make sure the well house door is always closed.

Once I get back upstairs with my colder than going-to-the-bathroom-after-the-fire-goes-out feet, Tash is in the living room looking out at Uncle Jim's truck. The camper isn't moving. He must've stayed up late last night, because I remember him being an early riser. Early rising is what Marines are supposed to do. Snow is coming down even harder now. It's a good thing Mom has already loaded up with milk and bread. Clarksville gets crazy when the weatherman mentions snow. Any mention of snow and we have to go to the grocery store quick. Bread and milk always empty out first.

Gallon jugs of water fly off the shelves, too. Apparently, other people have pipe-freezing problems during cold spells.

It's almost ten o'clock before Uncle Jim gets up. After a later than normal breakfast and warming up my feet by the fireplace, Tash and I go out to the side of the house. We get two of Granny's hand-me-down sleds. The wood slats are a mix of worn stain and weathered gray. The runners are a mix of rust and red paint.

Pop comes out and says, "Booger, go to my toolbox and get the wire brush. Ladybug, go find one of Mom's candles."

We do what we are told, having no idea what these things are going to be used for.

"You need to remove the rust off the runners. Then you need to wax 'em to make 'em slick," Pop informs us.

He cleans and waxes one runner. Tash and I do the others. Not used to the wire brush, we accidentally keep poking our fingertips and red dots of blood appear. We keep going. I replace a couple of rusted-out bolts that I 'borrowed' from the lawnmower handle. I've got to remember to put the bolts back before Spring. The sleds are slick and ready.

Tash and I rush back inside to get on our snow gear. Snow gear is wearing long johns under blue jeans, putting on an extra two shirts with a sweater, wearing any stocking cap we can find, and donning gloves with hopefully no holes in the fingers. The gloves don't have to match. They can be two right-handed gloves, too. Mom looks at us with our three pairs of socks on.

"Come here," she asks us in a nice tone. "When we were kids, we used bread bags."

Tash asks, "What for?"

Mom tells us to sit on the kitchen floor and out of the cabinet she removes a large paper bag full of bread bags. Some bags are Wonder

Bread, some are Roman Meal, and some are Jewish Rye bags. She takes off one pair of socks, installs the bread bags, and reinstalls the socks. It's instant heat. It feels as if there's a lightbulb duct-taped to each foot. I might need to put on bread bags with my pajamas at night before bed. Wow! Mom is smart. Tash and I run out the door to our own private sledding hill.

The hill next to our house quickly becomes tiresome. We soon get bored because the hill isn't long enough. The speed this hill can generate isn't enough. Tash and I take a break to go inside and warm up by the woodstove. Mom already has hangers nearby. We hang our socks, pants, and outer shirts and they begin to steam instantly.

I'm only partially thawed out when, *Ring. Ring. Ring.* I pick up the phone.

"Hello."

It's David, summoning me. "Dude, have you been sledding. The snow is awesome. I was just out in the cow pasture by our place. You know, next to the dam. We built ramps! Bring your sled and come meet us there this afternoon. I'll be there in an hour."

I have to ask permission from Mom or Pop. As long as they know where I'm going, they don't care. Though our clothes haven't quite dried enough, they're warm. Tash and I need new bread bags, too, since our old ones got holes in them. If one bread bag is warm, two must be better. I don them on my feet, happy they're warm.

It's tough going walking in the snow. There's just about one Budweiser bottle height of snow on the ground now. This snow doesn't stick together like some snows do. It isn't the snowman-making kind of snow. After our slogging, we finally get over to the cow pasture. There must be more than a dozen other kids there already. There are two sledding hills. One is a longer and less steep hill to the north. On the dam, there's a short, really steep hill. Partway down the long hill, there's a ramp. Just to the side of the ramp is a bucket of water. Apparently some of the teenage kids must've broke through the ice in the pond and carried water here. The water on the powdery snow, along with a couple pieces of wood, turned it to a stable ice ramp. To get extra speed, some of the older kids added water leading up to the ramp making it ice over. Ideal conditions for my re-waxed sled.

On the longer hill, I spy David, Jay, and Raymond, along with some teenagers. I watch David get a running start with his sled. He accelerates and hits the ramp fast. He must go a good two feet in the air. One of the teenage boys goes next in a giant tractor-trailer inner tube. When he lands, he bounces so hard that he flips over sideways, sliding on his Levi's to the bottom, laughing all the way. Next in line, I grab my sled and push off. I'm too scared to hit the ramp full on so I hit on the side and go airborne less than a foot. This is so fun.

At the bottom of the hill, I look about half-way back up the hill and notice Jay coming down fast. He intentionally misses the ramp, going for speed. He hits the bottom, coming fast at me. I try to jump out of the way, but he catches my leg. I spin vertically, almost doing a flip. He buries his feet into the ground to brake. It's too late. Jay becomes entangled in the old barb-wire fence.

I say to him approvingly, "Dude, you were the fastest one yet."

Jay, with his cold rosy cheeks, untangles. "Now that was fun! Didn't take out too many people. Too bad this fence is here or could have gone another fifty feet."

We go up and down at least a couple dozen more times. Before the day ends, David and I make a water run to the edge of the pond. We pour the water over the ramp, so it'll ice overnight. The sun is low, and the temperature is dropping. Time to head home.

Once home, we hang our clothes on various nails and a makeshift indoor clothesline surrounding the woodstove. Thirsty and hungry, we stomp upstairs in our partially wet wool socks. Mom has dinner boiling on the stove. I look on the counter where it looks like some of the snow made it into our house. Flour. That means part of our dinner is going to include some form of bread.

Mom proudly encouraging us. "I'll bet you two are hungry. Go get yourself a bowl. I made chicken n' dumplings."

Tash and I can't reach the cabinet, so we use a chair to reach the bowls. Half the pot is gone, so Pop, Uncle Jim, and Mom must've already eaten. There isn't any bread, just dumplings soaking in chicken juices. Mom gets after me for taking too many dumplings.

"Now, don't eat them all. Save some for later."

I eat one Maikel-sized bowl, which is equivalent to three Mom-sized bowls. After eating dinner and doing some repairs on the sled, I carry the sled downstairs where Uncle Jim is working on a square piece of leather. He's making a top for a wooden stool from Granny's. He is making a design showing three horses drinking from a trough.

"Hey, Uncle Jim. What did you do today?"

"Just some work on the camper and truck. Did you and Tash have fun sledding?"

"You bet we did. We had a ramp and jumped a lot. Some of my friends were there, too."

Uncle Jim fell quiet. We didn't have a lot of light down in the basement, and he only had one light turned on. I watch the shadows on his face. Uncle Jim looks sad, but I have some questions for him. We've hardly talked since he's gotten here.

"Uncle Jim. You left something from the last time you visited. I'll go get it."

I bring down my cedar box that has his Vietnam medals in it. He looks at them, just staring.

"Those aren't toys," he murmurs.

"I know, Uncle Jim. What's this one mean? What's a Sharpshooter?"

Uncle Jim explains his shooting abilities. I want to know more.

"How was it in Vietnam?"

He's quiet for a moment, then speaks. "There was lots of shooting. I remember one time, mortars were coming down. We had a bomb shelter dug into the ground. I could barely fit through the opening. Once I did, I dropped down six feet. The top was covered with steel plates and sandbags. Those explosions were loud and hit close, but we figured we were safe with the steel covering." Uncle Jim went quiet. "Son, I really don't want to talk about this. I'd like to be alone."

With the tone of Uncle Jim saying "Son," I know it's time to go. I walk back upstairs to let him be.

Pop is sitting in the living room. "Pop, is Uncle Jim okay? Was he hurt in Vietnam?"

Pop hesitates. After a few beers, Pop sometimes shares more information that he would otherwise.

"Booger, Uncle Jim had a hard time in Vietnam. You remember when he came to visit us at our last house? Well, he saw a lot of action. All those mortars and shooting scared the hell out of him. He saw too many friends die. But the reason he's here now is that he needed to get away for a while. He just needs some time to sort things out. Don't ask him about Vietnam no more. Give him a couple days, and he'll be all right."

For a few moments, I remembered when Uncle Jim visited our last house when I was three years old. I had so many questions for him back then, too.

I recalled when Uncle Jim looked at me seriously one day and said, "You know, you only have so much talk. If you ask all these questions now and keep talking, when you get my age, you'll run out of talk."

It took me a few days to figure out he was messing with me, but Uncle Jim said I sure was quiet for a spell.

I pull myself back from that memory. "Thanks, Pop."

After that, I didn't pin his medals on toys or on my shirts. I kept them in the cedar box. I never asked him again about Vietnam.

Uncle Jim's Vietnam Medals

The next day, with six layers of wax on each sled runner, I walk over to the sledding hill in the cow pasture by David's place. Before I leave the house, Mom's favorite candle is mutilated, mauled, and hidden so she can't find it. When I get to the cow pasture, David is already there at the top of the sledding hill.

"David, it sure got cold last night. Did you see the pond? It's all froze over."

Our minds think the same thing simultaneously. "Let's go on the pond. It should be frozen enough," David says.

Against our better judgment, we walk out onto the ice. We find that the ice is thick on the edge. We skate with our winter boots and fall a few times and the ice never breaks.

"Hey Maikel, I wonder if we can make it to the other side?"

"I don't know if we should, David. Pop told me to stay off the ice. But let's throw some rocks and sticks out there first and see how thick it is."

We throw and throw but not one of the rocks goes through. From the edge, David and I cautiously creep toward the center.

"David, how about we spread out a bit from each other so all of our weight ain't in one place," I suggest.

We keep going until we're about one-third away across the pond.

Crack! David and I see the largest crack ever shoot away. Striking its target, the crack races from my feet to David's feet to the drain of the pond next to the dam.

"Oh shit!" one of us yells.

We drop down flat on our bellies and start crawling back as fast as we can.

We hear a car horn beeping. A man gets out of his car yelling, "You boys get off that ice now!"

I think, *Oh shit, part two. We're busted!*

It's Mr. Cash from down the road. David and I creep more slowly back to the shoreline, but it's too late. About ten minutes later, Pop is running toward me down a gently sloped hill from Shiney Rock Road with only a short sleeve shirt on, and he's pissed off.

"What the hell did I tell you?" Silence. "What the hell did I tell you?!"

I know the answer. "Not to go on the ice."

"Get your ass in the truck." Pop looks over at David. "You! Go home right now! Your parents will be getting a phone call."

I run, dragging my sled like a scolded dog.

The drive home is only a half a mile, but he says to me, "Kids have died on that pond. Did you know that?"

Meekly, I say without volunteering any additional information, "No, sir."

We get home and Pop is all fired up. "Go to your room!"

I do what I'm told, knowing I'm going to get it. Soon, Pop comes into my bedroom. He unbuckles his brown leather belt and doubles it over.

Familiar with this routine and his words, he says, "This is going to hurt me more that it is going to hurt you."

He whips me ten times. I count the smacks. I start crying.

Pop's finishes with, "I'm disappointed in you, son." Then I'm informed, "You can't go sleigh riding anymore this week." Pop puts on his belt again and leaves.

I can take the whippin' part, but the "I'm disappointed" part is too much. I don't talk or make eye contact with Pop much during the next couple of days, but I wax my sled and have it ready, just in case.

Hospice Care (Day Four, Late Morning)

Saturday, February 24, 2007 – Can't Feed Mom.
Jack n' Jill Sign and Red-dyed Mop Wigs.

Mom's belly rumbles. Hunger pangs ensue.
I ain't supposed to feed you. What do I do?
I look into your eyes. Guilt eats at my heart.
I wish I could give you food. Death, I don't like this part.

Tash and I continue sorting through the items in the basement. We find a faded and flaked sign painted yellow and dark green. The sign reads, "Jack n' Jill Daycare Center." Mom fancied herself a painter. She painted this sign. It used to be an old Texaco gas station sign that she found over in one of Granny's barns. In a box next to the signs are mop heads dyed pink. The mop heads were once red. Time has made the makeshift wigs turn to a faded pink and dusty.

"Tash, do you remember these wigs?"

"I sure do. Mom made them for the Christmas parade. We all had to dress up as either Jack or Jill. Pop drove the lawnmower and towed Littl' Joe trailer he made into a float. You and I were mad that we had to be on the float because that meant we couldn't get any candy canes thrown out by the other floats."

"Tash, what should we do with all this stuff?"

"I don't know. Let's throw out the wigs and just set the sign to the side for now. We'll decide on it later."

"Maikel." Susan calls down to me. "Your Mom is awake now and is asking for you."

"Hey, Mom. What do you need?" Mom movements are slower. I can tell she's slowly degrading. Her eyes are not as alert. She can't lift her arms as high. Mom points to her mouth and then her belly.

"Mom. Are you thirsty?"

Mom taps twice.

"Are you hungry?"

Mom taps once. I hesitate and my eyes fill with tears. I have to look away from her gaze for a moment.

I remember what the hospice doctor said. "When Mrs. Wise is coherent, she can sip water. When she is unable to sip water, you should not give her water via her stomach tube. This can cause her lungs to fill up with water and she'll effectively drown in her own fluids. The morphine will help ease any hunger pangs. It is entirely up to you, but I would not feed her. That will prolong her suffering."

I remember that I had a hard time hearing these instructions. It's even harder looking into Mom's eyes and telling her. I'm trying to hold it together, but I can't.

"Mom, I'm sorry." I'm sobbing harder. "I can't give you anything to eat. The doctor said we weren't supposed to give you food. Let me give you some water."

Mom starts crying, too. Food is a big part of her life, for all of our lives. Even right after the tracheal tube was inserted into her throat, Mom would still eat solid food, although she was supposed to be on a strictly liquid diet. She fragilely sips the water. Then she grabs my arm and holds on.

It's the only way she can say, "I'm okay. You'll be okay. Thank you."

Slowly, Mom drifts off into her morphine nap.

Tash decides to stay home with Mom, while Susan and I take a few loads to the trash Dumpsters down the road. As we prepare to unload, we notice a poorer family there. I can tell by their beat-up

Impala and 1970's clothes. I don't know them. They pretend they are throwing away trash, but I can tell they are sorting through the trash, looking for anything they can salvage or use. I realize some items in their car are from what we just dropped off hours ago.

Susan walks right over and asks, "We're cleaning out a house, and we just don't have enough time to sort through the good stuff. Can you help? Can you take the stuff that shouldn't go into the trash?"

Without hesitation, the parents come over while their kid sinks in embarrassment in the back of their rusty Impala. I remember being embarrassed just like that kid probably is. His Mom and Dad are doing what it takes to survive just like Mom.

"That chair and those protein shakes?" The man asks.

"Absolutely."

Susan and I unload items right into their car without hesitation or judgement. I have more guilt than anything. Susan and I have been where this family is.

Susan says to them, "We have fifty more cases of these protein drinks. They're expired by up to two months but should still be good. When we finish unloading, we'll go home and come right back. We will bring them right here to you. In the next few days if there is something we think you might need, we'll leave it behind the right dumpster. We typically drop things off by late morning around ten to noon."

The man nods in approval and speaks. "Thank you."

Mom let so many of these drinks expire. It was further evidence she was not conforming to her strictly liquid diet. Stubborn Mama Mule. Susan and I return home and bring back the cases of expired protein drinks. In the last cases of protein drinks, I notice a small snakeskin wrapped in the cans. The man notices the skin, too.

"Don't worry 'bout it. It's too cold for snakes."

My Green Buddy and the Biting Kid

Thursday, May 13, 1976 – Seven Years Old. Second Grade.

Slither in the grass. Coil between my fingers.
Dropped. Lost. When Mom finds out, there'll be anger.
I told you once. Ain't going to tell you again.
Ouch! Now that's a taste of your own medicine.

It's 3:15 P.M. and we just got home from school.

Mom, anticipating my hunger, says, "Maikel, there are peanut butter and jelly sandwiches downstairs."

I gobble down two half sandwiches quickly before going outside. I walk down to the peppermint patch in the ditch, and something catches my eye. I watch it slither deeper into the Hall's-cough-drop-smelling damp vegetation. It's a green snake. Cool. I slowly drop to all fours and creep toward my prey. I reach out. The green worm with teeth slithers across the trickling water in the ditch. Too late. My determined hands shoot out with a faster snakelike strike.

"Gotcha!"

The beautiful green snake is about a foot long. It's none-too-happy to be captured and bites my hand a few times but eventually calms down. The skin around its head is molting, revealing fresh new skin underneath. I walk around showing the other kids. Most of the girls freak out and run away from me. I bring my new buddy inside, so we can bond. The green guy slithers and twists between my fingers trying to get away. I keep letting it weave between my minty-smelling digits. He bites my right index finger.

Ouch! I drop it. He lands on the floor. Faster than gossip spreading through a one-stoplight town, he slithers under the couch. I drop to my knees and peer under the couch. There's an abundance of dustballs and one of my missing wool socks. I hoist up the couch. He's wound tight around the dusty coils of the couch. Suddenly from the basement, I hear a kid scream like an arm was severed. I run downstairs to investigate the situation. It's Bill. He's bawling hard. Bill usually ain't the one crying.

Mom is next to him, "Now that doesn't feel good, does it? The only thing you should be biting is the peanut butter and jelly sandwiches I make for you."

Mom did it. She finally did it. Bill bit Mom and Mom bit back. She gave Bill a taste of his own medicine, a bitter bite. Ever since Mom started babysitting Bill, he's bitten at least one kid per day. After he bit me, I learned to keep my distance.

"Maikel, go get the peroxide."

"Sure. I can get the snake later."

"What snake?!"

"It's okay. He's comfortable and stuck in the couch springs."

"Now listen here, Maikel Lee Wise." I'm in real trouble when my middle name is used. "You get that thing out of the house NOW, and don't bring it back inside again!"

I do as I'm told. I'd rather catch a snake than have any body parts close to Bill's teeth. After a couple more tugs and several bites later, I remove the green snake from the couch. I take my green buddy back to the lush peppermint patch. He slithers away and disappears.

I walk back inside, and Bill is still sobbing holding his arm. A couple of weeks ago, I remember Mom talking to Bill's parents. "If you don't do something about Bill's biting, I can't let him stay here."

I didn't hear all the conversation, but Mom finally said, "I'll take care of it."

Most of the Burlington Mills and Russell Stover workers whose kids stay at the daycare pick up their children around 5:30 P.M. When Bill's parents come up to the basement side door, Bill is quiet.

Bill's Mom asks, "What's that bandage on his arm, Dolores?"

Mom says, "I bit him."

Stunned, Bill's Mom says, "You did what?"

Mom repeats, "I bit him. I took care of it."

Bill's Mom is outraged. "You have no right to bite my son's arm. We're taking him out of your daycare."

Like a preacher slamming a Bible on a pulpit to wake up a congregation, gossip spreads around Clarksville about Mom's biting incident. Some of the other parents let Mom clearly know that she can't bite their kid's arm. The phone rings quite a bit from concerned parents.

About a week later, the parents come back with Bill. I guess they couldn't find another childcare. "Mrs. Wise, please let Bill return to your daycare? Call us if he bites someone again, and please don't bite him."

Mom agrees. A few days go by, and Bill doesn't bite anyone. Every time Mom gets close to Bill, he covers his arms with his hands to protect them as he backs away. He's wary of Mom's mouth, and he knows the pain she will not hesitate to inflict if he bites anyone again. I can see Mom eyeballing him when he gets close to other kids, too. Billy has certainly changed. Mom did what she said she would do. She took care of it.

The next morning, I hear Mom yelling in the basement. I run to the top of the stairs and look down. She's holding a five-foot snakeskin in her hands. "Maikel Lee Wise. Did you bring another snake into the house?"

"No, ma'am. This one got in on his own. Don't fret, Mom. I think it's a black snakeskin. They usually don't bite people."

I don't have to worry. Mom can bite back.

Copper Tube Cannon and Fishtail Hogan

Saturday, May 22, 1976 – Poor Decisions and a Nickname.

A mouse fart sucks. Ain't much of a cannon.
Go get the gasoline. Let's see what happens.
Light the fuse. Stand back further.
Boom! Oh crap! I didn't mean to hurt ya.

My bike adventures take me farther from home. From my hub, I radiate outward in all directions, and I find a couple of brothers down the street. Curtis and Randall moved into the old farmhouse that is right on the Clarksville City limits. I think it's curious that half their house is in the city limits and the other half ain't. I wonder, if their foot is on the city limits side but their body is on the county side, could the Police Chief, Fishtail Hogan, still get them if they were up to no good? Something to ponder. Curtis, the older one, is hardly ever around. His brother Randall is the younger of the two but is still about three years older than me. Sometimes I see him walking in the cow pastures or at the ponds fishing. Stringy and long-legged, Randall can walk at his normal pace in the woods, while I have to run to keep up. I decide to ride my new Western Flyer bike up to Randall's house. I find him out back.

"Hey, Randall. What's going on?"

Bored, Randall replies, "Nothing. Just splitting some wood from the oak tree that blew down. I don't have to finish this today, though. I've got some firecrackers. Want to fire off a few?"

The soil around his farmhouse is sandy, and we soon find some anthills. *BANG!* Ants begin pouring out of the enlarged holes. A few crawl inside our pants and begin biting our ankles. We do crazy leg-swatting dances, smashing them against our tender skin, and move on.

Next, we find a beetle on some dog poop. *BANG!* Pieces of beetle and dog poop are blown into the sky. We give a new meaning to, "We blew that shit up."

Down by the barn, we spy Randall's cat. *BANG! BANG! BANG!* After getting a little too close and the cat jumping vertically three feet, the cat is nowhere to be seen the rest of the morning.

Disappointed, Randall says, "We used them all up. The package has a couple of fuses left though. What do you think we should do with them, Maikel?"

Enthusiastically, I respond, "Let's make a cannon. Are you sure you don't have no more firecrackers?"

"Let's go upstairs and see."

Rummaging under a pile of dirty clothes, Randall finds about three more firecrackers that had fallen on the floor.

"Randall, removing the powder is easy, but what kind of metal tube are we going to put it in?"

"Well, most cannons are made of iron, but we ain't got any. Let's go in the shed and see what we can find."

The shed contains mostly rough-cut lumber neatly stacked to prevent warping. Hung up on the walls are strands of wire and wire buckles. On the bench on the right side is a chainsaw missing the cutting chain. Back in the corner of the workbench, we find a couple of pipes leaning on the wall.

Randall explains, "This one is galvanized steel. I don't have no drill for the fuse hole. How are we going to get a fuse in it?"

My keen eyes spy another pipe lying on the dirt floor underneath the bench, "Randall, there's a pipe. Looks like copper tubing. Do you reckon that one'll work? It's not too thick, so we may hafta stand back after lighting the fuse. We can use a hammer and nail to make the fuse hole."

The tube is about eight feet long, so we bend about a one-foot section off. We nail two eight-penny nails through the flat end of the copper tube to an oak stump. Then we make a fuse hole and insert our firecracker powder with some cotton balls and some BB's. We light it and hardly anything happens. It's just a flash of light with a small poof, about the equivalent of an ignited mouse fart.

"Well, that sucked!" Randall disappointingly comments.

Undaunted by failure, I push on. "Randall, what we need is more powder. Do you know where we could get some?"

"I know! There are three twelve-gauge shotgun shells in the kitchen drawer. Since I lost my Buck knife, we'll have to use one of Mom's kitchen knives to open 'em. She don't like anyone using her knives. We'll have to be discrete."

Through trial and error, we discover that the bread knife with serrated edges cuts open the plastic shells the best. With three shell's worth of gunpowder, we figure we have something more than a mouse fart coming.

With dreams of a bigger gun, I ask Randall, "How about we get a longer tube?"

We repeat the process and move the oak stump farther from the house. This time, we add a few small nails and shotgun lead pellets along with BB's.

"Okay, Maikel, let's put in the fuse."

We forgot to make a hole for the fuse, so using a hammer and a nail, we carefully create a fuse hole, insert the fuse, and light it. Nothing. We try and try, but it just won't ignite.

"Maikel, go to the shed and get the gasoline."

I come back from the shed with a one-gallon red gas can in hand. I know we are going to set it off this time. With gas down the barrel and a drop or two in the fuse hole, we light it. There's a small flash. Spilled gas on the oak log creates a trail of flames back to the gas can. In a slow motion second, we watch the flame snake across the oak log down a wiggly gas trail headed to the can. *KABOOM!* A large fiery flash as the gas can rockets in the air. We hit the ground.

"Oops," one of us says.

Amazed, I say to Randall, "Look at the cannon. It's sitting there intact just smoldering and charring on the oak stump it's nailed to."

Disappointed and not hearing a response, I look over at Randall and gasp. His eyebrows are gone and his hair over his forehead is melted and still smoking. At least his two eyeballs are still in there. I feel my hands throbbing and look to see them red and burnt. *Uh-oh!*

"Randall, you smell like burnt dog."

"How do you know what burnt dog smells like?"

"It doesn't matter. Let's just say I know the smell and the dog wasn't too happy."

"You better get home, Maikel, and put some aloe on your hands. Better wash up, too, and get rid of that burnt dog smell. I'll get rid of the evidence. Maybe next time, we oughta think this through."

With all the noise, we worry that someone has seen the fireball and called the law. At least we are just on the other side of the city limits. Even so, I ride home as fast as I can.

I'm having a hard time holding onto the handlebars. With burnt hands, I just use my wrists to steer. Wobble-steering down the road, I hear a car haulin' ass with tires screeching and turning down Shiney Rock Road.

It's a good thing that I'm just off the road. The tires chirp in the first three gears. As it crests the hill, the driver of the white Camaro slams on the brakes, veering into our driveway and turning behind the house, stopping next to Mom's still struggling maple tree. It's my cousin Hank. I wonder why he's parked back there.

Then I hear it. Sirens from a police car that isn't far behind. Did someone see the gas can fireball and call the law? I see it's Police Chief Hogan and realize he's likely after Hank. Hank is always getting into trouble with Hogan. With the excitement dissipating, I feel my hands burning again. I slowly ride home across the top of our field on the uneven ground. When I walk in, Hank is already drinking a beer with Mom at the kitchen table. He may be in trouble being on this side of the city limits. My hands start throbbing even more.

"Mom, Mom, Mom. Do you have some aloe?"

Without hesitation, she knows. "Were you playing with fire?"

"Yes, ma'am."

We walk to the living room. She breaks a piece of aloe off one of her plants sitting on top of our Thomas Edison Gramophone. She rubs it on my burnt hands. "It might be sticky for a while, so don't go around touching things. Now how did you get your hands burnt?"

"Ah this is nothing. Randall lost his eyebrows and some of his hair."

Mom's voice rises. "What happened?!"

"We tried to make a cannon. Things didn't go so well after we added the gasoline."

"Now what did Pop say about that? He's told you two things not to do. Don't ever go out on the ice and never play with gasoline. I won't tell Pop, but don't do it again."

I'm relieved she isn't going to tell Pop because I'd surely get spanked. Mom is protecting me. As far as I know, it's not often she keeps secrets from him. I was okay with her keeping this one. Hank laughs and starts telling me a story about when he made a five-gallon gas explosion at Granny's. "You should have seen the fireball!" Mom gives him a disapproving look to not give me encouragement.

Since Hank is not in a hurry to get back on the road, I ask him a question that's been eating at me.

"Hank, why do you sometimes call Police Chief Hogan *Fishtail Hogan*?"

Hank starts twitching and smiling again. "Wayne Hogan and I went to high school together. We used to drag-race all the time. When we were younger, I got a '57 Chevy with a big block and I'd outrun his ass every time. So Wayne put a big block in his car. He used to brag how fast it was and that he could chirp the tires in the first three gears. But his car just didn't have enough power. So, when he hit third gear, he'd turn the steering wheel hard. He'd time it so the weight on the rear tire was less, and it chirped when he shifted. Sometimes he'd lose control with all that fishtailing. After that, we called him *Fishtail Hogan*. Now don't you go sayin' it to him. Wayne and I are friends. I just like messin' with him. He doesn't like that name, so I call him that to get him riled up. If you call him that, he might give you a ticket, young man."

Now I knew. I also knew better than to ever say *Fishtail* to him, too. That was between Hank and Wayne.

First Kiss

If you don't stop playing with it, you'll go blind.

Wednesday morning finds us at Granny's farm. Tash goes inside, but I walk straight to Granny, who is gently rocking on the porch.

"Granny, can I take your golf cart down to the potato barn?"

"Sure suga'. Don't run into anything."

I walk inside Granny's house looking for Tash. She's already playing post office on Granny's bureau writing desk.

I hear her mutter, "Now this one is our electric bill. This one is the house payment, and this one is for the doctor's office."

The bureau writing desk is old with a dark veneer. With a bookcase on top, it stands about six feet high. The glass doors in front of the bookcase have delicate panes. This desk would fit in perfectly in an old antique shop. The handles, knobs, and hinges are a lackluster brass color. The drawers and compartments hold all kinds of wondrous things—old military uniform buttons, .22 caliber bullets, 1940's coins, and outdated stamps. Granny keeps some of her old and important papers here, but it's mostly junk mail. I stand up on the edge of Granny's couch to see if anything is tucked away on top of the desk. Just behind the ornate leaf-carved molding, I find a couple of Playboy magazines and some Rough Rider condoms. I don't know who put them there, but suspect it was Hank, since the pictures in the magazine have naked women. Upon casual browsing, I find that Playboy magazines are so much better to look at than the

144

Christmas edition of the Sears Roebuck Catalogues. The mystery that was hidden behind women's undergarments is revealed.

"Maikel, you'd better put those back. You're gonna get in trouble."

"Hey Tash, let's go take Granny's golf cart down to the potato barn," I plead while staring sideways at a magazine one last time.

"Okay," she says as she checks out her last post office customer.

We whip the golf cart around, narrowly missing a wood pile. As we drive into the oak trees, the whole ground is covered with leaves and acorn shells from the previous fall. A fox squirrel darts out in front of us. The ground is dry and sandy. We brake hard to avoid the squirrel. The leaves reduce traction, and the three-wheeled golf cart slides a bit sideways. I remember Pop saying that three-wheeled golf carts aren't as stable as the four-wheeled ones. That didn't bother me, since the instability makes driving more adventuresome. We decide to chase the squirrel and accidentally clip a barn pole. We stop the chase to inspect the damage. There's one extra ding in Granny's golf cart. *Uh-oh.* Hopefully, no one will notice.

"Tash, let's do loops around the circle."

'The circle' is part of the road that goes around a giant oak tree. From our recent squirrel encounter, we know we can slide on it. Sometimes during dry spells, the sand becomes really loose. It's almost this loose now. Further pushing the limits, we keep going faster and faster around the circle. After about a half dozen loops, the golf cart spins out and we do a complete 180 slide.

"Whoa, Tash! Let's do it again!"

We keep going harder and find we can slide sideways without even hitting the brakes. The sand is getting looser and looser. Around and around the circle we go as the golf cart's rear drifts outward when we slam into the turns. We trade seats, since it's Tash's turn to drive.

"Faster, Tash! Faster!" I shout, dizzy from the loops.

We go around again and as we are turning; the golf cart catches onto something. Removal of all the sand from sliding exposes a root. We flip the cart on its side as Tash and I soar out. Superman and Superwoman momentarily fly before we harshly hit the ground. The seat on the golf cart flies off with us, smacking us on our legs.

"Oh, crap. I hope I didn't break it," Tash moans, pulling herself up from the leaves and sand.

We struggle to roll the golf cart back on its three wheels. As we do so, the batteries slide back into place. It's a good thing there's a bar holding the batteries partially in. We drive slowly back to Granny's. Whew, the golf cart isn't broken. It just has a few more scratches.

"Maikel, let's go inside and play post office. The worst we can get there is a paper cut." Tash darts inside.

After more post office, more Playboy gazing and more talking to Granny, we leave and go back home. Pop's new, used Suburban is loaded with jars of homemade pickles, stewed tomatoes, and black-eyed peas. I keep looking out the window thinking of those big boobies.

It's been over a year since Daniel and Charlene moved into the "For Sale" house beside Goddammit's place. Soon, Daniel and Charlene stay at Mom's Jack-n-Jill Daycare. One day, Daniel starts making fun of my name after Mom yells, "Maikel Lee Wise" at me.

Daniel taunts me. "Maikel Lee Wise. Ma Kelly Wise. Kelly. You have a girl's name."

I throw it right back at him. "Daniela. Daniela. You have a girl's name, too."

He doesn't like it, either. Eventually we both stop. After Daniel picking on me, and a few kids teasing me at school about my name, I got to thinking about people I call names. Goddammit up the street probably doesn't like it, either. I never called him that to his face, but now I start referring to him as Tom when I talk about him. I don't know if he minds the nickname, but since I don't like to be called names, I decide I'm not going to do it to him anymore. At least not out loud.

Daniel and Charlene go back home when their parents get home from work. With nothing else to do, I ride my bike over to my new friend's house, and yell, "Hey, Daniel. What are you and Charlene doing tonight?"

"Just hanging out. Come by after 7:00. We have company now. I still have some fireworks from the Fourth of July. I have a few Roman Candles, too."

Daniel looks a lot like his sister Charlene. Dirty blond hair and slim. I can just make out his ab muscles. So, when they come over and use the Slip-n-Slide, I hold my stomach in more to impress Charlene. Daniel is more a city kid than the local kids. He's fine going out in the woods, but he doesn't know much about hunting, fishing, fort building, or crawdad catchin'.

Tash and I sit on our front porch, waiting for 7:00 P.M. When we see the Jones's guests leave, we head to their place early.

Charlene comes running down her driveway to meet us. "Let's go play hide and seek. Who was it last time? Where is homebase?"

With the details out of the way, we get started, and I hide under a bough of tree limbs next to a pine tree. I cover myself partially with pine tags.

I hear my sister counting. "4…3…2…1…Ready or not. Here I come."

Someone runs toward my hiding space. It's Charlene, still looking for a place to hide. She has gorgeous dirty blond hair, cut-off blue jean shorts, a few freckles, and some long-striped tube socks that accentuate her legs. She reminds me of a young Farrah Fawcett. I never knew who Farrah Fawcett was until I saw the white bikini poster hanging up in the back room of Harrold Moore's Gas

Station. My heart pounds a little harder when Farrah Fawcett, I mean Charlene slides in beside me.

"Shh. Someone is coming," I whisper to her. I can smell her hair. It smells clean like Prell shampoo with a hint of pine. Tash walks by searching for someone to tag. She doesn't see us. We're safe.

"Maikel, I have something to ask you, but I'm nervous."

"Later," I tell her, dashing out to race towards homebase. We start over again. My sister is still *it*.

Charlene makes a beeline for the same hiding spot. I slide under the boughs, too, beside her. She moves closer and our arms touch.

"Maikel, would you kiss me?" She asks quietly.

I freeze. I've never kissed a girl before. Even though Charlene considers herself a tomboy, she's really cute. I never thought about kissing her. I'm shaking scared. I don't move. My stomach starts getting that feeling like driving over a hill too fast, going airborne, and almost losing your stomach. She leans in. Just before our lips touch, I inhale her Prell-infused pine-tag hair. My butterfly-filled stomach turns. I move closer toward her and our lips touch. The kiss lasts not even a second. I have the desire to hold her closer, but the butterflies are too much. The overwhelming wave of nervousness is more than I've ever experienced. We are so focused on the moment that we don't even see my sister getting ready to tag us.

Tash yells, "Got ya. I got ya before you made it to home base."

I was both mad and relieved. Mad that the moment had ended and mad that I didn't make it to second base. But I'm relieved that my tsunami of nerves is diminishing.

After Mom yells for us to go home, Tash and I leave, but I keep thinking about Charlene. I fall asleep fantasizing.

My stomach turns all night. I can't get Charlene out of my head. I wake up early. As I'm lying in bed, I fantasize about her kiss. Completely naked, I grab my second pillow and start kissing it, visualizing her, Farrah Fawcett, and the women in the Playboy magazines at Granny's. I roll over, imagining her soft skin next to mine while hugging the pillow. I hear the door creak open.

Mom quickly utters, "Sorry son," and then the door abruptly closes.

I'm mortified. Mom saw me naked and possibly my pee-pee. I throw the pillow off me and get under the covers, embarrassed and hiding in shame.

When I muster the nerve to go to the living room, Mom says, "It's okay. I won't tell anyone. I know you like that girl up the street. Pop needs to give you a talk about the 'Birds and Bees.'"

Tash, Scooter, and I at Granny's next to
Pop's new-used Suburban.

Hospice Care (Day Five)

Sunday, February 25, 2007 – Making Amends.

Littl' Joe trailer with wheels that are flat.
Given then withdrew by Mom, after they spat.
Granny's writing desk. Hand-carved wood and brass.
For Hank's daughter. I miss him. His crazy law-breaking ass.

Mom is losing weight. With only a diet of a small amount of water and an ample supply of morphine and Ativan, her body is consuming itself. Her legs have shrunk and are wrinkly. Mom's skin clings to skeletal cheeks, making them drawn in. It's painful to see her fade away. She's so strong and determined. My mind drifts to her inner strength as her body fails to keep up with her spirit. Death is about tired of waiting.

I hear a car pull up but dismiss it since I'm focusing on Mom. Soon, at the front screen door, I hear a gentle *knock, knock, knock*. The hospice nurse is here right on schedule. I didn't even hear her pull up. I wave her inside.

With the nicest, most sincere tone she asks, "Now how are you doing today, Dolores?"

There's no response, but Mom knows who she is. Nurse Johnson changes out my mother's catheter, adult diaper, and gives her a warm sponge bath. Mom always responds to touch. Like a house cat being spoiled and petted, she lazily closes her eyes with each stroke of washcloth. I walk to Mom's bathroom, grab her hairbrush, come back, and set it by her bed for later. Nurse Johnson is now rubbing

Mom's feet with the washcloth. Mom is in tactile heaven. I only know of two things that could make Mom calm—rubbing her feet and brushing her hair. I can eat all the ice cream, play with gasoline, and stop up the toilet. All I had to do was rub her feet or brush her hair. All would be forgiven.

I look over at Susan, "When Mom was a child, she'd get the eggs from the chicken coop barefoot. She said, 'The chicken poop gooshing between my toes felt good.'"

"That's gross." Susan winces.

"I agree, but she sure likes any form of foot rubbing or gooshing." The nurse laughs, "I've heard worse."

**The chicken coop where Mom liked
chicken poop gooshing between her toes.**

Nurse Johnson gently asks us a few routine questions about how we are doing and coping. I can tell she's seasoned. She can read our feelings, our stress, and our hardship with only a few questions and observing our body language.

"Maikel, I'm going to be here a while if y'all need a break. I have two hours before my next appointment. I'll sit with Dolores."

Susan, Tash, and I walk into the kitchen, humbled by her kindness and patience. The counters have more buckets of chicken, biscuits, and mashed potatoes.

I look out Mom's kitchen window through the wavy pane of glass and notice Tom (a.k.a. Goddammit) is cutting grass.

Sympathetically, I ask, "Tash, is there anything Mom has that Tom could use?"

"He and Mom had a fallout about her Littl' Joe trailer. Mom promised him the trailer, but they had a misunderstanding about something and that caused some tension between them. Mom changed her mind. He really likes that trailer."

"Tash, what about Granny's bureau writing desk in the garage? The one you used to play post office."

Tash recites the history. "Hank always wanted that desk. Mom wouldn't give it to him, either. I guess she had her reasons. You know, his daughter Pearl asked for it after Hank passed."

"Mmmm…I wonder if the Playboys hidden on top were his? If he wanted them back, too?"

We chuckle.

Susan says, "Let's make these things right. Let's give Tom the Littl' Joe trailer and Pearl the bureau writing desk." Deciding to act while Nurse Johnson is with Mom, we load up Granny's desk. It's awkward since the top part of the bureau writing desk has a bookcase with fragile glass panes. A couple of pieces of glass are held together with tape. The veneer is chipped with water spots on some of the horizontal surfaces.

When we are about a mile from Hank's place, I realize these relatives, his children, are strangers to me. I've been gone a long time. "Tash, I know these are my second cousins, but I don't know what any of them look like. Can you run interference for me and do most of the talking?"

"Sure, Cale."

I feel weird pulling up at Hank's house with no Hank there. I can see his old step-side truck in the driveway. There is still evidence of all the work he did on his place. His Camaro is long gone. I glaze over with memories. Trees are now all fully grown and will provide lots of shade when springtime comes. I remember drinking a beer with him on this porch. I miss him.

Pearl meets us outside. I remember when she was young. Now, I don't even recognize her. Part of me wants to tell Pearl and the others there the stories of growing up with Hank. Tell them all of the adventures, and the mishaps. When we arrive, though, everything seems so cold and distant. I don't have the energy to engage. I just don't have the emotional capacity to tell them anything. I shut down and deal with the task at hand.

We pass along Granny's bureau writing desk. "Hank and Mom would want it this way. You take care." She thanks us, and I can see the gleam of sentimental value in her eyes. I'm as kind as I can be. I miss Hank dearly, but just can't talk to them about him. We are silent on the drive back home.

Susan and Tash get out of the truck, and I pull down by the well house. I find Littl' Joe that caused such a dust-up between Mom and Tom. One tire is flat. I try to put air in it, but the tire is too old and dry-rotted. It won't hold air and needs to be replaced. I think about going downtown and getting new tires, but I just don't want to make the effort. It's too much. Susan walks down to check on me.

Sensing my frustration, Susan steps in. "Maikel. It is enough to give him the trailer. He can fix it."

Though I don't want to give him something partially broken, I know Susan is right. Using Tash's truck, I drag Littl' Joe to Tom's place. With all the scraping from the flat tires, Tom comes out of his house to see what's making all this ruckus.

"Hey, Tom. I know you and Mom feuded over this. Do you still want it?"

"Goddammit," he mutters.

"It's got a flat tire, and I don't have time to fix it. Here's forty dollars for a new tire."

Tom's eyes start watering up. Mine do, too.

Tom gives me a hug. "Goddammit."

For the first time ever, I understand him like my mom always did.

I open the passenger's door to Tash's truck, grab two bags of food, and hand it to him. He walks back in with two more buckets of Hardee's chicken with all the fixings. "Tom, do you mind if I walk around your yard?"

Tom's free arm shoots out with a Tourette's twitch signaling approval. I slowly walk around the yard. By an old telephone pole with a streetlamp, we used to watch bats go after the bugs. At the base of the pole is a discarded vodka bottle. Memories flood back. Motorcycles, lightning bugs, and forts made out of branches. This place was rich with adventure. I gaze upon the pine trees where the neighborhood kids made rope bridges. We'd climb the trees and see who could go the highest. One time, we raked up the pine tags and made a six-foot pile. Then we jumped off the tree from fifteen feet up. Another time, I played hide-n-seek and I had my first kiss. I close my eyes. It was yesterday.

Vodka Bottle Assault

Saturday, July 16, 1977 – Nine Years Old.

Wildlife Club with wine, song, and dance.
Don't get too close. Don't take a chance.
Mom's watching. Don't snuggle up to her Hub.
Hank protecting. He'll use anything. Anything as a club.

Mom and Pop decide to go to the Wildlife Club to a party with the Jones's. Mr. Jones is playing there with his rock band. Often, I hear Mr. Jones practicing his saxophone when he gets home from work. He looks like Zoot, the Muppet who plays the saxophone. He has thinning, receding hair and always wears mirrored Ray Ban sunglasses perched on a mighty schnozzle. He is so mellow that I never recall him ever raising his voice at Daniel or Charlene. His walk is kinda a "Hey Man" groove, simply flowing and relaxed as if he just smoked a joint.

All gussied-up, Mom says, "Now, we won't be too late. You can spend the night at Daniel and Charlene's house. We'll see you in the morning."

They head off for some partyin'. I'm grateful Mom tells me their plans. It's best to stay away from Pop when he's drunk. Sometimes, he gets as mean as a cornered tomcat.

With no adult supervision, Daniel, Charlene, Tash, and I tie a rope line between two pine trees next to their house. It's a bit higher than my comfort level. We keep trying to walk across it, but all of us fall with every attempt, cushioned by the six-foot high pine tag pile underneath. After hours of climbing and falling, we turn our attention to lightning bugs. After catching enough lightning bugs to write our bio-luminesces names on the concrete, we decide it's time for bed.

When we make pallets upstairs on the floor in their house, I ensure that my pallet is beside Charlene. I wait for Tash and Daniel to go to sleep by listening to their breathing. Soon, I touch Charlene's arm and find she's awake, too. She knows. She's waiting. I move closer, and she lets me kiss her again. This time it's longer and wetter with a touch of sweaty salt. I grew a bigger appreciation for salt at that moment. She lets me cuddle up against her and put my hands around her waist. I fall asleep wanting to touch her pre-emerging breasts.

RING! The phone abruptly wakes us up.

Charlene says, "It's your mom. She wants y'all home."

My morning kiss hopes ruined, Tash leads the way home, and I reluctantly follow.

Pop's Suburban is parked sideways in the driveway. Mom is anxiously waiting on the porch, pacing.

"Where's Pop?" Tash cautiously asks.

Hungover, she says, "Come to the kitchen and sit down." Her voice is hoarse, and eyes are bloodshot.

We know something's coming. Something bad. "Pop and I got in a fight. I didn't like how he was dancing with another woman. I walked up to Pop and he started hurting me. Then Hank hit Pop in the head with a vodka bottle. I ran out the door and came home as fast as I could."

Mom certainly didn't sugarcoat the story. Tash and I start crying. My imagination is on fire. I don't know if Pop is dead or alive. Will I ever see Pop again? Not even an hour later, I hear a car pull up in the driveway. I peek out a window and see Sugarfoot's truck with Pop riding shotgun. Mom doesn't go outside, but Tash and I run to meet Pop.

"Hey Ladybug. Hey Booger."

We start sobbing again. Pop's bloodshot eyes and bandages on his head look like he just got released from a M.A.S.H. unit. Blood has dried on his shirt.

"It's okay. Your Mom and I got in a fight. Don't cry, guys. I'm okay. Stay out here while I go talk to your mom."

After Pop argues with Mom, he climbs into his Suburban and flees. The tension in the air is as thick as gravy that stayed on the stovetop too long. A feeling of pain and dreariness lingers in the house.

Tash and I find comfort staying outside but don't stray far. That afternoon, Tash and I run into the house after finding another giant worm with teeth in the yard, eager to show Mom. Hank is at the kitchen table with Mom. We eavesdrop.

"Dolores, I'm glad you're okay. Are you sure Gary isn't mad at me?"

"He was mad at first. I told him you were looking out for me. Don't fret. I think you two are okay."

"Good. I like Gary, but I won't let him hurt you."

The floorboards creak under my feet. Mom and Hank catch us.

"You two shouldn't be listening to this but get in here and give your cousin a hug." Cousin Hank twitches.

Mom says, "But get that snake out of here first."

I ask Hank about the new 454 cubic inch engine in his '67 Camaro. He promises to give me a ride soon.

After Hank leaves, we listen for Pop's truck the rest of the day and all that night. Nothing. We don't know if he's coming back.

On Monday morning, Pop still isn't home. I grab the newspaper to read the comics as I sit on the front porch waiting for the school bus. I open the paper and right there, smack dab on the front page, are the words, *Vodka bottle assault at the Wildlife Club. No arrests or charges.* I feel like I'm going to throw up. I tuck the paper just inside the house as the school bus arrives.

I sit on the bus by myself. No names are mentioned in the newspaper article. It don't matter, though. In this small town, people will find out soon enough. When the bus arrives at school, I go to homeroom and place my head on the desk. I'm quiet and withdraw into myself. I avoid the hallway and socializing with my friends. I don't know if the other kids know about my parents. No one ever mentions a word.

When Tash and I get home from school, we see Pop's truck in the driveway. It looks like Mom forgave him again. That night, I hear Mom and Pop in their bedroom, wrastling and praying to God at the same time. "Oh God!"

The next morning with the sun just peeking up, it's early and I hear Pop's door creak open. Last night, I slept on the couch. He walks by and I say, "Good morning, Pop." He doesn't respond and keeps moving toward the door. Naked, he walks out the front door and down the road. Curious about where he's going, I step out onto the front porch. I look over and notice our neighbor Betsy is walking out her front door, too. She's getting her paper at the end of her driveway. At first, she doesn't notice him. Then she looks up and sees Pop. Bum naked, he's walking on Shiney Rock Road straight toward her. She quickly drops the newspaper, briskly walks back inside, and shuts her door.

I run back into the house and wake up Mom to fetch Pop. I've only been aware of Pop sleepwalking about five or six times since we moved here. He does seem to do it more when things are edgy. Seems like these days are always edgy, though. I think this is the first time he's been seen by a neighbor. I tell Mom what happened. She runs over and apologizes to Betsy and informs her of Pop's sleepwalking disorder.

Now that Pop is back, things return to normal.

At least, our form of normal.

Hospice Care (Day Six)

**Monday, February 26, 2007 – Bills. Spelling Bee Award.
Dented Sheetrock.**

*A little of this and a lot of that.
Save it all and be a good pack rat.*

Mom considered herself a pack rat and, well, she is. She keeps all manner of things. Each time Mom goes into her morphine-induced sleep, we sort through rooms and piles. We've removed enough to actually tackle the paperwork.

Overwhelmed, Susan, the organizer in our relationship, helps us. "Let's sort the piles. For example, electric bills in one pile, phone bills in another pile, and so forth."

Ninety percent of items we find are thrown away. As Tash and I discover outdated bills, we call the businesses to ensure all balances are paid in full. We log every conversation: date, time, account number, and whom we talk to. We have to. Our focus and memories are not reliable.

Among the papers crammed in one shoebox I find bank loan papers for $30,000 with a fairly recent date. I think, *Why would Mom take out a loan of this size and why isn't the money in her account?*

"Tash, what the hell is this?"

"Oh, that. Well, Mom got a balloon loan about the time you and Susan got married. She used the house as collateral."

Perplexed, I keep inquiring. "I didn't know she had bill problems. I wish she'd asked me for help."

Susan jumps in. "You know Mama Wise is too proud to do that."

Tash draws a deep breath. "Back before y'all got married, do you remember when Mom had her nervous breakdown? About 2001, I think. She stopped paying her bills. The electricity was cut off. She had DUI lawyer fees and medical bills. When she mentally broke down, she started buying things like a shed, a generator, and clothes. When a person is bipolar and depressed, they sometimes buy things to make them feel better. She went into buying overdrive."

There's a long silence with only the sound of paper rustling.

Finally, I speak up, "Tash, I didn't know. I knew she had some hard emotional times, but I didn't realize it was that bad."

"Yep, she was hurting. Just before the nervous breakdown, she had a couple of blood clots in her legs. She had to give herself injections in her stomach for blood thinning. She couldn't afford to go to the doctor's office for the daily injections. Mom did it herself at home. She took that needle and injected herself straight into her stomach. I couldn't do it. She's a hard woman...tough."

I don't know what to say. Mom always spoiled me, and I knew it. I just didn't know she was suffering. She hid it from me. It was one of her ways to protect me.

All morning, we continue to tackle the paperwork. The three of us keep saying, "She's a harrrddd woman. Harrrddd woman."

Tash hollers, "Hey, Maikel, I found your Fourth Grade Spelling Bee Award."

Bullies, Peas, and Spelling Bees

Friday, March 3, 1978 – Nine Years Old. Fourth Grade.

Crumpled sheetrock with the imprint of your back.
"You son-of-a-bitch!" Followed by a smack.
Drowning. Head held under water to get you to stop.
Mean ole cuss. I don't think much of Pop.
Focus on words, so I can't hear the screaming.
I wish it wasn't real. I wish I was dreaming.

Our fourth-grade English teacher announces, "Class, listen up. We are going to have an Elementary School Spelling Bee. Whoever wins will advance to the Mecklenburg County Spelling Bee. Here is a list of words each of you can study. This is your only assignment this weekend. Take this list home this weekend and be prepared for Monday."

I crudely fold the list and stick it into my pocket. I have biking plans with David and have no intention of studying. Class finishes, and we're off to recess.

I walk outside and notice that the softball team is already picked out. It doesn't matter—I don't have a glove to use, anyway. Nobody's playing dodgeball, since most of the basketball courts are being used for their intended purpose. I find a stray half-flat basketball and start playing HORSE by myself. Out of the corner of my eye, I see the bullies Cragley Kid and Wade, his partner in crime, moving toward me with a couple of their thug friends. I go into high alert. I'm hoping they stray off, but they walk right up to me.

"Hey, guys. You're welcome to jump in and play if you want," I say, trying to save myself from the torture I know is coming.

"Maikel, give us your lunch money," the Cragley Kid demands.

"Come on, guys. I only have enough for me. I need my lunch money." I know I'm about to be mugged.

"We ain't playing. Give us your damn money!"

The taller, stronger, and older kids surround me. I keep trying to play HORSE, ignoring what is about to happen. It's not the first time they've done this to me. Usually, they hang me upside down, drag me by my feet, or push me down until the money falls out of my pockets.

One of the other mercenary boys spurts, "You'd better listen to Cragley."

Two of the boys grab me by my feet, hang me upside-down, and start shaking me. I hear three quarters hit the pavement. A foot smacks as one quarter attempts to escape. They snatch it. I'm going hungry again today. There is nothing I can do. I am a fourth grader. They are seventh graders. They drop me on my head and move on to other soon-to-be victims.

Finally, it's lunchtime. David, my biking friend, has a table to himself. He lends me twenty-five cents. It's enough for a small container of chocolate milk.

Raymond and Jay sit down beside us.

After telling the guys what happened, David responds, "Yep. Those guys are assholes. That's why we try to hang out in groups of three or more. It's less likely they'll mess with three of us. I keep my change in my sock, too, just in case they come after me."

David graciously gives me his peas. I force them down with a pint of chocolate milk. I remind myself to keep my change in my sock from now on.

When I get home from school, the spelling list tucked in my pocket, Pop is already there.

"Hey, Pop. You're home early."

Not sleepwalking, he grunts, "It's been a long week. I'm plum tuckered out. We sandblasted and painted three bridges in five days."

He sits there drinking his Shlitz beer watching *The Andy Griffith Show*, a popular sitcom about a widowed sheriff in a nearby North Carolina town. I can tell it won't take much to set him off. I just leave him alone.

I grab a package of saltines to silence my hunger pangs. Not wanting to disturb Pop, I walk quietly back to my room to memorize my spelling bee words.

Pop's latest job is at a company called Bridge Painting out near the airport. Seems like every couple of years, Pop gets a new job. Each time, he makes a little more money. It's a stone's throw from Mr. Green's place where the barn collapsed on Pop a while back.

His new job requires him to travel to other towns every week. Sometimes he takes me to the main building to load up his equipment. The Bridge Painting building is nothing more than a giant garage with all kinds of tools lying around—paint guns, compressors, stirring motors, scrapers, and impact drivers. Anytime I knew Pop was there working, I would walk over to explore the tools and equipment.

One time after walking over to Bridge Painting, Cousin Hank outran Chief of Police Hogan and hid in the bushes behind the building. Hogan came zooming down the road a couple minutes later after him. Hogan, furious, yelled for Hank, but one of Pop's coworkers said in a calm voice, "Naw sir. We ain't seen Hank today." I remember Hank's Camaro engine was still hot and tinkling in the thick bushes. I thought fo' sure Hank was caught that time. He got away again. He outfoxed the coyote.

Mom has dinner ready. Pop has fallen asleep in front of the TV after drinking a six pack. Mom asks me to go wake him up. I hesitate but do as I'm told.

Mom, Pop, Tash, and I sit down at the kitchen table for dinner. Mmm…We are having chili hotdogs and peas. The hotdogs go first. Now all we have to eat are pearl onion infused peas. I really don't like peas, but Mom always says, "Y'all can't only eat meat and ice cream. You need your vegetables, too." Maybe so, but I think it wouldn't hurt to put a little bacon bits or sausage in the peas. Pop and Mom finish and get up from the table. Before leaving, Mom says, "You can't get up until you eat your peas." They leave Tash and me to stare at and suffer from our green balls of torment. Two doses of peas in one day is too much for anyone. On my suffering third nibble, a pea falls off my fork. It drops, bounces on my leg and lands on the floor. Scooter, our dog, is anxiously waiting for any scrap or handout. With one lick, the pea is gone.

I look at Tash and say, "Would you look at that? Scooter loves them."

Mom and Pop are nowhere in sight. I think of the recent song I just heard on the radio.

I look at Tash and sing a modified version of Johnny Paycheck's popular song *Take This Job and Shove It*. I substitute Pea for Job.

I place the pea up my right nostril and blow it on the floor. Anxiously waiting, Scooter quickly licks it up. Tash is rolling laughing. She starts shoving peas up her nose and singing the song. About two dozen peas later and after my nose starts dripping, my nostrils are getting sore. Plus, the excess pepper on the peas is causing me to sneeze. Tash and I decide to take our spoons and feed Scooter until all the peas are gone.

Not caught, we can now get up from the table and go to our bedrooms.

Tash, Scooter, and Maikel (about eight years old).

Shortly after, I hear a large thumping noise. I open my door further and see Mom lying on the floor. The sheetrock has collapsed above her where Pop picked her up and slammed her against it.

"Go to your damn room, or I'll give you something to cry about!" Pop hollers. I do as I'm told. I hear the shower turn on, and my Pop yelling, "That damn self-help Dale Carnegie course!"

I'm helpless. I can't do anything. I try not to listen as Mom gasps and begs for him to stop. I pick up my spelling bee word list and study. Teardrops hitting the word list, I repeat the spelling in my head as Mom cries, "STOP! STOP!"

Word number twenty-three, "Tenacious. T-e-n-a-c-i-o-u-s. Tenacious."

SMACK! Mom cries harder.

Word number twenty-four, "Dubious. D-u-b-i-o-u-s. Dubious."

The bathroom door flies open so hard that I hear the doorknob break more sheetrock.

Pop gets into the truck and leaves. Tash and I are still scared to leave our rooms until we are sure Pop is gone. We cautiously walk out and find Mom at the table. She's dripping wet with a welt forming on her cheek. We both hug her.

Tash asks, "Are you okay, Mom?"

"Yes Ladybug. I'm okay."

"Mom, what's Dale Carnegie?"

Mom cries but tries to remain strong, saying, "It was a course I took. Pop thinks it made me more stubborn. Don't worry about it."

Tash and I hug Mom again and hide back in our rooms. When Pop gets back, we don't know how mad he might be. We don't want to cross his path for any reason. For most of the weekend, I don't come out of my room. I study my words because it seems like the safe thing to do. I review my words over and over.

I was never so grateful for school to arrive than that Monday. I walk up to my English teacher on the stadium stage. She gives me a number to pin on my shirt. "Good luck, Maikel."

As ready as I'm ever going to be, it's time to start the spelling bee. I glance over at the honor roll kids and know in my heart one of them will win this. Word after word, we keep going. I'm grateful I don't get asked some words the other students get. Kids I thought would make it further drop out. Finally, it's down to Demetris Gregory and me. We go back and forth two more times correctly spelling our words. Then the judge says to me, "Shrewd."

"Shrewd...S...h...e...w...d...Shrewd."

I instantly know my mistake. I forgot the "r." Demetris spells her word and wins the spelling bee. I feel an overwhelming relief that

I don't have to represent our school in Mecklenburg County. Our teacher walks up and congratulates us.

"Good news. Both of you get to go to county spelling bee, but only Demetris can compete."

I'm excited for Demetris. I remember looking into her eyes and seeing how smart she was back when I first met her on the school bus. I can see it today. She looks the same but doesn't have cornrows and rubber bands in her hair anymore.

Two days later at the county spelling bee, Demetris wins. We return to English class and the teacher is dying to know the results. I run in first.

"What happened? What happened? How did Demetris do?" The teacher can hardly contain herself.

"She won! Demetris beat them all!"

The class goes wild with applause.

Hospice Care (Day Seven)

Tuesday, February 27, 2007 – Mrs. Vaughan vs Gladys's Chocolate Pies. Finding Boy Scout Klondike Derby Patch.

Ghostly image. You fell when you were shoved.
Hiding pain. Got back up. We're surely loved.
Victorious, Gladys's head held high.
I can't deprive. Just a little white lie.

The fried chicken in the fridge keeps growing like Viagra-infused rabbits. The neighbors, Betsy, Gladys, and Tom, take about one third of our stockpile. Another third is thrown away as the fridge has a finite capacity. I start to understand why all these folks bring food. When grieving, it is enough to just survive. A person doesn't need the added stress of shopping, preparing, and cooking. I'm drained from all the ongoing conversations from respectful friends to nosy people. I think back to all those folks who died when I lived here. I avoided them. After they died, I didn't do anything to help their families. I have to look inside myself and acknowledge that I could have done better.

At the same time, I recall what Scott, a friend of mine, told me. "You did the best you could with what you had." I think he's right. At least I tell myself that, so I don't feel so bad. Maybe I can do better in the future.

After my third cup of coffee, it's time for me to take a bathroom break. I walk to the bathroom, open the door, and look to the right. The sheetrock is still dented in. I remember the day this wall damage

169

happened. I try to hold it together in the bathroom, feeling somehow, I failed as a son. I sit on the toilet and try to rationalize the irrational.

My contemplation is broken by crunching gravel of another car pulling up in the driveway. An older lady pulls up in a car and gets out. I recognize her immediately—It's Mrs. Vaughan. She is the wife of Mr. Vaughan who owned the Vaughan grocery store years ago. I went to school with her three daughters. I also notice that across the street Gladys's curtain slides sideways ever so gently so she can see who's here.

We meet Mrs. Vaughan outside. "I made you a chocolate pie," she says in her most polite tone.

I remember Mrs. Vaughan when I was growing up. She was well-mannered, always polite and, unlike many I knew, nonjudgmental. She just seems to have a nice heart. If Clarksville had a royalty, Mrs. Vaughan would certainly qualify as the Queen. We invite her in to sit with Mom and Tash takes the pie to the kitchen.

"Are you doing okay?" Mrs. Vaughan reaches for Mom's hand and holds it gently.

"Yes ma'am. We are getting by. How are you and your daughters?"

In the most eloquent tone, she describes a little about them. Not too much, just a courteous amount. After about thirty minutes, Mrs. Vaughan gives us a hug. She seems more fragile than I remember. Not one minute after Mrs. Vaughan pulls out of the driveway, Gladys beelines it.

"Hey Gladys. That was Mrs. Vaughan."

"I saw that," Gladys responds promptly.

Tash, trying to stir up some competition adds, "Mrs. Vaughan brought us a chocolate pie."

With Gladys' curiosity satisfied, she says, "I just want to make sure you're doing okay." Then she heads back home.

She's barely down the front porch steps when we all head straight for the kitchen.

Susan says, "I'm trying that chocolate pie."

We all take a big slice. It's delicious. The pie is more refined and tastes better than Gladys's chocolate pie, but Gladys can never know.

The next morning, Gladys and Betsy come in around 8:30 A.M. They've been coming more and more to sit with Mom. I can't help it. I start chitchatting.

"Gladys, we have to tell you. Each one of us liked Mrs. Vaughan's pie. But we think your pie tastes better than Mrs. Vaughan's."

Gladys's eyes light up like a Christmas tree with an extra string of lights.

"Ahh, you think mine was better?"

"Fo' sho' it was."

We just made Gladys' day. I don't like fibbing to her because she has done a lot for us over the years, but what's a little white lie to make someone feel better?

Tash, smirking, says, "Now don't you go and tell Mrs. Vaughan. We don't want to hurt her feelings and stir up trouble. Give us a couple minutes to straighten up in the kitchen, and we'll be back."

Susan, Tash, and I race into the kitchen and finish up the last of Mrs. Vaughan's pie. Fortified, Tash and Susan join Gladys and Betsy to sit with Mom.

While they tend Mom, I start going through the clutter in my old bedroom. We've been here a week, and we haven't even touched the piles in this room. In an old cedar box, I come across my old Boy Scout hat and badges. I can remember working on some of the merit badges in the box. Among them, I find the Eagle Patrol badge and the numbers for Troop 7450. The First Aid and Canoeing merit badges took the most work to earn. There are fifteen of them in total. I have only a couple of regrets in life. Not getting my Eagle Scout is one of those regrets. I learned so much about respect, leadership, and the outdoors in Boy Scouts.

Troop 7450 and Klondike Derby

Saturday, February 3, 1979 – Ten Years Old. Fifth Grade.

Run like you stole something. Run with every intent.
Bloody, breathless. Just don't stop and consent.
Self-healing. Bimodal. Reattach if you can.
Gaining a bully's respect. Respecting me as a man.

Klondike Derby Patch and Occoneechee Indian Arrowheads

Our scout troop filters into Occoneechee State Park where our Scoutmaster, Fred Majors, awaits. Fred owns the *Bass Pro Shop* fishing store in Clarksville beside the Ford dealership where Pop was laid off. Fred is a little shorter than Pop and balder. Seems like he is always wearing a t-shirt or something with a fishing logo on it. I arrive at Occoneechee with our Assistant Scoutmaster, Wade Cobb, and his son Wade Jr., since he has to drive by my house anyway. Our other Assistant Scoutmaster, Billy Kearns, is there with his son Alec.

Fred starts the meeting. "Okay, scouts. I know we're a new troop, but we were invited to participate in a Klondike Derby. A Klondike Derby requires you make your own sled. At the completion, your scouting knowledge will be tested. Since we are such a large group, we will divide into our patrols. The Eagle Patrol and the Owl Patrol will each make their own sled. Here are some items you'll need: a saw, a knife, some rope, a tape measure, and pencil and paper. Any questions?"

Dead silence. I think about how we are going to accomplish this.

I'm in the Eagle Patrol. Mike Mills, a couple of years older and our patrol leader, takes charge. Whew. I don't have to make any decisions. "Listen up, guys. I've been thinking about how to build this sled for a couple of days. I have a list of items each sled has to carry. I'm guessing the sled won't have to carry over forty pounds. I reckon they'll want to test us on first aid. So, I suggest we make this sled long and strong enough to carry a person. We'll have to pull this thing like a sled, so we should bow up the front so it don't get stuck on nothin'."

We divide up the tasks. I go with Wade Jr., who is one of the bullies on my school bus. I think it's a good thing that I don't have any lunch money for him to steal. Our task is to find some new-growth hickory trees at least eight feet long.

"Leaves ain't out yet, Maikel. We have to look at the bark or at some dead leaves on the ground to make sure it's hickory."

I search the bare trees. "Hey Wade, here's a stand of them. There are some old hickory nuts from that bigger tree nearby." From my adventures with the bull, I know hickory nuts well. Wade and I cut down twice as many saplings as we think we'll need. We drag the saplings back to our meeting place to see that plans are well underway.

It's a good thing we brought back 10 twelve-foot pieces. When we try to curve up the front a little too high, some of the saplings break. Using our scout's guidebook, each one of us lashes and re-lashes every knot on our sled. Some of the younger scouts struggle with the bowline knot. Over and over, we tell them, "The rabbit comes out of the hole. Goes around the branch. Then, back in the hole." Eventually, everyone gets it. We fasten ropes on the front with loops so we can pull the sled like a pack of biped wolves. With the wood still green, our sled is a little on the heavy side, but it works. We made it ourselves. Our travois-like sled is ready for anything the competition throws at us. *Mush!*

When the derby finally arrives, the ride in the overpacked van is quiet. Looking out the fogged-up windows, we turn down a washboard road before the town of Boydton, heading to Eagle Point on the lake. We're all nervous and don't know what to expect. We're as green as our sled's saplings. We unload our gear at our assigned campsite and set up camp quickly. A few of us practice flint-and-steel fire starting to get rid of the cold dampness that envelops us. The wood is wet from drizzle, but almost anyone in our troop can start a fire anywhere. We have a couple of tricks that some of the city boys probably don't know about. We know things like using stringy cedar bark or fatwood lighter (the core of a half rotten pine tree).

Wood-smoke perfumed and as ready as we're ever going to be, all of us load up again in the van. We ride to check-in to have our sled inspected. There, lined up on the side of the dirt parking lot, are the sleds. These sleds are magnificent and fancy beyond belief. Some have gleaming stainless-steel runners. Many have three-inch holes drilled in thin plywood to make them lighter. Some sleds have runners with stained, laminated wood that is formed into elaborate curves. One sled is all aluminum and riveted with flames painted on the side.

We unload our primitive sleds from our mud-coated homemade trailer. Our sleds are unfinished hickory with frayed lashings. Some of the other troops start pointing at us and laughing. They are wearing ironed uniforms coated with awards and merit badges. We're wearing old t-shirts, blue jeans, and scout shirts with missing badges. I'm embarrassed. I lower my hat over my eyes to hide my humiliation. Some of the other scouts in our troop lower their eyes, too.

Our scoutmaster says in a volume loud enough for everyone to hear, "Looks like daddy helped these kids or did it for them. You boys listen here. You have a lot to be proud of. I didn't build. Wade Cobb didn't. Billy Kearns didn't. None of us made your sleds. You did it yourselves. I'm proud of you. I'm proud of you all! Now let's go register."

Straggling behind our leaders, we register and get another copy of the Derby rules, unsure of what tomorrow will bring.

That night, we run through the woods chasing each other like feral children, trying not to think about our fate tomorrow. That is, until we lie down. Morning comes sooner than expected, and we drag our sleds to the Klondike Derby starting point.

"Troop 7450, Eagle Patrol. Start at the First Aid Station," the referee directs. We jump into action as soon as we arrive at the first station. Alec makes a proper dressing for a wound. Mike handles a poison ivy rash. All of us make our sled into a litter and carry one of our scout-mates to the parking lot and back. We get all but the heat exhaustion question right. Since it is overcast and we can still see our breaths, it's too cold to worry about heat exhaustion today, anyway.

The next station requires us to extinguish a fire with a coffee can of water. We are not allowed to touch the can with our hands. We begin the technique we've practiced. Four of us pull in opposite directions allowing an elastic band to stretch big enough to go around the water can. Two people let go the elastic on opposite sides. The remaining two grab the can with the elongated rubber band and move it toward the fire. On our first try, we drop the can but get it right the second time and successfully put out the fire.

At the map orientation station, the referee instructs, "Use this map and compass. Navigate to find the treasure."

My heart races. I've only used a map and compass once before. Slowly, I align the map to magnetic north. I move to the first data point and find the first clue. Then, I repeat the same process for the next three data points. I stumble a bit on reorienting the map with the compass but figure it out. Finally, I find the silver dollar under a rock. *I did it!* I notice Mr. Kearns smiling at me. He had the same kind of smile when he taught me in Little League. He knows my self-induced stress and encourages me. "Good job, Maikel." I'm glad I didn't let the team down.

The last challenge is the time trial obstacle course. Our patrol has already scoped out this course during lunch. It's a crude trail along the shore of Buggs Island Lake, full of recently cut down trees. It's muddy, rocky, and stumpy. We put on our harnesses over our shoulders and line up at the starting line. Just like mush dogs in the Klondike, Mike, our patrol leader, is pulling back against us to keep us from taking off prematurely.

"READY! SET! GO!" the referee yells. As we start pulling our sled, it immediately catches on the tree stumps. We're stuck. Someone lifts the sled over the stump. We snag again. We aren't going anywhere fast!

Mike yells, "PICK IT UP! RUN!"

Instinctively, we do just that. We pick up our homemade non-daddy-made sled and run. We run like the ole bull is going to get us after we threw hickory nuts at him, and there's no barn to hide in. We run like an oak tree from hell is going to give us a devilish ass whippin'. Not only are we going to catch the train to the Second Coming; we're goin' to pass it. Somebody trips at front of the sled. We run over him, too.

Whoever the fallen, trampled person is, he gets back up, catches up, reattaches himself, and yells, "GO! GO! GO!"

I race forward with all my might. I feel someone step on the back of my knee. I'm immediately thrust down into the muck. I let go of the sled to use my hands to keep my face from hitting the dirt. My hands, sliding on the rocks and dirt, start to bleed. Then the boots run across my back. With so much adrenaline, I only feel subtle stomping and tenderizing.

I jump up, run, reattach to the sled and yell, "GO! GO! GO!"

Soon, someone else trips, falls, and gets trampled, but the single-focused scout-a-pede keeps going with a mind of its own. We lose a leg, run over it, it catches back up and reassembles itself to the body. With the finish line in sight, we hear the crowd yelling at us to go faster. We cross the line with everything we have. A couple more trampled, severed scouts cross just seconds behind us, ready to reattach. The clock stops.

We collapse. Out of breath, sweaty, muddy, and bleeding, we finish together. Wade Jr. is there, out of breath, too. I look over at him and see it in his eyes. Respect. I didn't quit. At that moment, I know he'll never again bully me, steal my lunch money, or hit me on the school bus.

The referee comes over, excited. "Wow! Wow! That was nearly a minute-and-a-half faster than anyone else so far! Wow!"

The other scouts are looking at us, but they aren't laughing anymore. Most of them are still in relatively clean uniforms. We are bleeding, muddy and a few of us have torn jeans in the knees. While the results are being calculated, we meander back to our camp to pack things up.

After about an hour, Fred says, "Troop 7450, gather around."

It takes a while to get everyone there and settle down. All the leaders are standing in front of us. Just arriving and standing with the leaders, Pop is there, too.

In a teary voice, Fred starts talking. "I don't know what to say. I'm proud of you." He turns around with watery eyes for a few moments trying to hold it together. "I couldn't have asked for anything more. Eagle Patrol, you tied for first place. Owl Patrol, you got third place." There are more moments of silence as Fred and the other leaders swallow the lumps of pride in their throats. "Just to let you know, they finally gave us plans on how to make a Klondike Derby sled. They forgot to mail it to us with the rules a few months ago. But honestly, I don't think you need it."

Hospice Care (Day Eight)

Wednesday, February 28, 2007 – Reverend Lyon.
Spaceship and Old Wheelchair.

Dust-covered toys and a rusty wheelchair.
Let's get rid of them. I'll go brush her hair.
Once a twig, planted when I was just past five.
It grew with us. That maple was part of our life.

"I don't know, Tash. Mom seemed to think these antiques are worth a lot of money. The problem is that she left them in the basement. Everything in that basement is rusty with all that humidity down there."

Susan steps in. "Why don't you call the local auction place? If they aren't interested, we'll donate it or throw it away."

More interested in the latter, I respond, "Okey dokey. Let me go check on Mom first."

Mom looks at me as I walk into the front room. She seems more detached now than a few days ago. She's less aware, but her eyes can still follow me. Tash, Susan, and I ensure every pile is out of her sight. We even hid a couple of the boxes behind her bed.

I pick up at her favorite turquois-handled black bristle brush and ask, "Mom, would you like me to brush your hair?"

She gently nods. Her eyes get more and more drowsy with each soft brush stroke. She has sleepy eyes just like after the morphine injections. After I caress her hair for about fifteen minutes, a white Lincoln pulls up in front of the house. A tall, slender woman gets out. It takes me a moment to recognize her. It's Reverend Jane Lyon, the funeral director's wife. A few days ago, Tash and I agreed to let Reverend Lyon speak during the funeral. I like that the reverend is a woman because around here it's usually men, some of whom I remember having clammy handshakes. I greet her at the front door before she knocks.

"Come in, Mrs. Lyon."

"Thank you, Maikel. I just want to see your mom and talk to you about a few things." Reverend Lyon walks over to Mom. "Hello, Mrs. Wise. How are you? I like all your flowers and balloons."

Mom is nearly comatose from my hair brushing. She gently closes her eyes. "Mrs. Lyon, let's go to the kitchen so she can sleep." She looks so small and fragile in the hospice bed.

Tash and Susan are in the kitchen drinking coffee. Mrs. Lyon and I join them.

"Tell me about your mom." I recount us moving here and Mom's jobs through the years. I only disclose some of her hardships. Mrs. Lyon takes some notes.

"She sounds like a tough woman."

I look over at Tash. "She's a hard woman."

Tash, Susan, and I crack up. Then we tell the Reverend about Mom injecting the needle into her own stomach. Mrs. Lyon doesn't cringe. She must be a hard woman, too.

"Mrs. Lyon, I have something you may like for the funeral." I hand her a poem that I wrote for Mom while I was in college.

We sit in silence so she can read it. "I like this, Maikel. A few days ago, you also mentioned a tree your mom planted. Was it this maple tree in the poem?"

"Yes ma'am. The tree was a silverleaf maple in the back yard. We'll show you."

181

We leave the kitchen and walk past the well house to the back yard. "That tree there. Here's a picture of Mom standing by the tree last year."

"Would you look at that? It's taller than your home."

Mrs. Lyon finds a fallen branch with new spring-growth leaves and picks it off the ground. She isn't rushing. She's taking in the moment. I feel the knot building in my stomach and find my eyes are starting to water again.

We say goodbye, and I go back inside. Mrs. Lyon stays for a while by the tree by herself. She embraces the spirit of the tree. I think to myself, *Yes. She is the right one for Mom's funeral.*

It's time to re-tackle the basement items again. Piles and clutter are dwindling, but it's taken a lot of work. I think, *When will this end?* Susan, Tash, and I are mentally scattered. We're in a mustier part of the basement. We decide to go into the dirt section, the unfinished part of the basement, and start pulling things out. We move several cans of solidified paint, oxidized copper pipes of various lengths, and dusty rolls of paint-splattered plastic to a trash pile. I pull out an old green-and-white bicycle with solid tires. The tassels at the end of the handlebars are nearly gone and look like short whiskers. I find one of my toys—a plastic spaceship from *The Empire Strikes Back*. It's covered in red iron-rich dust. Some parts are missing, and some stickers are gone or curled up on the edges. Behind everything, all the way back in the corner, coated in more dust and rust, is one of Pop's wheelchairs.

Mom in front of the Silverleaf Maple in 2006.
It was five feet (and ¾ inches) tall, the same height as Mom,
when she planted it.

A Wise Separation

I'm losing myself. I don't care about much.
Why even bother? To care and such.
Others smile. Sun shines, no bad weather.
Their families are happy. They're still together.

Our sixth-grade English teacher Mrs. Samford walks in a few minutes late and just in time. The class chitchat is reaching a roaring level.

"Settle down. Settle down. Hello class. Will you please pass your homework to the front?"

I reach around behind me and pretend to insert my nonexistent homework into the stack. It doesn't work. Mrs. Samford notices. I keep my head down. She collects the papers and goes through them.

She marches up to me. "Maikel, I don't see your homework. Do you have it?"

I hold tightly to the round polished edges of the desk, ignoring my fingertips as they press into the stuck gum underneath. The whole class can hear. I keep my response simple. "No ma'am."

"Why not?"

"I don't have it."

"Why? Why not?"

"I didn't do it."

I have no excuse. I just didn't do it. Some of the other students stare at me as I sink further under my desk. It doesn't seem to matter. At least it hadn't mattered until she'd verbalized it in front of the whole class. I'm ashamed, but there is nothing I can do about it now. The class ends, and Mrs. Samford calls me to her desk.

"Maikel, I know you can do better. You're in the school's Gifted and Talented program, but your grades are falling. I'll give you another day to finish your assignment."

I leave feeling relieved. I won't get an F. This time, I plan to do what I'm told. I don't want those judging eyes looking down on me again. All I want is to walk in the woods and sit and simply stare into the quietness.

When I get home from school, Mom is on the front porch mad and red-eyed. Surprisingly, Pop's Suburban is there, too. Usually, he isn't home until after 5:00 P.M.

"Maikel and Tash, go to your room!" I do as am told. I can't help it and sneak to a cracked window to look and listen. Mom is yelling at Pop "You son-of-a-bitch! This woman calls me and says you got her pregnant. Well, did you screw her?!"

Pop's face turns red, advertising his guilt. Pop doesn't say anything. He storms to their bedroom, and I hear clothes racks clinking and dresser drawers slamming.

I can hear Tash weeping in her bedroom. We hear Mom in the kitchen as wooden chair legs slide across the floor. She's sitting by the window smoking a cigarette and drinking her tea. She's crying.

Tash and I walk into the kitchen and Tash asks, "Mom, are you okay?"

"I will be. It's okay, but I don't know if Pop is coming back."

Tash and I give Mom a hug and try to comfort her. Mom continues to sob. There's nothing we can do. There's nothing we can say. We can't fix it.

I walk back to my bedroom and sit on my bed. Heartbroken, I reluctantly start on my overdue English homework. I'm required to write a one-page essay on: *Who is someone who inspires you?* I think long and hard about who inspires me. Eventually, my mind interprets the assignment as: *Who do I want and not want to be like?* I start writing.

The next day, I turn my paper in to Mrs. Samford early before most of the students arrive.

"Thank you, Maikel. I'll grade it now and hand it back to you before class starts." I sit down at my desk to work on my other homework that I was supposed to do last night. It only takes Mrs. Samford a few minutes to grade my paper.

"Here you go, Maikel. See, you did great. You would have gotten an A if you had turned it in on time."

I look over my paper and see the corrections. She was fair.

92

Good job! Minus one letter grade for being late. Watch your use of the word "ain't".   Who is someone that inspires you?

I've met plenty of folks in Clarksville. I've watched the news and seen heroes and

villains on TV. There really is no one person I've met that I can say that I would like to

be. There are things about my parents that are good and bad. I like how smart my

mom is. She calls it horse sense. She can make a good meal out of nothing. She just

keeps going. I don't like it how she smokes so much. It ain't supposed to be good for

you and doesn't smell great. I like how my Pop can fix a lawnmower or car. He can

repair anything. I don't like it when he yells at Mom and gets her crying. I like how
                                                              oxen -1 pt
strong Sugarfoot is. He's a nice man and strong as an ox. I hear oxe's are are strong

but ain't never seen one. I like my cousin Hank. He's always kind even after a few

beers and has a really cool motorcycle. I don't like my Uncle Henry. He's mean to his

workers and doesn't pay them much. They work hard for him. I think he's too
                          Spelling -1 pt
prejudace. I have black friends and don't think much of my uncle. When I was younger,

I wanted to be an astronaut but not so much now. Climbing up a top of an oak tree is

about as high as I wanna go. So there's not just one person that inspires me. There are

parts of people I like and some things I don't. I just don't wanna grow up and be a

mean old man.   *want to -1 pt*

Maikel Wise

Tash and I get off the school bus. In the front yard, Mom is handing out frozen treats to the daycare kids. Her homemade popsicles are made by pouring Kool-Aid into ice trays and adding toothpicks for handles. The kids consume all the toothpick popsicles in short order. Nearly all the kids have either a purple, orange, or red ring around their lips. Some kids have a rainbow of colors, so they must have consumed more than one. After a couple of ice cream headaches, Mom has some of the kids wash off their faces. Some of the kids escape the cleaning. Soon after the first shift ends, Burlington Mills and Russell Stover factory workers come to pick up their kids.

"Come on, Ladybug. Come on, son. Let's go upstairs." There's a seriousness in Mom's voice. "Sit down." Scooter, our dog, moves over to the side as Tash and I sit waiting to hear the bad news. "We both love you. Pop and I have decided to separate and get a divorce. You can choose who you want to live with. You don't have to choose right now."

Crying, Tash says, "Mom, we don't want to choose."

"I know, Ladybug. I wish things were different. Sometimes... sometimes the sun comes out, and sometimes it rains. This is one of those rainy days."

Tash and I start tearing up again. Seems like all we do these days is cry. We don't want to choose. We don't know why Pop is leaving us.

I ask, "Mom, did we do anything wrong? Can we do something to fix it?"

"No, son. Gary doesn't love me like he used to. It's nothing you did. Pop still loves you. I still love you." Even Mom starts sobbing. "You can skip school tomorrow if you like."

The next day, Tash and I do just that. All morning, I sit by the creek next to an oak tree in the cow pasture. I even see the bull looking at me, and I just don't care.

CLARKSVILLE ELEMENTARY SCHOOL
Clarksville, Virginia
1979-80

BETSY SAMFORD
Grade 6

Mrs. Sanders 6th Grade Class

Me, front row, second from left, in my Boy Scout uniform.

David, third row from bottom, fifth from left.

Talk About Sex, We Must

Friday, May 30, 1980 – Eleven Years Old. Sixth Grade.

Remember the butterflies of the first kiss.
A broken heart. That pain, I don't miss.
Remember the smells, the touch, and the taste.
Just in her presence, I feel my heart race.

A short time ago in what seems far away, Pop left his boilermaker job at Burlington Mills. His new boilermaker job requires him to travel to different cities to work on numerous power plants. It pays better and the company puts him up in hotels. After he left us, we haven't seen him much. When he does pick us up, he takes us to the *Penguin* for a hamburger or we go for a drive in Occoneechee.

One day, Pop unexpectantly pulls up in the driveway. He asks Tash and me to go with him for the weekend. Pop gets permission from Mom. However, Tash can't go because of ballet lessons. Pop and I load up in the Suburban and drive to Richmond.

"Hey, Booger. I thought we could go see the new *Star Wars* movie before going to the hotel. Get me another beer out of the cooler, will you?"

The first movie was great, and my friends told me the second one is even better. It wasn't often that I went to movie theaters. The closest one was about a half hour's drive away from our home.

"Pop, can I open your beer?"

Opening Pop's beer means I can have a sip or two. As I get older, the size of my sips grow. I gulp.

"Easy. That's enough."

As we turn onto the big rolling hills of Hwy 360 to Richmond, Pop takes his beer and tucks it between his legs each time we drive passed a Virginia Highway Patrolman. Two beers later, we pull into the theater.

Pop crawling into one of the boilers he worked on.

When we walk into the darkened theater, we find it isn't crowded. The movie starts, and I'm mesmerized by the spaceships, lasers, and special effects. I've never seen anything like it before except for the first *Star Wars*.

Part way through, one of the characters speaks. Pop and I start uncontrollably laughing. Every time he says something, we completely lose it. A lot of folks in the theater are getting annoyed and shushing us. Pop just ignores them, since he's at least twice their size. We hardly hear the dialogue in the movie each time after he talks.

The next day, Pop gets ready for work.

"Booger, you can go in the pool while I'm gone, but don't go in the deep end. Understand?"

"Yes, sir." Yes sir is my automatic response, but I plan on wearing out the diving board, anyway. How will he know?

When Pop gets back to the hotel, we laugh and laugh while eating dinner.

Pop gets serious. "Booger, come here." Since he called me Booger, I know I'm not in trouble but may have to bring him something. I jump off the bed and sit beside him at the table.

In a deep, gentle voice, he says, "I hear you like that Charlene girl."

I squirm. "Yes, sir. She's kinda cute."

Then an unexpected sledgehammer drops. "What do you know about sex?"

Nervous and a tad shaky, I say, "Just things I've heard from other kids at school. Some of the kids say they have 'done it.' Some of them show Playboys and condoms like at Gran...I mean behind the counter at the Hop-In store." *Whew*. I almost slipped up. I didn't want that Playboy magazine to disappear.

"Well, there's more to it."

Pop goes into detail explaining about sex and masturbation. He starts to fluster when talking about women's private parts. My mind drifts to the Playboys at Granny's house, to Charlene, and to teenage girls in bikinis at the pool earlier today. My stomach can't handle all those other things he tells me. Pop's sausage-finger examples and visual effects make me more curious but awfully uncomfortable. I don't think I'll be too keen for a back scratch for a while after seeing his animated fingers. Sometimes at church, the preacher talks about lust, and this seems to fall in that category.

On the last night at the hotel, I wake up to one of many Pop's beer-induced snores. I lie there at night wondering if this is how it's going to be. I miss Pop not being home and letting me help work on the cars and lawnmowers with him. I miss our trips to Occoneechee and swinging on vines after Sunday morning breakfast. This weekend has been fun, and we laugh all the time. It's good that he isn't hurting or fighting with Mom. It may not be so bad if he isn't home. That is, except for Mom. At home, she cries by herself almost every night. She's heartbroken, and I don't like her being so sad. At this moment, I think, *Sleep, you must.*

Pop races back to Clarksville the next day. As we pull into 119 Shiney Rock Road, I notice a sign on the yard of Daniel and Charlene's house. Pop speeds off and I go inside.

"Hey, Tash. What's the *For Sale* sign at Daniel and Charlene's place?"

"I just heard this morning. Their parents are getting a divorce, too. They've been packing up all weekend. I think they're leaving today."

My heart sinks. My crush is leaving, and I won't have any more kisses. I think, *Why do weekends have to end so shitty?* I look out the kitchen window—a rare moment, since Mom is usually perched here. I watch them load the U-Haul truck and trailer. I want to go take my love into the woods and hold her. I'm heartbroken. Then I see Daniel and Charlene making their way to our house at the top of our field.

Tash and I meet them in the front yard.

Charlene tells us, "I guess you've heard. Our parents are splitting up, too. We are moving to someplace in North Carolina."

Tash in her best Southern hospitality voice, "We'll miss y'all. If you come back this way, come visit."

We hug each other. I inhale a deep breath of Charlene's wondrous hair. I go downstairs and think, *See her again, I know not.*

With a broken heart, I walk into the kitchen and find Mom firmly planted in her perch. "Did Pop talk to you about the 'Birds and Bees'?"

I glance over my shoulder to ensure Tash isn't listening. "Yes, ma'am."

"Now remember, if God didn't want you to masturbate, he would have made your arms shorter. And don't read any of Pop's Penthouse Forums that he may have hidden around the house. They'll mess your head up."

Mom grabs my hand. She knows I'm in pain and have a broken heart. "I know, son. She was your first love. Don't fret. There will be others."

Pop's New Girlfriend

Friday, June 6, 1980 – Eleven Years Old. Sixth Grade.

Another woman holding on to my Pop.
He broke our family. Why doesn't he stop?
Preacher says make things right. Work it all out.
He's wrong, with the righteousness he touts.

"Pop called. He'd like to see you." Mom says sorely. "He's staying with a new girlfriend who has two daughters. They live over by Burlington Mills not too far from Hank. We talked to the judge. He says you get to visit him every two weeks and we'll alternate Christmases."

I can see the pain in Mom's eyes as she holds it together the best she can. "He'll be here at four o'clock to pick you up. Pack enough for the weekend."

Anxious and scared, we wait outside on the front porch steps. Pop pulls up at 4:45 P.M. He looks different. His mustache is thick across the top of his lip and turns down the side of his mouth. He's wearing a cowboy shirt. I notice there is a cowboy hat in the back seat with a headband made of bobwhite quail feathers. Somehow, I missed the memo that Pop was changing his appearance, or maybe this new woman is forging him into something she wants him to be.

"Hey Booger. Hey Ladybug. Hop on in."

"We missed you, Pop," Tash says.

After turning right on Highway 15, Pop says, "I missed you, too. I'm staying with a lady over near Burlington Mills. You'll like her."

Not knowing how to respond, Tash and I remain quiet. We pass the Russell Stover candy factory and Burlington Mills factory. We drive down the old highway 15, the Old Sudan road, toward Merrifield. Just a short way down the road past the railroad tracks, Pop turns left. He drives slowly down a washboard gravel road following a power line. I've seen this road before but have never gone down it since there are private road signs posted. As the crow flies, this place is close to Hank's. At the end of a gravel road paralleling power lines, there's a nice two-story house nestled in an oak forest. As we approach the house, I'm completely shaking and nervously sweaty.

Like refugees looking for a place to sleep, Tash and I get out of the truck with our weekend paper bags of clothes. A woman walks towards us. "Hello, Natasha and Maikel. I'm Jolene." She has curly brown hair and oversized glasses like Elton John wears. Her breasts are bigger than Mom's, too. My mind goes to a dark place. I think, *Is she going to be mean to us?* She was mean to my family by having an affair with Pop.

We walk inside her home. After a few games of Yahtzee, the tension is gone. Then Pop kisses and hugs this other woman. The awkwardness returns. I don't like it. She isn't Mom. I decide to be polite to this woman but nothing more. She took Pop away from us, but Pop made a choice, too.

On Sunday afternoon, Pop drops Tash and me back home. Mom is there with Jane, one of her friends. The conversation looks serious. We make peanut butter and jelly sandwiches while they talk and we eavesdrop.

"Jane, I talked to the preacher. I told him that things weren't working out with Gary, that he got another woman pregnant. Now he has a new girlfriend. Anyway, I said I wanted to get a divorce and might need some help. Do you know what he told me? He said to *work it out*. Can you believe it?"

"Dolores, I wonder if he would *work it out* if his wife slept with someone else."

"I know, right? I don't want my kids going to that church again. I think I'll find another church."

Tash and I heard part of our soon-to-be-future. It's not like Mom, Tash, and I ever went to church on a regular basis. However, it sure sounded as if we were going to a new place and may have to be "churched-up" more frequently.

Pop and Mom before they separated.

The Accident

Friday, June 20, 1980 – Pop Showing Off.

You were supposed to pick us up that day.
You didn't care. Drinking your troubles away.
Your judgment was off. You made a mistake.
What's going to happen? What is your fate?

It's 5:00 P.M., and as usual, Pop is late to pick us up. Tash and I wait for an hour on the front porch with our overnight bags. We finally tell Mom, and she tries to phone Pop. No answer. We keep waiting. Sirens blare in the distance. Minutes later, I hear a firetruck on Highway 15 going past Shiney Rock Road and heading south. Soon several emergency vehicles follow. The phone rings. Mom picks up the phone.

She runs out of the house, nearly slamming the door into us. "You two! Go to Betsy's! NOW!"

Mom races to her Pinto, heading in the same direction as the emergency vehicles.

When she returns two hours later, Mom's red-tainted eyes advertise her pain. She asks us to come to the living room and sit on our shaggy-brown couch. Tash and I know something is coming. Something bad.

"Pop had an accident. It's really awful. I followed the ambulance to South Boston. We had some problems. The ambulance ran out of gas, so I got some gas for them. Then, they got a flat tire. Finally, Pop made it to the hospital. They had to fly him to Duke University

198

Hospital for specialists. He has some type of chest injury. I'm sorry this had to happen to you two."

All I heard was "accident," "bad," and "hospital."

Numbly, Mom says, "Go get ready. We are going to the hospital."

I'm filled with deep sadness not knowing what dark place we are driving toward. When we arrive in the waiting room, we wait. Tash and I glance at pictures in magazines while Mom takes dozens of smoke breaks. After what seems like an eternity, a doctor comes out.

"Are you Mrs. Wise?"

"Yes, doctor."

"We had to operate on Mr. Wise's heart. When the truck landed on top of him, his aorta ruptured. He lost several pints of blood. He also broke his back and pelvis in several places. He broke an arm and a leg. There's severe head trauma, and as a result, extreme swelling. He'll be in ICU for quite some time, and we don't know if he will survive."

"Can we see him, doctor?"

"Not tonight. He's in a coma. We'll know more in the morning."

We drag ourselves back to the waiting room to find a couch. We sleep the best we can. About 9:00 the next morning, Pop's girlfriend Jolene and her two daughters arrive. They sit as far away from Mom as they can and avoid any eye contact with her. A couple of hours later, the doctor comes out. He lets Mom, Tash, and me know we can visit him for only five minutes. We walk into the room and see Pop's hips are suspended in a contraption that looks like a swing. Tubes connect to his chest, nose, and mouth. Bandages wrap his chest. His right leg is elevated and in a cast. His left arm is in a cast, as well. I hear the beep of his heart mimicked by a machine. Pop's head and closed eyes are extremely swollen. His eyes remind me of those bulging goldfish eyes I've seen in pet stores. We cry and cry. There is nothing we can do.

Off and on for a couple of weeks, we visit Pop. Each time, the swelling in his eyes lessens. At the end of the second week, Pop's eyes finally open, but they look weird.

"Hey, Pop. You look better."

He's still not all there. He looks towards me but not at me.

We hear him mumble, "I want to go to top of a mountain and drink cool Jell-O through a straw."

He keeps repeating it. We ask the nurse if they have any Jell-O and straws, but Pop can't eat food yet. We leave feeling better that Pop may survive but know he's not out of the woods yet. I don't understand all that mumbling about Jell-O and straws. Maybe he has brain damage, or he's drugged up. I can't figure it out.

On the drive home, Mom starts preparing us. She pulls over in a *Piggly Wiggly* parking lot. "I have something to tell you two. Pop's accident was bad. He lost too much blood and now he's blind. They don't know if he'll permanently lose his sight. He broke his back and may not be able to walk again."

I'm numb. Overwhelming and deep sadness takes over. I think of the things we can't do with Pop anymore. No more swinging on vines in Occoneechee. No more fishing in the remote coves on Buggs Island Lake. No more walks in the woods. No more Boy Scout camping trips together. No more drives down the Old Sudan Highway. There's nothing to do but look out the window and think how things will never be the same again.

Hit the Road, Pop

Wednesday, December 25, 1980 – Twelve Years Old.
Seventh Grade.

I don't know total darkness. A day without light.
Other senses amplified, with the loss of your sight.
To stand upright. To stand tall once again.
Tables turned. Now you must depend on your friends.

Pop spent nearly three months recovering in the Duke University Hospital, then another two months in rehabilitation. Now he's back in Clarksville living with his girlfriend. He's learning how to adjust to his blindness and paralysis. Mom says we can spend Christmas with Pop. On a cold, gray December day, we reluctantly go to the Pop's girlfriend's place. Jolene's front porch steps are covered with a new, unpainted wheelchair ramp that still has the smell of fresh-cut pine. The well-built ramp looks solid but would be slick as snot if it snowed. Tash and I walk up the ramp. Pop waits inside the stuffy house and gives us a hug as we enter. It's odd to hug Pop with him sitting in a wheelchair. A short time ago at this same spot, I recall Pop giving me a big ole bear hug and lifting me so high that I hit his cowboy hat. He was standing tall and strong back then.

He's excited for us to open our presents before lunch. Tash and I each get a vest. Mine is navy blue and Tash's is Tarheel blue. In the middle of each folded vest is a replica of a Rubik's Cube. I've seen these toys downtown in some of the stores by the checkout stands. These cheap knock offs are about half the price of the original Rubik's brand and don't turn as easily. My second present is a spaceship from *The Empire Strikes Back*. Cool! Tash is equally excited getting a Tanya Tucker cassette. Jolene yells, "It's time to eat."

Lunch sucks. Jolene prepared mostly prepackaged, undercooked food. It lacks the excess grease and butter that Mom uses. No soppin' this shit up with a biscuit.

I put on my new navy-blue puffy vest and walk outside into the woods nearby. There's a bite to the air, and I'm grateful for the vest, even though it's a size too big. I can tuck my arms inside to stay warmer, but I look like an armless biped. There is enough space inside for me to tuck my spaceship gift under it, too. I remember laughing at with Pop not that long ago in the movie theater in a place that seems so distant. It's good to get out of the house. It's too toasty. Pop needs to have the house warmer since the circulation in his legs was affected by the accident. I feel weird looking down at him when I listen to him talk about his rehabilitation. Pop's fight in life has changed. Now, his fight is to walk and see again. It's no longer fighting with Mom. I still fear him losing his temper, but things are different. Pop is completely dependent on help. He seems vulnerable and even humble.

After twenty minutes outside, I notice a fender-rusted, red Chevy Silverado truck rolling down the driveway. I move to a better spot with no trees in the way to see who is pulling up. A Clarksville, wanna-be cowboy man gets out with his black hat and Wranglers a size too small. I don't recognize him. In some ways, this stranger reminds me of Pop before the accident. He's tall, sporting a little beer belly and is about the same age as Pop, but this dime-store cowboy has dark hair with a dark mustache. I walk back to Jolene's house, curious who this outsider is.

Jolene introduces us. "Hey Maikel and Natasha. This is Jerry. He's a friend of mine."

I say "hi" back but get an odd feeling. Something is out-of-place. There's something she isn't saying, and she seems to be flirting with him, too. I don't think Pop would approve if he could see; however, I notice a crease deepens between his eyebrows when Jerry gets nearby. After a few awkward games of Yahtzee, we are rescued when Mom comes by to take us back home.

On the drive back, Mom asks curiously, "Well, how was your Christmas?"

Tash unenthusiastically says, "It was all right. Jolene's girls got a LOT of presents including new bikes. Pop got a typewriter and Ugg boots. Jolene got tons of clothes, a TV, and a washer and dryer."

Mom wasn't digging for information, but she sure didn't refuse any intel.

Mom vigorously cuts Tash off. "That son-of-a-bitch!"

Mom's abruptness makes me curious. "What, Mom?"

"Well, you're old enough to know. Pop got over $40,000 from insurance from the accident. He's supposed to pay his hospital bills. Last week, he told me he signed the check over to his girlfriend. Sounds like she took it all for herself. I asked him to save anything left over for your college."

Mom is fuming, and I decide not to give her any more intel for the moment.

We unload out of the Pinto, happy to be home. Inside, we open Mom's presents to us. Tash gets a tape recorder and I get a Casio watch.

December 25, 1980 Christmas. Tash got a tape recorder
and a Tanya Tucker cassette.

Pop getting a typewriter for his first Christmas after the accident.

Since we only nibbled on Jolene's Christmas dinner, we're starving. Tash asks, "Mom, what are we having for dinner?"

"Chinese noodles."

Mom's Chinese noodles aren't even close to what I've seen on TV commercials. Having never been to a Chinese restaurant, I have no idea what authentic is, anyway. She simply uses what's in the cabinets. Typically, Chinese noodles were angel-hair pasta with Lipton Onion soup mix, a sliced boiled egg, and soy sauce. Simply delicious and never undercooked!

After two helpings, Tash and I are lying around and playing quietly. The phone rings. It's Pop, and he's upset. "Hey, Booger. Can I speak to your mother?"

"Are you okay, Pop?"

"I really need to talk to her."

I yell, "Mommmmmm."

The black, spiral phone cord isn't long enough to drag it to the kitchen even with me tugging on it. Mom comes to the phone, leaving her tea and smoldering cigarette on the kitchen table. I hand the phone to Mom, and she shoos me away. After a few minutes, Mom hangs up and calls our cousin Hank. As soon as Hank arrives, they drive off together. When they get back, Pop is riding shotgun in the front seat.

Tash and I dash out the front door. "Pop! Pop! Pop!"

There is an awkward silence with Mom, Pop, and Hank. Hank starts unloading Pop's clothes, wheelchairs, and things, carrying them to the house. Mom leads Tash and me under the apple tree in the front yard, while Hank pushes Pop to the back porch.

My cousin Hank and Mom.

With weary eyes, Mom says, "Pop is going to stay with us a while."

Tash asks the question that's on my mind. "Are you two getting back together?"

Mom firmly responds, "NO. Pop's girlfriend has someone else living with her now. She doesn't want Pop anymore."

Mom's expression is confusing. She seems like she's happy that Pop's relationship failed but is angry that she has to pick up the pieces.

I unintentionally give more intel. "Oh, you mean Jerry. We met him."

Mom gives a disapproving look. She's steaming mad.

We spend the next week with Pop on the enclosed back porch. The plastic stapled to the screen windows flaps a little when there's wind. One night the wind and flapping picks up as an out-of-season thunderstorm approaches. Tash, Pop, and I listen to the rain and thunder. Water rushes and gurgles through the gutters above us. We sit there together in the blindness of night.

When the lightning flashes, we ask Pop, "Did you see that?"

Pop isn't sure but thinks he did. His blindness is nearly a hundred percent, but sometimes he sees shadows or flashes. We hope one day his sight will return.

In a serious tone, Pop says, "I want to tell you both something. I'm sorry for what you two have to live with. I still love your mother. I know she tells you it's all my fault, but your mother isn't innocent, either. When we get into a fight, she just doesn't stop. She gets right in my face. It's that damn Dale Carnegie Course. I try to get away, and she gets right in front of me again. I've had to push her a few times. All I wanted to do was get away."

Tash and I don't say a thing. Pop's mind is made up, and we ain't changing it. I want to believe Pop, but Mom is the one who takes care of us. Mom always handles things. It seems like Pop is trying to blame Mom for all that happened and claim everything isn't his fault. It doesn't matter because my mind is already made up. I believe Mom. We eventually drift off to sleep on our pallets on the floor beside Pop's bed as the storm moves away.

The next day, we have a visitor from Richmond. She's a professionally-dressed representative from Pop's rehabilitation facility. The lady explains that they would like Pop to come back and continue his rehabilitation. They taught Pop how to cook, clean, and become more independent.

Pop says, "They even taught me how to cook bacon."

Tash and I are shocked.

Tash asks, "What if it pops and splatters? Won't you hurt your eyes, since you're sitting in your wheelchair so close to the pan?"

Pop chuckles. "It doesn't matter. I'm already blind."

We all laugh together. Pop is thrilled to continue his rehabilitation. They have openings now, and he can go as soon as he wants.

On our last night together, Tash and I sit with Pop on the back porch. Pop asks us to fill out his request forms for books on tape.

Tash reads the questions out loud. "Do you want religious or nonreligious books?"

"Nonreligious."

"Check. Do you want violence or nonviolence?"

"Violence."

She struggles, "Ex...Explic...Explicit language or not?"

"Explicit."

"Fiction or nonfiction?"

"Either."

"I don't see a check box for *either*, so I'll check both. I take it you prefer western, sci-fi, and fantasy?"

"Yes, Ladybug."

"I assume the same for sexual? You'd prefer sexual?"

"Yes, please."

It was interesting how Pop's preferences for reading also summed up his life.

The next morning, anxious to get rid of him, Mom loads up the Pinto with all of Pop's possessions. The back of the car sags as we drive off. We can only carry one of his wheelchairs, so we leave the other one in the basement.

The drive to Richmond is quiet. Tash and I try to make conversation, but it fizzles out and silence follows. Pop has run out of options of places to stay and people to take care of him, and he has only one place to go. After getting lost in the big city for nearly an hour, we finally find the rehabilitation facility. Some of the staff meet us and remember Pop. "Hey, Gary! I'm glad you're back!" He's wanted and missed here. Like a light switch, Pop's mood changes to the happiest mood I've seen from him in a while. There are many others there just like him here. Some are blind with Ray Charles-type glasses and long white canes with red tips. Some are in wheelchairs and are paralyzed or missing their legs.

One of the scrub-dressed nurses escorts us to Pop's room. His room is big and painted a blinding sterile hospital white. The handicapped-accessorized room has its own bathroom and is about twice the size of my room at home. Outside, all the sidewalks are flat and wide with no uneven surfaces with handrails everywhere. I feel calmer knowing he'll be safe here. We say goodbye and walk back to the Pinto. We don't know when we'll see Pop again.

After many phone calls and two months later, Pop is doing great. When we finally see him, we notice he's lost weight and is stronger. Part of his rehabilitation includes braces for his legs. We watch him stand and walk using handrails. He struggles with wobbly arms and stiff shoulders but manages to walk twenty feet to the end of the rails and back. Now Pop is as big and tall as I remember. We walk back to his room. His kitchen has dirty pans from him cooking. His maid hasn't been by this week. Brail books are scattered about on his nightstand. After he locks his wheelchair brakes, Pop readjusts his half-full bladder bag. His pants ride up on his leg, revealing what looks like women's panty hose.

Inquisitively, I ask, "Why are you wearing women's panty hose, Pop?"

"These are called, Ted Hose. They help my leg circulation, but sometimes I wear panty hose, too. They keep my legs warmer."

I remember Pop always wearing worn steel-toed boots but not socks with slippers. By his bed, I spy something that looks like a two-handed sander.

"Why do you need a sander by your bed, Pop?"

He explains that he uses it to reduce fluid buildup in his legs. This massager happens to do more than reduce fluid buildup. It's the Harley Davidson of all massagers. This oversized-cam massager-from-hell is a great back massager. Pop uses it on our backs when we watch TV at night. When he rubs Tash's back, I look over at him. Pop seems happier here and is really improving. He's becoming more independent and gaining his confidence back. Maybe I was wrong about some of the things I thought we would never do again. Pop can't lift us over his head on a swinging vine. Pop can't drive us down the Old Sudan Road, but we can hike on a sidewalk and go camping again.

Before we leave, Pop looks at us, not directly at our eyes, and says, "Ladybug, I'm proud of you. Booger, you are the man of house now. You both take good care of Mom. Understand?"

"Yes sir. I understand."

"Hey guys, my stay here is almost done. I'm moving to the apartments across the cow pasture from you. The new ones next to Clarksville Primary School. You can come visit me."

"Great, Pop. It'll be fun."

On the way out, Pop hands us a bookmark describing his accident and progress.

Front side of Pop's bookmark.

GARY WISE

At age 37, Gary Wise of Clarksville, Virginia, was employed as a boilermaker and spent his spare time on woodworking projects, as an outdoorsman or with his fiancee.

But all this was interrupted last spring when an automobile accident left Gary blind and paralyzed from the waist down. After three months at Duke University Medical Center, he began comprehensive physical rehabilitation at Sheltering Arms.

"There," Gary says, "I learned how to start life over. I discovered the meaning of patience and understanding."

He credits Sheltering Arms with teaching him how to cope physically, mentally and emotionally with his disability. Independence in self-care and everyday activities is being regained. And Gary has quickly picked up skills such as typing, reading Braille and even playing the guitar.

This month, he returned to Sheltering Arms for an evaluation of his progress and to plan for vocational training at the Woodrow Wilson Rehabilitation Center or the Virginia Rehabilitation Center for the Blind. Other future plans include getting married in November, setting up a woodworking shop at home and Gary adds, "I think I'd like to learn to fish again."

Back side of Pop's bookmark.

211

Tired of Living

Saturday, February 28, 1981 – Twelve Years Old. Seventh Grade.

Loneliness is my buddy. Sadness is a friend.
I'm tired of living. I just want it all to end.
You don't know what it's like, in darkness all day.
I'm less of a man. I'm pulling the trigger. Just go away.

Pop's new apartment is about a country-mile away, if I take the shortcut through the cow pasture behind our house. There's one creek crossing that I can usually hop, if the water ain't too high. It takes me nearly thirty minutes to walk there, if I don't have to take the long way around to avoid the bull.

Pop's place is sparse and doesn't need much furnishing. It's just more obstacles for his wheelchair to bump into. He keeps it fairly tidy but has a maid come in about once a week. On his nightstand are dozens of books on cassette tape. Pop often listens to them in the afternoons and at night before snoozing off. Proud of his blind cooking skills, he cooks us bacon making the "I'm already blind" joke when we visit him. Cousin Hank comes by and helps him with various tasks. Hank helps with things like an uneven table or a fridge door that won't quite close properly. Pop is especially sensitive to squeaky doors and hinges and always has a can of WD-40 nearby. I think it's a place that's closer than Mama Johnson's for Hank to escape and drink a beer or two.

I'm at home and hear the phone ring. It's not even eight o'clock on Saturday morning and a little early for a phone call. I pick it up.

Pop softly, dismally says, "Hello, Booger. I love you."

I instinctively respond, "What's wrong, Pop?"

Silence.

I'm concerned. "Pop? What's wrong?"

"I'm tired of living. Tell your sister I love her. Tell your Mom I love her. You take care."

"What's wrong? STOP! I'll be right there!"

I throw down the corded phone and blast out the front door. Running full speed, I hop over the first fence and step on the electric wire. I barely feel the jolt. I run as fast as I can. I hope I'm not too late. "Run faster!" I scream at myself. Leaping over the swollen creek in one bound, I run past the red-eyed bull, not even looking to see if he chases me. I race up the second big hill, completely out of breath. The stiff, dry, golden-yellow grass hides the lumpiness of the ground. I trip a few times. About halfway up the second hill, I slow down because the pace is too much. The hill flattens out, and I catch my breath. I pick up the pace again and don't stop until I get to Pop's front door. It's unlocked. I burst inside. Pop has a gun in his hand. The revolver's trigger is pulled back.

"It's okay, Pop! I'm here! I'm here!"

"I'm so tired of living. I don't want to hurt you or your sister, but I'm in so much pain. Please go. I don't want you to see this."

I can't think of anything to say. I walk toward Pop. He lowers the gun. I bend down to hug him. He completely breaks down emotionally. The gun drops to the floor. I pick up the 22-caliber revolver, relieved it didn't go off. I point the gun away from Pop, putting the trigger back to a safer position. I set it out of his reach. I call Mom because I don't know what else to do.

Mom and Tash get there in minutes. Accustomed to being with

Pop in difficult situations, Mom calms Pop down. He's still bumming, but his voice holds a sprinkle of hope.

With his gun safely stowed in Mom's purse, Mom drives us home. Mom pulls out a notebook full of addresses and phone numbers. She is on the phone for hours. She calls long distance and talks to different people whose names I don't recognize. Shortly afterward, she sits us down for one of those serious talks.

"Pop is going to move out west with his family. He has relatives to help take care of him."

I ask, "Can we go visit him there?"

"Yes. Maybe in the summertime. He'll be happier there. I can't take care of Pop anymore. I just can't do it."

Trying to get Pop up early in the morning to cook some bacon.

Churchin' Up (Part One), Bigfoot, and Moonshining

Monday, June 22, 1981 – Twelve Years Old.

A giant gold ring. A cologne-filled van.
I don't like it much. Those sinful clammy hands.
Pressure to walk. To the preacher's pulpit.
Pulling of my strings. I'm a sinner. I'm a puppet.

Pop's been gone for months. When Tash and I talk with him, he seems to be doing great. His new place in Utah sounds better than red-eyed gravy on one of Granny's biscuits. Hard to imagine such a place. But you never know with Pop. He always thinks things are great when they're new.

He tells Tash and me things from a blind and paralyzed perspective. Emphasis is placed on sounds, smells, and touch. Supposedly, his apartment is draft-free. That's great and means I won't have to hear him continuously saying, "Shut the door!" or "There's a window open." When I explain things to him, I try to add sounds, smells, and touch to the descriptions to help him better relate.

Pop tells us he's met some kind Mormon folks and occasionally goes to church with them when he isn't in too much pain. I don't know hardly anything about Mormons. Some of the Baptist folks around here actually believe some Mormons have horns on their heads. That doesn't seem likely. Every phone conversation with Pop finishes up with, "Y'all need to come out and visit me."

These days, Mom's fatigue is perpetual. Tiredness drags her and tries to pull her down every day. She finally gets around to finding a new church for us: Light in the Woods Baptist Church on Hwy 58. It isn't far from Aaron's Creek. The area near Aaron's Creek has a reputation for having magical springs. In the olden days, people came for miles to get therapeutic spring water from Buffalo Springs. I remember Granny loading up with gallons of the elixir water and storing it on the back porch.

Aaron's Creek is also known for its excellent but illegal moonshine. One year, Southern Virginia had weeks of spring rains. Bugg's Island Lake filled to the brim. The inlets flooded, which made for excellent canoeing and fishing higher up into the creeks. That allowed some local teenagers to paddle way up and unknowingly get a little too close to a moonshine still. Shortly afterward, the alcohol refinery specialists cut some Bigfoot feet out of plywood and strapped them to their boots. Bigfoot tracks appeared along the creek to scare the kids away. The kids told their parents, who then told the police. A few days later, the newspaper informed the entire town what happened. Even so, I still look for Bigfoot tracks whenever I go walking in the woods. Just because a human made those particular tracks doesn't mean Bigfoot ain't real. I believe.

The new church Tash and I are required to attend has its own van to pick up us sinners. After a clammy handshake with the preacher, my evil sister and I pile into the van with the other perpetrators. On the way to Baptist Revival Week, the preacher/van driver eagerly waves to every single car we pass. There ain't no way he knows every single person, but he keeps waving. The preacher seems friendly enough but could have gone easier on the aftershave. I crack my window to get fresh air. His big ole gold ring on his clammy hands glares in the sunshine as he grasps the steering wheel. When we cross the Bigfoot Creek, I wonder if any of those local alcohol refinery specialists go to this church. I suppose it's okay to make moonshine as long as they pray for forgiveness after they make a batch. We finally get to the church and separate into different age groups.

Every day that week, I read Scriptures and sing hymns. I'm grateful when they let us skip the third verse to make the hymn shorter. I'm constantly reminded of the error of my ways. Seems like we sinners can't do nothing right. On Friday, the last day, they make all of us younger ones congregate in the main hall. The lights dim as a film starts. I'm disappointed that it's not science-fiction. This peculiar film shows two teenagers drinking and partying with friends—a definite sin. The two boys get into the car, drive fast, crash, and die. They go to hell and are condemned to an eternity of damnation. The film shows their flesh burning, followed by worms eating them consuming the remains. Then the lights turn on.

The preacher begins, "Feel the spirit. You don't want this to happen to you. Feel the spirit move you." His arms reach out to the unbaptized worm-fodder sinners.

As he preaches, people younger and older than me walk up to the pulpit. They must've felt the spirit, but I ain't feeling nothin'. I don't want to go. I see the preacher put his hands on their heads. He grabs some of them hard, and I wonder if that big ole gold ring leaves a goose egg on their noggins.

"Is there anyone else who is moved by the spirit?" His arms appear to grow outward toward us, pulling us in.

He looks right at me! I know and he knows that I'm not baptized. "Come forth and be saved."

He turns to look at others that I know aren't baptized, either. Finally, not wanting to be an outsider, I get up, slowly walking to the pulpit. I do what is expected of me. I don't want to burn and have worms eating me, especially worms with teeth. He baptizes me. I'm expecting to feel cleansed, but instead feel tainted by clammy hands and aftershave. I'm uncomfortable and don't know why.

Tash and I take the church van home now filled with righteous folk. All I want to do is get away from these people. Mom is home, and we tell her we got baptized but don't want to go to that church anymore.

"Tell me what happened."

Tash and I go through the events, and she abruptly stops us after our description of the film.

"Stay here!"

Mom is gone for over an hour and comes back home. Tash and I meet her at the door.

"Where did you go, Mom?"

"I told that preacher that he ain't going to brainwash my kids. He can go straight to hell. If I ever find out he's playing that film again in front of children, I'm going to the police." Mom is fuming mad. "You're not going to that church ever again!"

I'm relieved. Playing in the cow pasture and catching bream and crappie seems more churchlike for me, anyway. As far as I know, worms are made for catching fish or putting down people's pants. They aren't for eating people, but I guess they have to eat, too.

I'm still infused with a going-to-hell mindset. "But Mom, you just told a preacher off. Ain't you worried about the wrath of God?"

"No. What's He going to do that hasn't been done to me already? All I have to do is what the preacher said, 'Pray about it, and all will be forgiven.'"

Hospice Care (Day Nine)

Thursday, March 1, 2007 – These are my favorite things. Story behind "One-Beer Daisy". Twelve buckets of chicken. Old prison uniforms.

What are Mom's favorite things?
What songs make her laugh and sing?
What songs make her cry and dance?
I should've asked sooner. Now, I've missed my chance.

Mom's eyes are glassy and unfocused now. She can't click on the side rail for "yes" or "no" anymore. She can't write or read. I know it won't be long now. I offer to fill up her plastic cigarette, but she just looks at me with distant, watery eyes. I grab her favorite turquois-colored hairbrush and start brushing her hair. Just barely, I can see those sleepy eyes again, so I know she's aware of what I'm doing and is enjoying it. Tash joins me in the room with her cup of steamy hazelnut crème with coffee.

"Tash, there are so many questions I have for Mom but can't ask her now. I'm too late. I think she can hear me, but she can't respond. What's her favorite movie? What's her favorite song? What was her favorite flower? I'm too late. I'll never know."

"It's okay, Cale. I know some of those answers. She really liked *The Sound of Music* movie. When Sheryl Crow would come on the radio, she'd dance and make me dance with her. You remember how she would move her shoulders? There's another song—gimme a minute. Let me look it up. Hmmm…Sheryl Crow singing *All I Want to*

219

Do. Sometimes that song *Shake, Shake, Shake* by KC and the Sunshine Band would come on. Mom had no coordination, but she would 'Shake, Shake, Shake.' You know a song she likes that I could never figure out? *Brass in my Pocket.* I never got that one. I didn't know she'd like the Pretenders until it came on the radio. That was one of those shoulder-movin' dances, too. What was the other question?"

I ask, "So what is her favorite flower?"

"Oh, she likes daffodils and daisies."

I know that. I don't know why I asked. I glance at the daffodils she planted between the two pine trees toward Betsy's house. Cozied by a layer of pine tags, the fresh green stalks of flowers are waking up from their winter slumber.

"Tash, do you remember that guy who started Darryl's restaurant in Raleigh? Pop and Mom helped him set up his first restaurant. He would make us those wonderful Garbage Pizzas with all the fixings. When the restaurant would close, Mom, Pop, and Darryl would sit around and drink beer. They used to call her, 'One-Beer Daisy.' Back then, Mom couldn't hold her alcohol, so she'd start slurring after one beer."

"Oh yeah, I remember. Well, before this hospice thing happened, she wasn't One-Beer Daisy anymore. More like a Six-Gin Geranium."

"Tash, you're right about that. I get it, though. She was in a lot of pain. We're still finding bottles everywhere in the cabinets. Mom has had a hard life. I get it."

At lunch time, we hear another car pull up in the driveway. I walk to the front porch steps before they can even knock on the door. I watch an elderly lady unload another Hardee's family pack of chicken from her silver Buick. I should have bought Hardee's fried chicken stock futures.

"Hello, I'm so-and-so. I just want to drop some food off for y'all. I have to get going back to the church."

All I can say is, "Thank you. You are too kind."

Mrs. So-and-so leaves as I take the food inside. We throw away a few older buckets of chicken and side dishes. These new buckets go in the fridge in their place. Now, we have a piece of paper taped to the fridge. I add another tick to keep track of our buckets of chicken. This makes twelve buckets of chicken. Even Tom can't take any more.

Last time we offered him some, his "Goddammit" response sounded like, "I can't eat another damn bite. I'm chickened out."

I appreciate the generosity of this lady and others from the Roanoke River Baptist Church. Although I wasn't necessarily against the church folks, my experiences in the past have made me wary. Two of my three experiences with churches weren't favorable. My last experience with the Mormon Church wasn't encouraging, nor was my time at the Light in the Woods Baptist Church. I did have a good youth experience at the Roanoke River Baptist Church, though. Some of these folks are helping out with Mom, and they certainly don't have to. I'm reminded not to judge. A few bad individuals doesn't mean everyone in that group is that way. I have to keep reminding myself of that.

With dread, I open the door to Mom's room to resume the cleaning and sorting. I know all the clothes and sentimental items in her room will turn me into an emotional whirlwind. They are personal. They are her. Tash and I have to do it. We both walk in and turn on the light. The light bulb in the ceiling is out and there is only a shadeless nightstand light. When the smoke-infused dusty curtains open, we have enough light to see the innards of the room. The walls are yellowed from the smoke, and a film seems to cover everything. The light-switch cover has grime from hands. When I think of how to describe this place, dingy, painful, and full of sorrow comes to mind. Dingy from all the smoke. Painful because I have a strong feeling of Mom's suffering in this room. Full of sorrow because of all the ghosts she hid and carried with her through life. I can feel how she cried herself to sleep in this room so many nights alone. The overflowing ashtrays, disarray of clothing, and lack of cleanliness shows it, too. This room feels like the ashes of her life.

I start with the clothes hanging in her closet. I pull them to my nose. I want to remember what she smells like, but all I breathe in is cigarette smoke. This is part of what she smells like. Tash and I place the clothing one-by-one into garbage bags. I find one of my Iomega work shirts tucked deep, hidden between two thick sweatshirts. I remember when she stole this particular shirt from me. She liked that shirt. We fought because she just took it without asking. Now in hindsight, I wish I had bought and given her a dozen of these shirts. She only wanted it because she was proud of me and wanted to wear it to show others. That fight seems so long ago.

Rack by rack, I make my way to the end of the closet. In the cold, dark depths, I find two of her old prison guard uniforms. Mom's last job was as a prison guard before she went on disability. The shirts are stained and timeworn from the day she left the prison. These uniforms are shrouds of sadness and pain from her own prison. These uniforms are a reminder of her humiliation, discrimination, and abuse.

Penny-filled Tube Socks and the
Famous Sunflower

Monday, September 7, 1981 – Thirteen Years Old. Eighth Grade.

Granny and me from a stovetop perspective.

Word gets around Clarksville quickly when the construction of a prison starts in the nearby town of Boydton. The money is supposed to be good and the benefits too. After Pop's accident, Mom doesn't have any health insurance for Tash and me. She applies for the prison job and gets accepted. Five years after starting her business, Mom gives up the Jack-n-Jill Daycare. Even though Mom watches over thirty kids a week during the summer, she makes less money when school starts. When she has over twenty kids, she has to pay another adult to supervise, too. For guard training, she has to go to

Waynesboro for several weeks. Tash and I stay at Granny's while Mom is away.

Granny gets after us to get up every morning.

"Get up! Your breakfast is getting cold. You're gonna miss the bus."

Granny gets tired of saying it after the first couple days, so one morning wakeup call is accompanied by a broom. After a couple of smacks, Tash and I get up immediately. We don't have to be nagged ever again.

We rarely have sugar-infused cereal each morning at Granny's. She gets up to make eggs, bacon or sausage, and biscuits. I still pull out the Kellogg's cereal box and read it: Calories 120, Iron 30%, and Thiamine 45%. I don't know if Jimmy Dean sausage has Thiamine as high as cereal, but I'm sure it makes up for it with more calories and fat.

Every couple of nights, Mom calls us to tell us how things are going. She has to retake a few written tests and is struggling to pass the AR-15 target test. Mom isn't into gun shooting at all. Since she's small, I try to imagine her shooting a 12-gauge shotgun with buckshot. I'm sure her right shoulder is bruised, but I know she won't quit.

It's Tuesday morning after the first week at Granny's, and I have to go to the bathroom. Everyone avoids the outhouse after finding a five-foot long snakeskin in it earlier in the summer. That, the bees, and the spiders make it a place to avoid. There's something terrifying about pulling my pants down, putting my privates into a dark hole and hoping something doesn't fly out, bite me, or pull me in. It's none too appealing. Even for Granny, instead of using the outhouse, she has a five-gallon bucket set up on the back porch.

The snake, spider, and bee-infested outhouse.

I open the door to the back porch and watch Granny lowering on the bucket. As she squats, I see Granny's breasts are hanging down between her legs. They look like penny-filled tube socks. Those mammary tubes look to be over a foot long just dangling. I see her pick them up and set the danglers on the outside of her legs before her first big food-exiting push.

She looks up, "Whew! Shut the door!"

I do as I'm told and wait for my turn. Granny finishes and washes her hands in her kitchen sink. Just two years ago, Pop and Travis added a water pump to her well, so Granny didn't have to pull up water from the well one bucket at a time. Granny has running water in one sink and her washer machine. That's it. There's no toilet, but the bucket is fine with me.

"Granny. I ate too much cheese. I haven't gone to the bathroom in a week," I moan.

"Lord, child! It ain't good to have all that stuff stopped up inside you. Go use the bucket."

"I'm just joking, Granny."

She smacks me on the bottom as I walk away and mutters, "Well bless your heart."

"Bless your heart" has all kind of meanings for us. Some folks said it instead of "you idiot," "that was foolish," or "I ain't going to tell you what I really think." It's the Christian thing to do, I reckon.

Granny hollers through the closed door, "Honey, would you empty the bucket when you're done?"

"Yes, Granny."

I finish my morning business and walk out the back porch door near the old fig bush. The fig bush was cut down earlier in the year, since it was gettin' out of hand. This year taking its place are a patch of giant sunflowers. Since I regularly eat salted sunflower seeds and sometimes swallow the seeds whole, I wonder if I sowed these behemoths. I empty the contents of the bucket at the base of the sunflowers. I can't believe how tall they've gotten. Seems like they've grown even more while Tash and I have been staying here. I reckon they are at least three times taller than Granny. I spray out the bucket and return to the back porch. I put it under the two Smithfield hams shrouded in cheesecloth hanging from the ceiling and under the gallon jugs of Buffalo Springs elixir water on the shelf.

After a day of learning, our school bus drops us beside Granny's ten gallon-sized rusty mailbox. Earlier this summer, even three of my firecrackers weren't powerful enough to do any damage to it. I reach slowly and carefully inside the mailbox trying to not disturb the wasp nest underneath. Granny usually sits on the front porch waiting for us as we get off the bus. Today, we find her sitting at the dining room table and hand Granny her mail.

Tash says, "Let's sit on the porch."

We hold the front screen door open for Granny. She beelines to her favorite rocking chair. Tash and I sit next to her on the porch swing. The chains and wood creak as we gently swing. The dark green paint on Granny's porch furniture is starting to flake off and reveal the weathered wood underneath. It's best not to slide and possibly get a splinter on the bucket side of our bodies.

We can tell Granny is a little excited and wants to tell us something.

"I went to the garden and picked some vegetables. I stewed and canned a few jars of tomatoes. Best get what I can before the first frost comes."

"And the paper called today. They heard about my giant sunflower. They want to come by tomorrow and take a picture."

I say to her, "Granny, it sure is the biggest sunflower we'd ever seen. Are you going to tell them how it got to be so huge?"

Granny is unsure of what I'm asking. "What you talkin' about, honey?"

"Well, you did have some special fertilizer. Isn't that the same place we throw the bucket?"

"Now, don't you go around telling anyone about that. They don't need to know. They just have to mind where they step. Since you brought it up, why don't you get a shovel and cover all that bucket stuff up with some dirt? Git going."

The next day, the paper, The Mecklenburg Sun, came out to take Granny's picture. Granny is so proud. Tash and I laugh when the picture comes out a couple days later. We know why that sunflower got so big.

Tash says, "Looky here. The caption under the picture says, 'Mrs. Ruby Yancey of Forest Hill Street in Clarksville, poses beside this 25' sunflower plant which voluntarily grew in her yard this year.'"

Granny looks at me. "Sug', maybe volunteer isn't the right word. Highly encouraged sounds better."

We all crack up laughing as the porch swing creaks.

GIANT SUNFLOWER PLANT--Mrs. Ruby Yancey of Forest Hill Street in Clarksville, poses beside this 25' sunflower plant which voluntarily grew in her yard this year. (Staff Photo by Carrie Clark)

Granny Ruby beside the "voluntarily"

giant bucket-fed sunflower.

(Photo from Mecklenburg Sun Newspaper)

Ice Cream Air Bubbles and
Redneck Engineering

**Sunday, October 4, 1981 – Mom vs My Size Bowls.
Hank's Ingenuity.**

*A stolen stop sign. A couple of bricks.
Fire and flame. Ain't nothin' my cuz can't fix.*

Mom picks Tash and me up from Granny's a day later than she'd planned. She's happy to see us and seems a bit more confident. From Granny's shelves and freezer, Mom gathers a few Mason jars and frozen quart-sized bags of food. We're now stocked with future sunflower fertilizer: corn, beans, and tomatoes. Thanking Granny, we load it all into the car.

On the ride home, Tash asks, "How did it go, Mom? Was it hard?"

"Ladybug, it was hard. I retook a few tests. I didn't think I'd pass the gun parts. It took me a few times. I got through it, though." I hear the dog-tiredness in her voice. Mom wasn't the academic-type, and learning new skills in any type of school would certainly wear her down.

When we pull into the driveway, I know what I have to do. The grass needs cutting, and leaves need raking. Pinecones and branches need picking up. I look over at the ditch and see our neighbor, George graciously cut our side of it. Cutting the ditch is a constant rivalry between Mom and George. George often says, "Dolores, the property line is on my side of the ditch. You should be cutting the grass in the ditch." Mom always responds, "The line goes down the middle.

We own one side each." Even so, if George cuts his grass before us, he always cuts all of the ditch. If I get to it before him, I cut all of the ditch. I compose a variation of Robert Frost's poem in my head, *Mending Wall*, "Well-cut ditches make ..." Sometimes, I think they argue with each other to see whose blood pressure rises first. Tash gets onto the riding mower, and I start with the old worn-out push mower.

Mom perches inside the whole time peering out the kitchen window, comforted with sweetened iced tea and a cigarette. The bottom of the kitchen window is cracked, and I notice a wisp of smoke exiting the house. After twenty minutes or so, Mom yells, "I'm going to the grocery store. I'll be right back. I'm going to get us a treat."

She returns with a full-sized brown paper bag. My mind speculates on the mystery treat content in the bag. I think, *Could it be Little Debbie Cakes* or *Cinnamon Rolls?* Whatever it is, I hope it's something sweet. I know how valuable this treat is because she hasn't had extra money in several weeks. She calls us in, and we make a beeline to the sweet hive of the paper bag. We're not disappointed. It's Neapolitan ice cream.

She says to Tash and me, "Thank y'all for helping out around the house. I can't do it all by myself. I appreciate it."

She scoops three equal portions into our chipped ceramic bowls. When Mom hands her bowl to Tash, she notices a redness around Tash's recent ear piercings. They go to the bathroom to put some peroxide on it, since it looks a little infected.

This is my chance. Stealthily, I flip the box of half-gallon ice cream over. I open the bottom and quickly inhale several Maikel-size scoops from the bottom. That way, Mom won't know how much ice cream I've eaten. Mmm...strawberry, vanilla, and chocolate. I listen for the oak hardwood floor creaking, knowing they'll return before their treat melts much more. The bathroom door squeaks open. Thank goodness for the settling of the house and uneven door alignments. I quickly reclose the bottom of the box and place the now top-heavy box of ice cream goodness back in the freezer. I'm safe.

The next afternoon, we're home from school for about one hour before Mom returns from her first day as an official prison guard. Tash and I make peanut butter and jelly sandwiches and watch Looney Tunes.

"Maikel, it's your turn to wash the dishes."

I'm on my second sandwich. "Tash," I plead, "I'll pay you fifty cents to do them for me."

"Okay, but you already owe me fifty cents. You'd better pay me."

Tash goes into the kitchen to do my chores while I begin to fret. I don't have fifty cents, or even a dollar. I try to think about how I'm going to pay her, but quickly get distracted watching the Coyote chase after the Roadrunner in a race car.

Mom walks in. She is slurring-her-words tired.

"I need to ask you two something. I'm going to set up my bedroom downstairs. Please keep quiet. I need to sleep."

With Mom setting up her bedroom, I ask Tash, "Seems like Mom is always tired, even before we stayed at Granny's. Do you think she's depressed?"

"I don't know, Cale. Maybe. She's been through a lot with Pop leaving and his accident. She started a new job, and things are uncertain. I know I'd be frettin'."

Mom is in bed by seven o'clock.

When Mom wakes up around 9:00 P.M., she goes to the kitchen to get something to eat. Tash and I are in the living room glued to the TV.

Mom yells, "Maikel, come here! NOW!"

Mom is making herself a small bowl of ice cream, and she turns the box of Neapolitan ice cream toward me. I see the hole breaking through the top layer of ice cream revealing the large empty void below.

"Mom, it looks like this ice cream box has a giant air bubble," I suggest.

"Don't give me that. I can see where your spoon left marks. Look! No more for you. The rest belongs to your sister and me."

Shoulders drooping, I return to the living room to climb back onto the couch with Tash. I'm more disappointed that I can't have any ice cream than being upset by getting caught.

"Tash, the next time you get a bowl of ice cream, if you give me some, I'll give you twenty-five cents," I promise.

Leaves are starting to fall, and it's an opportunity to make money by raking leaves. At the cost of only two blisters on my hand, I earn fifteen dollars over the next two weeks.

Tash eyeballs my money. "That'll be $2.50, please."

"$2.50? How'd you figure?"

"Interest."

I pay up and remember it's my turn for dishes again. "Tash, I'll pay you fifty cents to do dishes for me."

"Nope. I'll do for a dollar, though."

"Why more now?"

"'Cause you have it. You have more than fifty cents."

Just getting off third shift on a Saturday morning, Mom says, "One of the guards I worked with says the newspaper is looking for some extra help."

With only two newspaper options in our small town, Tash asks, "Which one?"

"The Mecklenburg Sun."

"I stopped by on my way back from the prison today, and they hired me on the spot. It's part-time, but this will give us a little more money. I'm really going to need you two to help me out. I can't do this by myself. Tomorrow, we have to go to Henderson and pick up the papers from the press."

"Dang," I mutter under my breath. I had been planning on repairing my motorcycle. Now I'm delivering newspapers to help pay the bills. I respond with a "Sure, Mom," but hold my tongue on how I really feel. I decide to start now instead of tomorrow. I open the garage doors, propping each giant wooden door open with a cinder block. It's time to do some work on my Yamaha YZ80 motorcycle. My yellow two-stroke beast of a motocross bike was looking funny when I left it here. I don't know what happened, but after jumping the ramp in our field, the bike felt off after my last landing. I didn't think much of it at the time, but now I take the time to really examine it. The shocks work. The front wheel turns freely side-to-side.

Then, I see it. The front wheel is sticking out too much from the frame. I'd cracked the frame. I say out loud to myself, "Dammit!" I roll the motorcycle closer to the garage door opening with more light and find there is a quarter inch gap where the fork attaches to the frame. I don't know what to do or if it can be fixed. I sit there moping, and Mom sees my despair.

"What's wrong, son?"

"My motorcycle. The frame is cracked, and I don't know how to fix it."

"Why don't you call Cousin Hank? He's one of the best welders around."

I call Hank and he picks up, a rare event. "Hey Hank. How are you?"

"Good. What's up, cuz?"

"I cracked the frame on my Yamaha."

"Bring it over. I'll take a look at it. I'm helping Travis with his Chevelle today, too."

Excited that not all may be lost, I top off my gas tank and ride the motorcycle on the railroad tracks to Hank's place. All that jarring from the railroad ties diminishes once I pick up speed to about 35 mph. I'd like to go faster, but the front half of my bike might fall off. I keep looking back to make sure a train isn't sneaking up behind me. When I arrive at Hank's, he's there with Cousin Travis. Freshly waxed, Travis's silver '68 Chevelle gleams with two newly-painted black racing stripes on the hood.

"Hey, those racing stripes look good. What y'all doing to the Chevelle?"

While rolling out his blow torch equipment, Hank says, "Travis wants to drop the front end a couple of inches." Hank's nose and mouth twitches.

"I don't get it. How're you going to do it with that torch?"

"Come under the car with me, and I'll show ya."

I glance at a large area of red on the floorboard of the passenger's side. A cutup stop sign fills in the rusted-out hole so a passenger's feet won't poke through. I wonder if this is the stolen stop sign from Granny's street. Apparently, a redneck engineer has been here before. Hank takes a weathered red brick and places it under the right front wheel's swing arm. He measures about three inches with the tape measure and moves the brick to another place on the swing arm that only has about a two-inch gap. Next, he moves the brick to the other side and repeats the process. Intrigued, I keep watching, still not knowing what he's going to do next.

Hank lights up the torch with a loud *pop* as the gas ignites and tunes the flame to a sharp blue point. About midway up with the brick underneath, he starts heating part of the spring going back and forth a few inches at a time. Dirt and rust flames yellow as it burns and blows off the spring steel. After about a minute, the spring starts turning cherry red. Hank double checks that the brick has a solid footing on the ground. Slowly, the spring fatigues and bends. The heated side of the front end starts to drop toward the brick. He's slow and careful not to overheat the spring. Once the swing arm touches the brick, Hank turns off the torch and then repeats the process on the other side. I witness redneck engineering firsthand.

"That's really cool, Hank. I ain't never seen anything like that before."

Travis stands at the wheel wells to ensure there is enough space and that the tires won't rub. His car is more wedge-shaped now and looks even faster. Satisfied, he stammers, "Tha, tha, thanks, man. Lo, looks good." He glances at me and says, "Motorcycle Man."

Travis was fond of calling me a name of an object, which was then followed by *Man*. If I was on the tractor, I'd be called Tractor Man. A bicycle, then I'd be Bicycle Man. I like Travis with all his eccentricities.

"Hey, Travis. I heard you lost your job at Burlington Mills. You find something else?"

"Ye, ye, yes. I was a school bus driver for a day, but they let me go after I backed into a car on the first day."

I fight hard not to laugh, but I'm sure he sees my grin.

"I g, g, got a job building those prefab houses in Boydton. I like it all right. I ge, ge, ge, get to stand up more. The money's good." Travis's discussion turns to Hank. "Ho, ho, how much you want for your Camaro? I heard you want to sell it." Travis is envious of his brother's faster car.

Hank matches his twitches to Travis's stutters and half-heartedly says, "$3,500." This Camaro is Hank's baby, and he doesn't want to get rid of it, even though he needs the money.

"Mmm. Tha, tha, that's a bit high. I can't pay you that much. Le, le, let me know if you want to sell it cheaper. Th, thanks. See y'all." Trying to impress his older brother, Travis speeds off but misses second gear and the engine whines. His Chevelle leaves a smell like it's burning a little too rich.

With a twitch and a chuckle at his brother trying to show off, Hank turns to me. It's ten in the morning, and he opens his first can of Bud. At our house, the rule is noon before you open a can of beer. "Whatcha got here, Maikel?" Hank looks over my motorcycle frame and checks for play in the crack. He responds to his own question. "It ain't that bad. I can fix it. We gotta turn your bike upside down. Hold on."

Hank walks back inside his modified two-room add-on trailer house. The screen door slams as he exits. He has Saran Wrap and a come-a-long winch in one hand. A fresh second beer occupies the other. I eagerly watch, waiting for the next magic trick of redneck engineering. Hank takes off the gas cap, covers the opening with Saran wrap, and screws the gas cap back on.

"See that? You have a breather hose. Gas fumes will leak out of it. This should seal it up good enough from the sparks. Don't want it to explode while we weld it."

Hank easily flips over the motorcycle with the wheels up in the air, a position this bike has seen more than once with me thrown off to the side. He wraps the cables of the come-a-long around the wheel's aluminum rims and hooks them in place.

"Maikel, what's your wheelbase supposed to be?"

I have all the specs of my Yamaha YZ80 memorized. "Forty-seven and a half inches."

Hank measures the wheelbase. It's four inches longer than it's supposed to be. "Pop!" The torch ignites and the flame is tuned. Skillfully, with one hand holding the torch, he heats up the frame around the crack. After it turns a glowing cherry red, he takes his other hand and gently pulls the come-a-long winch.

"Maikel, hold the tape measure in place and let me know when we're there."

One ratchet click. A second. A third. "STOP!" I yell at Hank.

Hank covers the yellow plastic gas tank with an old pair of Levi's to keep it from melting from the sparks. It seems odd to me that he didn't protect the gas tank sooner. No boom or loss of hair yet. Hank rolls his welder closer. With the wheelbase set to the proper specs, the crack is barely visible. He adds three welding rods, securing it shut. Impressive redneck engineering surpasses graduate level. Hank is now a PhD candidate.

"Thanks, Hank. That's amazing. How can I repay you? Is there anything I can do?"

"Don't worry 'bout it. Who knows. One day I may need your help! If it breaks again, bring it by."

Hank in the Slammer

Wednesday, November 4, 1981 – Thirteen Years Old.
Eighth Grade.

It's really late when the phone rings in the House of Wise. It must be sometime after midnight. When the phone rings this late, usually someone is drunk, or bad news is coming.

I hear Tash stumble into the kitchen to answer. "Hello."

Moments pass before I hear Tash yell, "Moooommmmm. Wake up. It's Hank."

Mom, usually a deep sleeper, hops right out of bed. I peek out of my bedroom. Now that we have a longer phone cord, Mom moves the phone to the kitchen table.

"Hank. Where are you? I'll be right there."

And then she hangs up. "You two go back to bed."

"What's wrong, Mom?"

"It's Hank. He got arrested for speeding, drinking, and driving. Y'all have school in the morning. Go back to bed."

Mom leaves and goes to the police station.

When she comes back, we're still awake. She updates us. Hank said that Police Chief Hogan got him for a DUI and speeding. His bail is $1,000 dollars. He's asked Mom for money to pay for it, but she doesn't have it. We can barely pay the electric bill. Hank may have to spend a night in the slammer.

Hank just helped me with my motorcycle. Is he expecting me to return the favor? I think of ways to break him out. I can go get his torch that he used on my motorcycle.

With the kitchen light on all night, Mom can't sleep and putzes around as quietly as she can. I hear her exactly at 6:00 A.M. making her first phone call. Unlike normal, we willingly get out of bed. Mom calls Granny, and then Hank's sister Clarabelle and brother Travis to chip in for help with the bail. I overhear some of their comments. *"He shouldn't been drinking and driving." "I knew they'd catch him, eventually." "Hank loves his Budweiser."* Hank helped each person Mom called. There's only silence or the sound of crickets now. None of them want to return the favors. Who are they going to call for help if he stays in jail forever?

Thinking it may come to me busting Hank out, I ask, "Mom, is anyone going to help Hank?"

"Nope. They say he gets hammered all the time, and it's 'bout time he got nailed. You kids get ready for school. I want to stop by the jail to see Hank before work."

We quickly do as we're told. We know it's not a time to mess around.

I'm at school all day wondering what's going to happen to Hank. In between classes, I find Tash and ask if she's heard anything. Nothing. At the end of the day when we jump off the bus, to our surprise, Hank is sitting right there on our front porch!

"Hank! Hank! You got out of jail!" We race to give him hugs.

With a sheepish look, he replies, "Yep, 'bout two hours ago. I sold my '67 Camaro to Travis for $1,500."

"I thought he said he don't have no money."

"He has it if he wants something. He said he'll sell it back to me later."

"Come inside. We can make you a peanut butter and jelly sandwich," I offer, hoping to soothe him. I know our sandwiches have to be better than jail food. "Hank, we were thinking of ways to break you out."

Hank pats me on the shoulder, "I appreciate you thinking of me."

A short time later, Mom arrives, happy that Hank made it out. Hank is anxious to get back home, so Mom chauffeurs him back where surely a reprimand is waiting to greet him from his wife. Tash and I quickly try to clean up the house before Mom gets back.

With worried lines etched on her face, Mom says, "I'm tired. I didn't get much sleep last night. I'm going to bed early. Can you keep the ruckus down and try to stay quiet?"

"Yes, ma'am." We know it's important to be quiet tonight.

Not long after she goes to bed, I hear a siren coming down Shiney Rock Road. The whine is coming over the hill heading toward Grassy Creek. I'm not fast enough to see out the front window if there was a car leading the chase. Hogan speeds by, focused on the road ahead.

I wonder if it's Travis racing Hank's Camaro. I think, *wouldn't it be funny if Hogan catches Travis and throws him in the slammer? Then, he calls Hank for a favor.*

Hospice Care (Day 10)

Friday, March 2, 2007 – Finding the Trophy. Pop Bruising Me. Rich Faucett Prejudice. Eighth Grade Report Card.

My flip cell phone rings at 8:01 A.M. I recognize the number. It's work.

"Hey, Maikel. This is Jeff. How are things?"

"Just taking care of Mom. She's slowing down. I don't think it will be long now."

"Take all the time you need. Is there anything you need?"

"No, we're doing fine. Just cleaning up and getting things ready. When Susan and I leave here, my sister Tash will have a lot to do. Susan and I are just trying to make it as easy for her as we can."

"All right, Maikel. Holler if you need anything. Later."

It's a dry conversation. I don't have much to say to Jeff, although we've been friends for almost ten years and he's now my boss. My superficial conversation is because it's hard for me to talk about what's happening with Mom. The situation is too painful.

Susan walks in and sits beside Mom. Susan picks up Mom's favorite brush and strokes Mom's hair.

"I see you looking at me, Mama Wise. Just relax," she coos.

Standing up, I turn to Susan. "I'm going to clean up some more of those boxes in my old bedroom. There's no telling what Mom saved in them."

I walk into the darkened bedroom. This room only has two windows. One's dark from facing the inside of the garage, and the other is dark from facing the enclosed back porch. We've replaced the burnt-out lights. I turn on the lights and notice my two-foot-tall blue and gold motorcycle trophy. Mom proudly positioned it in

241

the room for all who entered. This accolade is from the only race I've ever won. I remember Mom getting me a new motorcycle after starting her second job at the newspaper. She'd begun dating Ed of Ed's Honda and Yamaha. Every now and then after that, Ed would show up at the house. They'd slip away for a few hours. I suspected it was a "booty call" for both of them but never asked.

Gazing at the trophy, I remember in high school when Mom said to me, "You needed that motorcycle. You took all your frustrations out on it. It was how you coped with things."

I walk to the kitchen where Tash is having a cup of coffee.

"Tash, remember that motorcycle Mom got me?"

"Of course, I do."

"It doesn't seem fair that Mom got me that and didn't get you anything equivalent."

Tash's eyes get serious, and she calls me another nickname, one she reserves for when she's compassionate. "It's okay, Cale. You had it tougher than me."

Perplexed, I ask, "What do you mean?"

"I know you may not believe it, but Pop used to beat and shake you when you were a baby. When you were born, you cried and cried for days on end. Mom said that when you came out, your mouth opened and didn't shut for two years. Pop couldn't stand it. He'd shake you and hit you in your crib. If Mom took you to town, she'd wrap you up in a blanket so no one could see the bruises.

"When I was born, Mom adamantly told Pop, 'You are not going to hurt this one.'"

Quietly, I say to my sister, "I didn't know."

Moments pass and Tash repeats, "I know you had it rougher than me."

I wonder if this is why I was so fearful of Pop at such a young age.

Maybe it was one of those unconscious things ingrained in me at an early age. Though I was too young to remember being beaten, I have to accept that maybe it's true. While waiting for Susan, I continue to wonder how these events made me who I am today.

When Susan returns from a morning grocery store run to get more coffee creamer, she asks, "What is up with all these angry people?"

"Honey, what are you talking about?"

"Everybody is angry. White people. Black people. They're all mad and angry. I remember you telling about how racism and prejudice is still a big issue down in the South. You weren't kidding. I've heard the 'N word' more times this week than in my whole life."

I narrow my gaze on Susan and speak. "I was aware of the prejudice as a kid growing up here; however, I really opened up my eyes in the Navy. You remember my friend Rich Faucett?"

"Yep."

"He gave me a glimpse of what it's like to be black in the South. Let me tell you. We were on the ship one day. Rich walked by me and angrily said, 'He's racist.' Rich was mad after a comment by one of the other sailors."

I tell Rich's story:

> So, I ask Rich what the sailor said. Rich replied, "You chicken watermelon-eatin' people, blah, blah, blah." I told Rich I knew what he meant. Having been raised in the South, I knew all about racism and prejudice. He responded, "What do you think you know? You don't know shit!" I told him there was no reason to get angry at me.
>
> Rich was fired up but calmed down later toward the end of the day. After work, he asked me to go with him to the store. We drove to a pharmacy in Chesapeake a couple of blocks from his house.
>
> Before we walked in, he said, "We'll walk in together. Watch who they watch."

We entered, and I immediately noticed that the manager didn't take his eyes off Rich. We paid for our items and walked out.

Rich asked me to imagine I was him. "If you're black, everything you do is judged. You're never trusted. Your kids are suspects everywhere they go. School, work, and the grocery store, it doesn't matter. When I'd walked down the street, folks would go to the other side because they thought I might jump them. The police shoot us and ask questions later."

"Rich, shooting seems a little extreme."

Then he told me one of my friends had been shot last week!

I couldn't say anything. When Rich went places, it was as if he was contaminated with a disease that people would watch and avoid. I was oblivious to prejudice, yet I thought I knew all about it. We wore the same types of clothes and the same brand of shoes. The pharmacy worker only watched him because he was black. I'd just had a small glimpse into his everyday life. I couldn't fully know what it was like because that cloud wasn't over me every single day.

Ever since then, I notice this behavior nearly everywhere I go. I understand why some folks are angry. They are judged, scrutinized, and mistrusted every time they walk out of their home. As for white people, I remember growing up and hearing the prejudice within some of my family on Granny's side. They were angry. I think it's taught and gets passed down from parents; like-minded friends fuel the hatred, and the prejudice fire grows. I decided a while back that I don't want to be that way.

Susan takes in what I just said for a few moments.

I finish, "Rich is right. We white people have no idea. How can we?"

After sharing my story, I turn back to the cleaning. With the need to keep at it, I walk back to my bedroom and find another box underneath the bed. This box contains most of my report cards from elementary and high school. I never paid much attention to my grades in the past, but as I flip through them, I can see where they abruptly dropped after sixth grade when Pop's accident left our family in dire straits. Among them, I find an eighth-grade report card. I see it's from Mrs. Dawson's English class. Oh, I remember Mrs. Dawson.

Rich Faucett. A man who gave me a small glimpse of what it's like to live with prejudice every day. (Rich Faucett Photo)

I Won. I Think.

Friday, March 12, 1982 – Thirteen Years Old. Eighth Grade.

It's been ten months since Mom got me my motorcycle. She worked hours of overtime to get me this luxury. I'm still testing the Yamaha YZ80 and my limits. It's so fast! Sometimes we go out to the Goodyear place or The Greenhouse to find new places to jump. This morning, I call David and ride over to his place to meet him.

I pull up slowly to the beginning of his driveway so as not to upset his dad. I turn off the engine and push the bike up the driveway. Most folks in town call David's dad Buck. I just play it safe. "Good morning, Mr. Buchanan." He nods at me and keeps fiddling on his primer gray step-side truck.

"Let's go to the Goodyear place," I suggest.

We wind through woods, cross edges of spring-plowed fields, and race down a windy back road. Always the competitors, we push each other to jump higher and go faster.

"David, let's see if we can jump that big hill and make it out to that bush."

The jumping hill is nothing more than a cutout from a hill. At nearly thirty feet high, it's flat at the base, which makes for some good speed.

"Let's try to make it to that bush," David says.

That bush is a good 75 feet out from the hilltop. It's a long way. David goes first. He winds it up and hits the Goodyear hill fast—too fast. He leaves the ground at the top of the hill and keeps gaining altitude. He goes so high that his helmet hits the telephone line, nearly knocking him off the bike mid-air. For a moment, his feet are

246

off the motorcycle with only his hands holding on. It's as if he was bucked by a bull. He manages to hold on. Just like the old primary school swing days, David sets the standard. He lands on the targeted small bush.

"Okay, David, it's my turn. You're going down, Charlie Brown."

I hit the bottom of the hill faster than David but then slow down a little in order to avoid hitting the telephone line with my helmet. I come up several feet short.

"Let me try your bike," I say.

After a couple of practice jumps to get the feel of his bike, I tie David's record.

He looks at me. "Maikel, you should try racing again. You've gotten faster. They've reopened the Rip-Rap race course down near Highway 49 in Virgilina. I hear there's a race this weekend."

"Dude, that was fun. I will try racing again. I have to ask, but I think Mom will take me to the race on Sunday."

David and I have freedom on our motorcycles. In those moments, we are free of the bullies and all the other crap with which life has beat us over the head. We are happy. After a couple of hours and several crashes later, David and I ride home. I ask Mom if I can race, and she agrees. She calls the newspaper, and they let her take a camera for pictures for a write up in the newspaper.

On Sunday, I load up in her Ford Pinto. Because the motorcycle barely fits, I have to put my weight on the front wheel to keep the motorcycle from falling out the back. I drain the gas, so it doesn't spill in the back of the car. Mom drives down Highway 49 and takes a right to the Rip-Rap race course near the community of Virgilina. Soon, the pavement ends and turns into a dusty washboard gravel road going into a deep old forest.

We approach the infamous *One-Lane Bridge*. I've heard of this place but ain't never seen it. The flaking silver painted on the rusting bridge is all beat up from cars side-swiping into the side rails. A small creek trickles down below. Mom slows down, watching to ensure no cars are coming the other way before crossing.

"Mom, is this the bridge I've heard about?"

"What have you heard?"

"I heard the Klan used to hang people down here."

"You shouldn't know about these things. But yes, that's what I've heard, too. When I was younger, we were warned never to come down to these parts, especially after nightfall."

"Does this kind of thing still happen?"

"I don't know. You shouldn't worry about it." Mom gets a troubled look upon her face.

The *One-Lane Bridge* is an eerie place. The woods are dark, and it's daytime. The dense tree canopy shields the sky and the moon, hiding whatever happens here at night. Just back down the road where we came from is a white building where I heard the Klan meet.

"Mom, I wouldn't be around these parts at night." The look on her face lets me know to stop talking or asking any more questions.

Mom and I arrive at the Rip-Rap race course. She parks by a big old yellow Caterpillar bulldozer beside the racetrack. The smoke from the revving of two-stroke engines fills the air. My stomach has a whole swarm of butterflies. Some of the racers here have sponsors who provide them with two bikes and trailers full of spare tires, chains, and helmets. I tuck my carpet padding back inside my yellow helmet to look less scruffy. I notice the Ward Kid is here too. The Ward Kid, sponsored by Kawasaki, gets two new bikes a year along with gear. He always wins, and he beat me the last time I was here. I'm nervous for nearly one hour as I watch the first two races. Now it's time for the 80cc class to start.

I pull up to the line. The Ward Kid and I are the only ones in our category. At least I'll get second place if I don't crash, I rationalize. From experience, I know that the Ward Kid usually wins the hole shot or first turn and then continues to pull away each lap. We start revving our engines. I glance at him enviously. He confidently looks back at me. I notice he's sitting on a brand-new water-cooled motorcycle with brand new tires. I glance down at my half bald rear tire. Now I wish I'd cut a few more yards and earned enough money to get a new rear tire.

Our heads turn forward. 3...2...1...*Snap!* The elastic starting band shoots across our motorcycle front tires, signaling to go like a scalded cat. I start in second gear and dirt flies behind my tire. The Ward Kid and I speed straight for the first left turn, neither of us yielding. I've been practicing my takeoffs with David. I find I'm holding against the Ward Kid into the first turn. I decide to be more aggressive than the last time he kicked my ass. If he wants this, he's going to have to squeeze between me and first corner cone. I'm not going to yield! The cone rapidly approaches. The Ward Kid tries to go inside and cut me off. I hold my line. I try to win this small battle, even knowing he's going to win the war. I reach the cone first, but somehow, he ends up in front of me. He accelerates away from me. And once again, I'm eating his dust and smoke. I think, *Second place is not bad.*

After about two laps, I notice Mom at the sidelines jumping and waving her hands. "GO! GO! YOU'RE WINNING!"

I don't understand. How can I be winning? He beat me on the first corner, pulled away, and is out of sight. I don't understand. I hope he doesn't lap me. My engine and skills are maxed out. I pass the checkered flag and see the Ward Kid about one-quarter lap behind me. Then he passes the finish line with the checkered flag. I ride up by the Pinto and look at Mom. She's got a big ole proud smile on her face and shakes her right fist with joy.

"He got penalized on that first corner. He cut inside the cone! You won!"

I can't believe it. I actually won! Chin held high and chest sticking out a bit more, I enter the trophy room to see the race referee.

"Good job, Maikel. He may have cut that corner, but it don't matter. You won. See all these trophies? You can pick any one of these three."

"If I can pick, then I'll take the biggest one."

I grab the blue and gold trophy and line up outside. I'm grinning from ear to ear. I glance at the other two winners and notice they aren't smiling. I mimic their expressionless faces as Mom proudly snaps a picture for the paper. I stroll back to my motorcycle and load it into back of the Pinto. I re-inspect Hank's near perfect welds. They're holding strong.

Monday morning, I confidently walk up David in the school hallway.

"Hey, Maikel. How'd you do?"

"I won. I beat the Ward Kid."

I don't volunteer that he got penalized. I get one of those rare *you-are-a-badass* look of approval from David.

"Totally awesome! See, Maikel, I told you that you're faster."

The bell rings. It's time to go to English class. I sit down as Mrs. Dawson stands up. There is a smell of fresh mimeograph printed paper in the air.

"Okay, students. Here's your test. Please pass them back."

"Oh crap, a test," I moan quietly. I was so focused on the race this past weekend that I totally forgot about my English test. I'm visualizing the red ink markups that will cut and bleed into the purple-blue ink on the test. I give it my best attempt and turn in my test, knowing that I probably failed.

The next day, Mrs. Dawson walks the graded tests to each student.

She hands me mine and announces, "This is what happens when you don't study."

I'm mortified and sit there and stew. My initial embarrassment turns to anger. Mrs. Dawson is right that I didn't study, but she didn't have to tell the whole class. I plot how I can get even, something that would be just as embarrassing.

Lunch arrives and I join David, who's always one of the first ones to sit at the lunch table. Between David and me, I'm sure we can think of something to get even with Mrs. Dawson.

"David, do you know Mrs. Dawson?"

"You mean, Mrs. Dawson the English teacher? I sure do. She lives right across the street from me. On that outside corner lot with all those pine trees with the railroad tracks on the other side."

I know the house. David and I have shortcutted through her yard more than once over the years.

"I need to get even. Any ideas?"

With David and me, we didn't have to ask the cause for the retaliation. We simply assumed that whoever crossed us was wrong and that was that. We had each other's backs.

"She has all those trees. We could roll her yard with toilet paper. Kinda like a Christmas come early decoration of the trees. Let's wait until Saturday night."

"Great. Let's meet at the tracks where the trail crosses at 9:00. My parents are closely watching me, so I may have to sneak out my window. If I'm not there after fifteen minutes, go ahead without me."

We have a plan. I can always count on David.

Me after unloading my bike from the Pinto before the motocross race. The yellow helmet with carpet padding.

Maikel's first and only motocross win.

English Toilet Paper Etiquette

Saturday, March 20, 1982 – Thirteen Years Old. Eighth Grade.

Throw it up. Damn, it came up too short.
Try again and heave. Car comin', abort!
Higher in the trees. Unfurl every roll.
We got that yard good. We achieved my goal.

I don't see David Thursday or Friday at school. I assume our toilet paper plans are still on. Unexpectedly on Saturday, our old neighbors Daniel and Charlene visit us. They want and are allowed to spend a night with Tash and me. We haven't seen them since they moved to North Carolina. I've missed my crush Charlene and haven't kissed a girl since. She's more gorgeous than ever.

I worry that my plans tonight might not happen, but I ask them to join me, hoping for the best. "Daniel and Charlene. Want to roll a yard tonight?"

Immediately, Charlene responds, "Sure. Who is it?"

While staring at Charlene's soft lips, I explain what happened. Daniel and Charlene are more than enthusiastic about helping. I realize I made one big mistake and didn't plan my attack properly. I check under the bathroom sink and in the linen closet and we only have six rolls of toilet paper. I grab all but one roll and walk out to hide them in my backpack. Mom catches me on the way out of the bathroom.

"I see. Did you leave any toilet paper for us?"

Surprised, I stammer, "I left one roll."

"We need two rolls. Put one back. I'll go to the store and buy you some more."

Mom comes back with a twelve pack she found on sale. She hands me the package of Scott toilet paper. Scott toilet paper is wound so tight on the cardboard tubes that we call it "perpetual rolls." Those rolls never seem to run out. That's a good thing too. We'll get more mileage per roll with Scott's relative to Charmin.

"Here you go. Take ten rolls and don't get caught."

On the way out the front door with our rolls of ammunition in hand, Charlene is amazed. "Our Mom would have sent us straight to our rooms. Your Mom is so cool."

Tash, Charlene, Daniel, and I arrive at our meeting spot on the railroad tracks five minutes late. David is already there, nervously waiting. I find that I'm stressed out too. I have the same butterflies as before kissing Charlene and at the beginning of a motocross race. I can't get caught.

I turn to David. "Mom bought us more toilet paper. Can you believe it?"

David is uncharacteristically anxious. These days, he's constantly under his parents' watchful eyes. He keeps looking over his shoulders toward his house. We trudge down the tracks a bit and follow an overgrown trail to the south side of Mrs. Dawson's yard. About five minutes later after the last light goes off, we sneak forward and cautiously start throwing toilet paper into the smaller pine trees on the edge. As our confidence grows, we gradually move to the bigger trees and bushes closer to the house. A car drives by. We drop flat on the ground to hide. The car keeps going. The driver ignores us. *Whew!* We throw and throw until every roll is unfurled. My revenge for my embarrassment is fulfilled. Justice.

All of us walk back to the tracks laughing and relieved we didn't get caught. David runs home ahead of us, hoping his parents didn't notice he was out. I see him crawl through the window and no lights come on. Seems like he made it without getting caught. Charlene and I fall back on the walk home. She grabs my hand, and I'm in heaven once again. This night could not be more perfect.

The next morning, David calls me around noon. I have a question for David. Worried that I'd embarrass him, I didn't want to ask it last night.

"Hey David. Where were you last week? I didn't see you in school Thursday or Friday."

"My parents pulled me out of public school. They're sending me to a military academy."

"What for?"

"They found a pack of cigarettes and a beer can. They think the military academy will straighten me out. They say I'm headin' down the wrong path," he grumbles.

I respond, "You seem okay to me. I don't care for smoking, but it don't bother me if that's what you want to do. I like beer too, but ain't never had more than a couple swallows at a time. Seems like if they can do it, why can't you?"

David doesn't want to talk about it. I know his dad is tough and expects a lot out of him.

Changing the subject, he perks up. "Dude, you won't believe it. I got on my bike and rode up and down the road to wait for the Dawson's to wake up. We got their yard good. They came outside and just kept looking around. Guess they were shocked. There was a heavy dew last night, and the toilet paper came apart. They got brooms, and rakes out, but when they tried to pull it down, it kept falling into smaller pieces. Then they waved me over. They said that they would pay me to clean it up. I got ten dollars for cleaning up a mess that I helped make. Plus, I didn't have to go to church."

We laugh and laugh. "I don't know what's better. The extra money or getting out of church."

**My friend David Buchanan in
military school to "straighten him out."
(Marie Buchanan Photo)**

Hospice Care (Day 10, Afternoon)

Friday, March 2, 2007 – Parachute Pants, ATARI, and Grandpa's Sheriff Report.

Susan, Tash, and I drop the stairs and climb up in the attic for another round of decluttering. The rickety steps creak but hold our weight as we ascend into chaos. Like a family of prairie dogs, one by one our heads pop up through the ceiling hole into the attic. In the cold attic air, we're overwhelmed and completely surrounded by piles of clothes and boxes of Christmas decorations. The mounds of clutter extend to the unfinished walls in all directions for the entire length and width of the house.

Susan gasps. It's the first time she's seen the piles. Using humor to cope, I respond to the look on her face. "Look here, Susan. I've always said we have so many clothes in the attic that we didn't need to add insulation."

There's a huge collection of at least two dozen plastic bags. I grab the closest one. It's labeled *Kids Clothes*. Inside the bag, the patterns and colors of these clothes are familiar. I remember the green slacks and the polo shirts with hand sewn Izod patches. Legitimate Izod shirts were expensive. One of Mom's friends gave her a couple of dozen old, stained Izod shirts. Mom cut the Izod patches off the worn-out shirts. Then she bought cheaper unlabeled polo-type shirts from the Peebles clothing store downtown. She hand-sewed the Izod patches on them. That way, Tash and I could fit in with the other kids.

One time a kid at school said, "Your alligator is crooked."

It was. As tired as she was, Mom fixed it that night when I told her. She didn't want us to be embarrassed.

Tash reminisced, "Mom kept all our old clothes. She wanted to make each of us a quilt out of these."

I sort through the clothes, but my attention is drawn to something wrapped in a shirt.

I pull out an ATARI Pong game that's well used. I remember Tash and me playing this for hours. Right beside the ATARI is a water-stained cardboard box. Written on top with a Sharpie, I read, "TRS-80 Computer."

"Cale, do you remember when Mom bought this for us?"

"Kinda."

"This computer went on sale at Radio Shack for $299. Mom knew computers were going to be big, and she wanted us to have a head start learning about them. She worked a lot of overtime to get it for us."

"Incredible. How do you remember it was $299?"

"The price tag here, silly." I rarely see price tags on items anymore. Technology has changed so much. Items are scanned these days.

The year she got it, I remember telling her about a computer class at high school that I couldn't register to take. Mecklenburg County had twelve Apple II computers arranged on a small school bus that traveled to all schools in the county. Only twelve people in my high school could get in. I wasn't one of them.

"Tash, now I remember! She didn't want us to have it as hard as her life."

Mom made another sacrifice getting us this computer. My memories flood back. I only wrote one program in BASIC on it but played games for weeks. Lying just under it was something else I hadn't seen since the 80's—parachute pants.

"Would you look at that? My waist was 26 inches. I can't fit into these things anymore."

We laugh, knowing we have *character* now from eating chocolate pies and Hardee's chicken.

Tash, Susan, and I carry several loads of 70's and 80's nostalgic shirts, pants, and jackets back down the creaking attic steps. Nearly all of these items are going to be donated to the Goodwill. We lack the enthusiasm to wash them before donating. Under several piles of clothes, I find a cardboard shoebox marked *IMPORTANT*. I open the box and read a letter on top.

"Tash, I found a racist letter that I can't figure out. Why did Grandpa pay for this man's parole? Why is the sheriff looking for a subject? Do you know anything about it?"

Maikel L. Wise

TOWN OF CLARKSVILLE

Clarksville, Virginia

February, XX, XXX

Sheriff of XXXXX County

XXXXX, North Carolina

Dear Sir,

Mr. J. L. Yancey of Clarksville, Virginia has informed me that XXXXX male, colored, about five feet, one hundred forty-five pounds, twenty-five years old, dark skin is residing in the vicinity of XXXXX County, North Carolina on XXXXX between XXXXX and XXXXX.

This subject is paroled from XXXXX, Virginia XXXXX XXXXX. Mr. J. L. Yancey has signed for subject's parole. Please check county and see if this subject can be found. Please notify me if subject is found and Mr. J. L. Yancey will send for him.

Your cooperation in this matter will be greatly appreciated.

Verify truly yours,

XXXXX

Chief of Police

Dear Sir,

I have check and found that the above subject is in XXXXX county and staying with Mr. XXXXX. We will be glad to help pick up subject and whenever you send for him.

Yours truly,

XXXXX

XXXXX, Sheriff

Redacted letter to my grandpa, Jimmy Lou Yancey.

"Yeah, I do. Cale, do you know what happened to Mom when she was young?"

"No. What are you talking about?"

Tash struggles and tells me something new about Mom. "Cale, Mom was raped when she was young."

There are a few moments of stillness.

"One of the people who helped our grandparents on their farm raped her. The man ran off, but they found him. After they brought him back to the farm, they never saw him again."

"Tash, are you saying Grandpa did something bad to him?"

"Mom seemed to think so, but that's not all. Right after it happened, Grandma and Grandpa held Mom down, poured bleach on her and scrubbed her with a brush until she was raw. Mom told me she screamed and screamed but Grandpa wouldn't stop."

"How do you know this? She never said anything to me."

Tearing up, Tash says, "Mom told me how it has upset her all these years."

I sit down, experiencing an overwhelming wave of sadness for what happened and what's happening to Mom. I'm furious at the man who hurt Mom. Anger swells at my grandpa, Jimmy Lou.

"Tash, I had no idea." Venting my anger in a raised voice, I say, "Why am I finding out about this today?"

The room is dead quiet.

"I'm sorry. It's not you. It's just..." I stop not knowing how to finish my sentence.

"Do you remember what Mom used to say? 'I want to raise you right and not hate anyone.' She didn't want us to be like some of our relatives. Mom thought she knew what happened to that man. All her life, she's lived with that guilt."

"Tash, I didn't know. I knew she had some ghosts but didn't know this happened to her. I wonder if that's why she would stare out the window and sometimes weep. I never knew she carried this heavy burden all these years."

Susan chimes in. "So nothing ever happened to your grandpa? Did they investigate?"

Tash responds, "I don't know. Mom didn't say, but she told me he wasn't arrested. I don't think we can do anything about it now. She can't speak now, and all we have is her word. We don't have any other proof."

Tash is right about one thing. We aren't perfect, but we aren't like some of my hateful, prejudiced family. For that, I'm grateful to Mom.

Stage Ten Hemorrhage

Monday, July 12, 1982 – Fourteen Years Old.

July is heating up and encouraging shorts, but I still like wearing my parachute pants even though they're warm in the humid summer sunshine. Careful not to spill any gas, I load the push mower into the back of the Pinto. Mom drops me off with it down on College Street. I cut two yards and earn twenty-two dollars. After finishing the last yard, I recount my cash and look at one of the ten-dollar bills. It looks weird.

Mom can't pick me up, so I push the lawnmower down the sidewalk back home just like Possum the town drunk does. Except my lawn mower isn't running, a pack of dogs ain't following me, and I'm sober.

"Tash, look at this. Do you think this ten-dollar bill is counterfeit?"

"I know what that is. That's one of those silver certificate bills. It might be worth some money. You'd better hold onto it."

I walk back to my bedroom and tuck the rare bill into one of outdated Britannica Encyclopedia books. In the kitchen, I hear Tash turn on the radio to WRAL, a popular station out of Raleigh.

The announcer blares, "This is Tommy Tutone's, *867-5309/Jenny.*" Great, now this song is stuck in my head.

"Tash, they have a new video game down at the Hop-In store. Wanna go?"

"Nah. You go ahead. I'm gonna watch music videos."

There's still some cut grass stuck on the bottom of my black parachute pants. I use a washcloth to get the green blades off. My nylon black-sheen britches quickly dry, and I walk down Shiney

Rock back to College Street. I find myself humming the stuck song. I try to find another song to replace it, but it's too late. I walk into the Hop-In convenience store and notice the new Galaga game has a player perched in front of it. I recognize him. It's Troy, and my friend David is standing beside him. I know Troy but don't really hang out with him. He's a nice enough fella, though.

"Hey, guys."

David says, "Hey," back, but he's watching Troy focusing on getting a new high score. I watch Troy masterfully play the new game. This spacer shooter game is more sophisticated and has better graphics than the Asteroids game it replaced. Plus, the *Asteroids* game had a sticky fire button. Mrs. Pacman, the game beside them, is open, so I start on it. *Wonka, Wonka, Wonka.* I die quickly. The high score is in no danger of seeing my initials.

Ding, ding the front door chimes. I notice the Cragley Kid stroll in heading our way. At least we're in public, I'm around three friends, and it's daytime, so I think I'm safe. Even so, I discretely move some of my cash into one of my lower pockets in my parachute pants and zip it shut. I'm too big for him to hold me upside down anymore, but that won't stop him from mugging me. At least part of my money is dispersed if he threatens me.

In a malicious tone, the Cragley Kid says, "You colored people are always on the games."

I'm really uncomfortable. I back up a bit, waiting for vengeance to be unleashed.

Stage 10 on Galaga ends.

Bap!

With lightning speed, Troy turns from the game and pops the Cragley Kid in the nose. His head rolls back and snaps forward again. He stumbles backward. Blood trickles out of his left nostril.

The Cragley Kid, who is fair skinned, is now bright red. Unconcerned about retaliation, Troy turns right back to the game and continues to Stage 11. The Cragley Kid whimpers away, looking like a squashed tomato.

I think, *Who's colored now?*

After several more minutes of playing, Troy enters his initials in first place on the high score board. It's David and my turn to try the new game. We play for at least an hour until a hefty chunk of my money is *Wonka-upped* in this new game machine. I make top ten, but I'm a long way off from Troy's first place initials.

Although he's not smoking, I can smell the Marlboro smoke on David's clothes. Like many in town, including my mom, he started smoking young. I'm used to the smell, since Mom inhales and releases similar toxins daily.

"Maikel, can I borrow a couple of dollars? I'm outta cigarettes," David asks.

"Sure. I have $2.50 left, but you can have a couple of bucks. Do you think they'll sell them to you, since you're underage?"

"Yep. That lady did yesterday, as long as there are no other adults in the store."

David waits and then goes up to the counter, and she sells him a pack. We walk outside under the shade of the tree at the back of the store, and he lights one up.

After he deeply inhales and exhales, I ask David, "How's your summer going?"

"It's all right. I fight a lot with my parents. They're always wanting me to work around the house and help Grandpa. They found another pack of my cigarettes in the heat vent and had a fit. I'm running out of hiding places. They watch my every move."

"At least you're not in the military academy now. Let's go get our motorcycles and ride."

David walks back to his house, and I walk back to mine.

Mom is home when I walk through the front door. "Son, did you get paid for cutting grass today? I need some money for gas for the car. I'll pay you back this Friday."

"I have a ten-dollar bill left, but it's a special ten-dollar bill."

Hidden in the encyclopedia on my shelf in my bedroom, I grab the ten-dollar silver certificate and bring it to Mom. I'm disappointed, not knowing if this bill is worth more than ten dollars.

I check the gas can in the garage and realize now I'm the one out of fuel.

I walk back and disappointedly call David. "I can't go biking. I'm out of gas."

"Dude. I'll give you some. I just filled up my gas can yesterday. Do you have enough to make it over to my house?"

"I'm on fumes, but I can push it if it runs out."

Mom hears me talking to David.

Mom offers help. "I'm gonna call around and see if we can get you some more yards to mow. And maybe you can help your uncle with the tobacco harvest."

Above the Law

Sunday, August 1, 1982 – Fourteen Years Old.

Mom is preparing to take a nap, since working multiple jobs is sucking the life out of her. "I might need your help with newspapers tomorrow morning. I know it's a school morning, but you'll only have to wake up an hour earlier."

Tash and I say in near unison, "Okey dokey." We know how hard Mom's been working to hold us together.

When the alarm goes off at 5:00 A.M., we walk to the kitchen, but Mom is nowhere to be seen. There's a note on the counter with biscuits holding it down. "I can take care of the newspapers this morning. Don't forget your lunch money. Don't miss the bus. Love, Mom."

Mom's routes for delivering newspapers take her to Boydton, Chase City, Clarksville, and a few places in between. Sometimes we join her before school to help out. It's kind of tight in the back seat of the two door Ford Pinto with the stacks of newspapers, but we manage. I'm thankful I don't have to help today since I get motion sickness from all the twisty, turny roads.

Arriving at school, I hear over the intercom, "Maikel Wise, would you please come to the office?"

Am I in trouble? I wonder. I can't think of anything. I didn't swear at anyone of consequence that I can think of. I walk into the office, sit down, and wait until I'm called. I can see the paddle with air holes hanging on the wall by the principal's office. Air holes are drilled into the wood to make it go faster as the spanker smacks the spankee. I'm thinking I should have worn thicker britches. Tash walks in a couple of minutes later.

"Natasha and Maikel, would you come into my office?"

I'm trembling. The principal seems serious, and I am formulating excuses for something I haven't yet been accused of.

"Maikel, Natasha, your mom was in a car accident."

My eyes start watering up. All I can think about is Pop's car accident. I don't know if Mom is dead or in the hospital hooked up to tubes. I hope the ambulance didn't run out of gas or get a flat tire like it did with Pop's accident.

Tash and I are fearing the worst. The principal reassures us. "It's okay. She's fine. She's fine. Her car got hit hard, but your mom is okay."

I feel better but still expect the worse.

When Tash and I get home, Mom is recovering on the couch with a sore neck and a couple of scrapes on her forehead. She tells us what happened, and we can see she's uncomfortable. About thirty minutes later, the sheriff's deputy comes over to review the police report. After I let him in, Tash and I sit by Mom.

"Mrs. Wise, I have the report from the accident. You mind if I read it to you and ask you a couple questions?"

"Go ahead."

Mom is lying down with lots of pillows behind her, so she isn't quite flat. She sits up a little more.

"On the morning July 31st, Mrs. Dolores Wise of Clarksville, Virginia was rear-ended in a 1972 Ford Pinto registered to Mrs. Dolores Wise. Mrs. Wise was delivering newspapers for the Mecklenburg Sun Newspaper to Triangle Grocery store at approximately 5:45 A.M. near Boydton, Virginia. The vehicle of the unidentified car proceeded to leave the scene of the accident without consulting Mrs. Wise or local law enforcement. Mrs. Wise had just entered her vehicle and had not yet started her vehicle nor fastened her seatbelt. After the accident, Mrs. Wise walked to a nearby pay phone, called 911, and waited for an officer and ambulance to arrive. Statement signed by Mr. George Jamison, Sheriff."

"Mrs. Wise, the individual who hit you has turned himself in to us. His name is John Jamison."

"Really? That's good news. Wait. Jamison. Jamison? Is he related to the sheriff?"

"Yes, ma'am. As a matter of fact, he is. He's the sheriff's nephew. The sheriff wants to know if you are going to press charges. The other thing is that the owner of the store would like your car moved. I know it's to the side of the building, but it's damaged. You are going to have to move it."

"I didn't fall off the turnip truck. Of course, I want to press charges! I'll bet he was drunk when he left the scene. The man who hit me should move my car. It was his fault!"

The officer shrugs. "Please have it removed by the end of today. Thank you for your time."

The deputy leaves, and Mom is sourer than an unripe green apple.

Talking more to herself than to either of us, Mom says, "I know how this works. The sheriff's nephew will probably get out of this. I'm out a paycheck. Out a car. What's going to happen next?"

I chime in, "Mom, it's a good thing you had that gas tank safety plate installed. Pintos are known for blowing up in rear-end crashes."

"Yes. I'm lucky, but now I need a car."

"Travis has three cars and a motorcycle. Why don't you ask him?" I suggest.

She calls Travis, and he says, "No." Travis is funny about lending stuff, and he's tight with his money, too. Travis could give Mom a paper bag of steaks, and he'd want the paper bag back. I saw it firsthand when he wouldn't help his own brother get out of jail. Travis bought Hank's car cheap when Hank needed bail money and never sold it back to him like he'd promised.

Unlike his brother, Hank comes through for Mom. He always comes through. Hank doesn't just lend Mom one of his cars but does one better. He helps Mom buy another car the next day. Mom is now the proud owner of a slightly used four-door Chevy Chevette with air conditioning. It's no Cadillac, but I feel like we are living the high life. As I'm admiring Mom's snow white four-door hatchback gleaming in the driveway, I hear the phone ring in the background.

Mom hollers for me. I go inside and Mom says, "That was Aunt Abigail. Uncle Henry could use some help pickin' tobacco leaves tomorrow. Make sure you're ready and out front at 5:30 A.M."

"Okey dokey. I'll be ready. Do I need to bring anything to eat for lunch?"

"Nope. Aunt Abigail will take care of food."

I go to bed early. I know what's coming. Uncle Henry is always complaining, yelling, or bitchin' about something or someone. I just hope I don't fall into the crosshairs. I feel ready for tobacco picking after helping on Granny's farm, but with this hot spell it may get tough in the afternoon.

Primin' Tobacco and Segregated Tables

Tuesday, August 3, 1982 – Fourteen Years Old.

My aching back. Tobacco wax in the eyes.
I'm slow as a slug. Juan, well, he flies.
My racist Uncle saying things out of spite.
In his house, I'm ashamed to be white.

I never like being late for anything. I know my ride is picking me up at 5:30 A.M., but I'm ready and waiting by our mailbox just after 5:00 A.M. I hear the Bobwhite's singing their name *bobwhite, bobwhite, bobwhite* at the bottom of our field, and the sky starts to wake up. I glance over at our poor mailbox post. It was knocked over again last Saturday night by a car speeding down Shiney Rock. It's likely from a drunk driver leaving the *Pizza Pub* or the *Buffalo Inn Lounge*. Some mornings we'd wake up and find pieces of our mailbox or the neighbor's mailboxes down the road. When Pop was here, he embedded a steel U-channel post into a foot of concrete. After this latest hit, the steel post is bent over at a right angle, rendering it unusable. My repair, not as good as Pop's, is temporary, with some cinder blocks and the old mailbox's four-by-four post. It leans over, but it's good enough for now. If a drunk is going to take out our mailbox again, I want to ensure it does some damage. Concrete and steel ensure that.

I anxiously look at my watch. It's 5:14 A.M., and I hear a vehicle with a V-8 coming down the road. By the left headlight, I can tell it's a Chevy half-ton truck, even with the right front driving light out.

271

Uncle Henry stops in the middle of the road. The truck is well-used, and I realize it's been neglected when the oil smoke exhaust from the worn engine drifts by me. He tells me, "Git in boy." After slamming the door three times to get it to shut, he backs up in our driveway and heads back down the road.

"Maikel, you ready for some real work? Most folks around here don't know what hard work is."

"Yes, sir. I help Granny on her farm, but I have to admit that I ain't never picked tobacco before."

"Yankees call it picking tobacco. We call it priming tobacco. After the first row, you'll have it down. You have to move fast, though. It's hard to keep up with the Mexicans and Coloreds."

This is going to be a long day. The day is already starting out justifying why my uncle is an asshole. I wasn't used to calling people *Coloreds*. Some of the people I know use the *"N" word*, but I don't like it. *Coloreds* seems to fall into that same category. I reason that if black people are called Coloreds, it seems only fair to call us white people *Colorless*.

On our ride to Aunt Abigail's place, I get to thinking about Uncle Henry. Now, if Grandma Ruby's sister is Aunt Abigail, shouldn't that be Great Aunt Abigail? Then that would make Uncle Henry my Great Uncle Henry. Then who would I be to him? Would I be his Great Grand Nephew? Am I his Second Cousin? I'm on the verge of figuring out my relationship status from his perspective when we pull into his driveway. We climb out of the truck, and he introduces me.

"This is Jimmy Lou's grandson Maikel. You boys show him how to prime." In our town, you were always somebodies' boy or grandson. It's like you don't matter until you've established yourself.

Uncle Henry goes back inside his house. Most likely, he's going in to gather more insults.

A man with a heavy Spanish accent walks up to me. "Buenos Días, Maikel. I'm Juan. Follow me and do what I do."

At a brisk pace, Juan heads toward the large tobacco field across from Aunt Abigail's place. I have to run to keep up.

He changes my name and starts tutoring me. "Miguelito, these tobacco leaves ripen from the bottom up. Just pick the bottom two or three leaves that are a little more yellowed. Put them under your arm. Move to the next plant. When you can't hold any more, place them in the cart behind the tractor at the end of the row. Don't rub your eyes. ¿Comprende?"

I don't know what *comprende* means but automatically respond, "Yes, sir."

The leaves are all soaked in heavy dew. My shirt quickly becomes soaked as I tuck the big tobacco leaves under my arm.

"Señor Miguelito. ¡*Más rápido!* ¡*Más rápido!*" Juan hollers. Juan is already at the end of his row, and I'm only halfway done.

I don't know what ¡*Más rápido!* means, either, but I certainly know by his tone that I'd better get my ass in gear. I start priming as fast as I can. I run with my armful of leaves to the trailer and back. I glance up. It appears that Juan and the others are picking up the pace. They're so fast that it's impossible for me to keep up. Instead of priming two or three leaves per plant, I prime one or two. That way, I can go faster.

Juan notices what I'm doing. "Señor, you need to get these, too."

He helps me by alternating priming his row and mine. I appreciate him not telling my uncle about my inability to keep up.

Throughout the morning, my uncle yells, "You boys had better hurry up if you want to get paid," and "I ain't got all damn day." Yet more confirmation that my uncle is an asshole.

At least three hours go by, and the day is heating up. I'm glad I'm not wearing my new parachute pants. My shirt, armpits, and arms are covered with tobacco wax. A stream of salty sweat runs into my eye. I rub it. Too late, I remember Juan's instructions. My eye starts burning as if someone has poured a full bottle of Tabasco sauce in it. I rub my eye with a non-contaminated tobacco portion of my shirt that only has salty sweat on it. The burning is still there but dissipates, leaving only salt in the wound.

"¡Más rápido!"

I try to go faster. My back is aching, but I keep going. Then I see them. Giant Japanese hornets! But I can't stop. I'm already the slowest worker in the field. I carefully pick the two bottom leaves on the plants so the whole stalk doesn't sway. The hornets move a little but don't strike. *Whew!* I keep going, pushing through one of my worst fears and doing my best to not disappoint Juan. Juan's opinion means more than my uncle's.

Our crew finishes up priming by 11:00. It's time for lunch. My back is in knots, I'm dehydrated, and my eyes are burning. We all wash up with the water hose in the back yard, but I just can't get all the tobacco wax off. Even dish soap with a stiff bristle plastic brush doesn't budge it all off. I walk inside through the back porch and see Juan sitting at one of the tables. I promptly sit beside him on one of the chairs covered in plastic. After all these years visiting Aunt Abigail, I now finally know why the chairs are covered.

"Thank you, Juan, for helping me today. I've never primed tobacco before. You were flying out there."

"*No hay problema, Miguelito.*"

All of the other field workers join us at our table.

My uncle yells, "Maikel, get in here. That's where the help sits."

"I am the help."

"Don't get smart with me! Mexicans and Coloreds sit there. You sit here."

I'm embarrassed and ashamed. I move to the segregated table full of colorless people with real ceramic plates instead of paper ones. I am the help. The other white guy at the table who I don't know is also the help. It seems more appropriate that I sit on the front porch steps than at either of these tables. I certainly didn't work as hard as the *help* table. I don't want to be associated with the colorless table, either. We bow our heads as Uncle Henry's words smack God's face with typical Southern Baptist grace.

After a full meal, I am ready to go home, but Uncle Henry directs me otherwise. "All right, y'all. 'Nuf lounging around. To the barn."

I'd thought we were done. I shouldn't have eaten that extra hotdog. Sitting on Aunt Abigail's front porch swing for half an hour would be agreeable right now. All the tobacco we'd picked this morning is stacked up next to the barn and overflowing in several trailers. The weathered-gray log tobacco barn is similar to the one at Granny's where we stored potatoes in the winter but is more like the barn the bull chased us into after throwing hickory nuts at him. To the east side of the barn, close to a conveyor, there's a huge pile of dried grayed sticks.

"Maikel, you help your Aunt Abigail on the conveyor. And keep up!"

Juan and the rest of the men form a line going from the conveyor to the top of the barn. Some of those in the barn are standing on the horizontal logs that go end to end from the barn. Looks like the workers are up on the logs trying to get away from the mean old bull down below—Uncle Henry. The conveyor starts as I look over Aunt Abigail's shoulder.

In her strong Deep South voice, Aunt Abigail says, "Now see here. Place leaves on the bottom like this. Place the stick over that. Then place more leaves on the top. The machine will stitch them together. Then hand them off."

I watch about a half dozen sticks stitch to tobacco leaves and figure it out. Aunt Abigail moves behind me, and I take over.

Juan and the rest of the men have no trouble keeping up with the machine. Some of them even toss the filled tobacco sticks. It only takes about two more hours to fill up the barn. Uncle Henry starts up the heaters to cure the tobacco and closes the door.

Finally, we're done!

It's pay time. Juan and each of the other men get a $100 dollar bill. I don't know if I am "helping a relative" or getting paid. Uncle Henry hesitantly hands me two twenty-dollar bills. He's fair. I'm glad I wasn't paid as much as the other workers. They'd earned it. I walk over to Juan and shake his tobacco-stained calloused hand. I almost give him one of my twenty-dollar bills, but I know I'd have an embarrassing moment again with my uncle. Uncle Henry drives me back home, and I collapse on the living room floor still wearing my sweaty, dirty clothes. I'm rich but too tired to spend any of it.

I hear Mom slowly getting ready for work. She's still sore and bruised from her hit-and-run car accident.

She asks from the bathroom, "How did it go today at Aunt Abigail's?"

"Fine, I suppose. Mom, it sure seems like Uncle Henry is prejudiced. You and Pop have black friends. I don't reckon Uncle Henry does, though."

"Why do you say that?"

"He says things like 'Mexicans this' and 'Colored folks that.' You ain't that way. Tash and I ain't that way. Why is that?"

Walking out of the bathroom, Mom rubs her sore neck and says, "Sit down."

I do as I'm told, since I know this conversation is about to get serious.

Sitting beside me, she tells me, "When I was growing up, we had black people living on Granny's farm. They used to help us out. Grandpa would pay them. There's something that happened when I was younger. I said that I wouldn't raise you the way my grandpa and Uncle Henry raised their kids."

"What happened?"

"It doesn't matter. I don't want you to grow up hating someone just because they're different. Understand?"

"Yes, ma'am." A few moments pass. "Mom, I don't like Uncle Henry. Do I have to help him again?"

"You're a young man. You can do what you want. Now go get cleaned up."

Churchin' Up (Part 2) and Stop Cussin'

Sunday, September 12, 1982 – Fourteen Years Old. Ninth Grade.

I swear all the time. It's just who I am.
Influenced by others. To be a better man.
I think I'll read the Bible. See what it's about.
My friend leaving. Hard life coming, no doubt.

Mom is working as much overtime as the prison will give her. Although she won't admit it, she's exhausted. She needs Tash and me to go to church to give her a break when she's home. Moreover, she doesn't want us to have too much idle time—a pathway to evilness. In the last church, Mom condemned the preacher to hell. Mom won't have no part of that *y'all goin' to hell* place. I don't fancy meeting that preacher again, either, especially in hell. I wonder what kind of film he'd show his congregation once he gets down there. I can envision some of the titles: *101 Ways to Eat Worms that are Eating You* and *Cooking with Hell's Flames from Simmer to Broil.* When I think of those days, I'm still traumatized.

With Granny riding shotgun, Mom is taking us back to our former church, the Roanoke River Baptist Church. We enter and duck into the back pews with the less righteous folk. Our neighbor Betsy is already there hiding. If this were a high school class, this would be the C- or D student desks. I pretend to sing the hymns, and I'm overjoyed when we skip the third verse. Betsy lets out a snore as her head nods off. I wonder if all the churches skip the third verse. All the hairspray, aftershave, and perfume from the gussied-up congregants keeps me taking shallow breaths. In addition to their sins, I wonder what else those folks are covering up as they sit in the polished wooden pews. As the service ends, Betsy instantly wakes up. There is only one exit, and the preacher is guarding it like the Doberman guard dogs at *Bowman's Garage and Junkyard*. We have to pass by him and I hope his words don't bite.

"I haven't seen you in a while, Mrs. Wise. Where have you been?"

Mom squeaks out, "I've been working a lot."

She isn't afraid of the preacher, but she doesn't fully trust him. The real reason she hasn't been to this church is the last conversation they had when Pop was cheating. "Work it out. You need to learn to forgive and be a good wife..." is what the preacher had said. It's still taking Mom a while to get over that.

"Mrs. Wise, did you know we have a new youth minister? The youth group meets here at 5:00 P.M. First, they usually play softball, and then they have a meeting. We'd love to have your children join us tonight."

Sounds like my evening is being planned out. I think, *Dammit, I've got shit to do.* It's truly amazing how the tasks I've been procrastinating on have suddenly become a priority.

Mom responds, "I'll think about it." She doesn't commit but says it in a manner to ensure the preacher knows she's in control, that he can't bully her again.

We pile in the car and deliver Granny home to her front porch steps. Driving back down Forest Hill Road toward home, Mom asks us, "Just try it. The church's youth group does trips, too, and you may like it. Please." Mom looks drained. We don't want to, but we do as we're asked.

Later that day, Mom drops us off at the church early at 4:30 P.M. Tash and I take our skateboards since Roanoke River Baptist Church has one of the smoothest parking lots in town. They take care of their black asphalt. The cracks in the asphalt are always filled and weeds aren't welcomed. We skate down the slightly sloping parking lot a few times but stop after cars start showing up for the youth group. Tash and I skate over to the back side of the church and consider not participating in the youth group. Instead, we continue our up and downhill runs, but our plans for escape are cut short when the youth minister spots us and direct us to the softball field.

I'm not looking forward to playing softball because I suck at all ball games. I remember in Little League baseball when they'd put me in right outfield. I was smart enough to know that the really bad players were always put out in right field. As such, the batters would purposefully hit their balls toward me. Even though I couldn't hit, throw, or catch the ball, my coach, Mr. Kearns, kept encouraging me. I decided not to play anymore and quit Little League.

Heads down, Tash and I trudge out to the field. I recognize a few of my high school friends, and there are other folks I've never seen before. Next to home plate, everyone introduces themselves, and the two captains start picking teams. Like a flashback from my traumatized Little League days, I'm almost the last one picked on a team.

My mind fights to find something wrong with this group. I search for any excuse to justify not coming back. With self-induced misery, I depressingly suffer through the innings. When it's my turn at bat, I actually hit the ball and make it to second base. I think to myself, *Amazing! Unbelievable! Maybe I don't suck all that much.* On my next batting turn, instead of people walking infield, they back up, knowing I can hit. I start feeling a little better about being here. Now all I have to do is improve on catching the ball. The game ends with me feeling that I may have a place where I fit in.

The flock gathers their possessions and migrates to the church's basement for the next inning of righteousness. A few of us are called to read verses in The Bible. I'm one of them. I'm not good at reading out loud. I only slip up twice with foul language after mispronouncing a couple words. No one reprimands me. I'm starting to feel a little better about being here. Plus, we haven't been offered tainted Kool-Aid or worm-eating films. Andy, the youth minister, smiles and says, "For next week, I want you to read the Book of John."

Ah, great. More homework. This is bullshit! I think. At least I don't say it out loud. Maybe this youth group thing ain't so great after all.

The good news about us participating in the youth group is that Mom doesn't require us to go to morning services, too. Another benefit is that I don't have to be subjected to all those toxic perfume smells. Churching up one time a week is good enough for Mom. After about four weeks of being around so many church folks, I find that I'm minimizing my cussing. Soon, I start substituting with words like "crap" and "dang-it." It's still not proper, but I don't get the stares like I did when I used the real bad words. About every few weeks, someone new joins the youth group. If the newbie returns, I notice the same changes in most of them, too. We're being tamed and domesticated bit-by-bit.

After two months of youth grouping, Andy announces, "We are going to have a Saturday night sleepover at the church. We'll camp out in the basement and have snacks, play games, and study Scripture. All you need is your sleeping bag and pillow."

A sleepover sounds fun. There are some cute girls in our group. Even though I feel they are out of my league, two of my high school crushes are there. Maybe I could finagle a "Holy Kiss" from one of them during our sleepover.

Saturday night arrives. Mom drops Tash and me off at the church around back at the basement doors. A few of my friends bring their boomboxes in addition to their sleeping gear. Still timid, I scurry through the basement door and cower in a corner of the room by myself. Just a few moments later, to my shock, my friend David Buchanan walks in. I haven't seen him since his dad sent him away to military school. His hair is Marine-short, and he looks fit. I guess he needs some churching up, too. He walks right over to me, finding refuge.

"David, man! How've you been?"

"Okay. Military school is tough. It's tougher than Bluestone. There are always room inspections, uniform inspections, and physical fitness tests. I'm glad to get away from that place."

"I'll bet. Sounds tough." I glance down at his cassette case.

"Maikel, I brought some tunes."

David picks up his high-end silver Panasonic boombox and his loaded cassette case and places it between us. I unzip the black double-layered case. He has various tapes of Asia, Black Sabbath, AC/DC, KISS, and, to my surprise, a less evil John Cougar tape. We listen to the evil jams and talk about our adventures since the last time we met. Even though the last church said this music had subliminal messages, we don't feel sinister. As long as we don't turn it up too loud, no one seems to mind what we're listening to.

David and I decide to explore around the church before our Scripture lessons begin. The church is spooky at night. Long, dark shadows replace the reflections with no Sunday morning sunshine. Finding our way using only the dim streetlights shining through the stained-glass windows, David and I sneak up to the baptism pool and sit beside it. All the times I've sat in the pews looking up at the preacher perched behind his pulpit, I never knew this pool was behind him. The pool has steps on both sides and is about three feet wide and eight feet long. David tries to spit to the other side of the pool. He doesn't quite make the eight-foot distance but goes farther than me. I'm accustomed to David winning, and he beats me again, spitting farther. No worries. The chlorine radiating from the pool will likely kill any germs. If anyone enters this pool, they'll get cleansed more than one way—baptized and sanitized.

David is quieter than he used to be. I can tell he has something on his mind. He speaks in a subdued tone. "Dude, I'm thinking about leaving."

"Leaving what?"

In a serious tone, he responds, "Dropping out of school and leaving home."

Now I know why he wanted to escape the basement room full of people.

"What? Where would you go, man?"

"I can get a job doing construction work. I can stay in the old barn behind the Price's place. The one where we hung up the Playboy centerfolds."

"Man, I don't know. Leaves will be changing soon and it's 'bout to get cold."

"All I know is that I don't want to go back to the military academy, and I can't go back home."

"You can always stop by our place, and I'll give you food if we have it. If it gets too cold, you can sneak into our basement. Do you remember which one of our basement doors doesn't lock?"

"I remember. Thanks, dude."

It's quiet for a long time. I break the silence. "Why are you leaving? Is it because you're adopted?"

In a low voice David discloses, "I just don't get along with my dad."

I don't want to push him or ask him any more questions.

Before standing up, I sing the song *Big Balls* we'd been listening to earlier. David and I bust out laughing at the AC/DC song reference. "We'd better git back before anyone notices we're gone. We need some churchin' up."

Hospice Care (Day 11)

Saturday, March 3, 2007 – Basement Bathroom.

A place of refuge. Dark, damp, and cold.
Hiding from life. From the pain that it unfolds.

Tash is in the upstairs bathroom and is taking her own sweet time. The coffee inside me is percolating. I've got to go NOW. I run downstairs to the hardly-ever-used basement bathroom. The red, white, and blue '76 bicentennial wallpaper is peeling up at the edges. Still traumatized from Granny's outhouse in my youth, I look under the toilet for any creepy crawlies. There's a spider web below the tank covered with condensation, so I lean down to verify it's not a Black Widow. The tank turns on and off as I sit. I know what's wrong and think that maybe I should replace the toilet flapper flush valve.

I remember when Mom remodeled this bathroom. It needed fixing up to pass health care inspection since Mom needed a second full bathroom for her daycare business. While Pop was working, she fixed the sink plumbing and duct-taped anything else that was hanging by a thread. Mom added sheetrock to this bathroom and wallpapered it with discounted '76 bicentennial wallpaper that she found on a sale table at Sears in 1977. She even fixed the boiler room ceiling so it would meet fire code. It was a damn ugly job, but it passed inspection. Mom was resourceful.

When she finished the project, she immediately got on the phone with the inspector to set up an appointment. I thought it seemed like an opportunity to put worms down Mom's pants. She kept talking to the inspector on the phone while squirming and giving me the evil eye. Immediately after the phone call, I had to clean the entire basement, including this bathroom, before the inspector arrived.

As I sit on my porcelain perch, another memory flashes back to me. Mom hired a maid, Josephine, to help clean the house. Josephine lived down the road out by the sawmill. When we visited her, Tash and I would run off to the nearby sawdust piles and jump off the top. Sometimes we dug holes to feel the warmth radiate from the cores of mulched wood. While we played, Mom and Josephine would bicker about the cost. In the end, Mom always managed to get Josephine to come help clean our house.

Sometimes Josephine would say, "Mrs. Wise, I'll help you today for forty dollars."

"That's too much."

Mom always talked her down to twenty dollars. When Josephine came over, she'd sit on this toilet midafternoon and try to take a nap. It was possible compensation for being underpaid or exhaustion for working so many jobs on top of taking care of her own family. Tash and I would peek in and see her nodding off.

"Now y'all go on now. Leave me be," Josephine would scold.

Tash and I would laugh, running off for other mischief.

After she gave up the daycare business, I recall Mom coming down here when she was working third shift at the South Piedmont Correctional Facility in Boydton. Even today, I can still picture her sitting on this same toilet seat, thinking she could wean herself off nicotine. She tried smoking pipes and cigars, chewing Nicorette gum, and chewing regular gum. None of her efforts to stop smoking worked. Sometimes she'd throw the packs of cigarettes away only to retrieve them thirty minutes later. Tash and I threw them away too, begging her to stop. Sometimes she'd get mad at us because they were expensive. Other times she teared up because she knew we'd pitched them because we loved her. We feared what would eventually happen.

It's happening now.

Mom had a lot of jobs—Jack and Jill's Daycare, biscuits for auctions, a newspaper job, and as a prison guard. Out of all her jobs, being a prison guard was the hardest, and it took its toll on her. Even with so much darkness during that time in her life, Mom made new friends at the prison. She lost one, too.

Prison Discrimination

Saturday, May 26, 1984 – Fifteen Years Old. Tenth Grade.

Make fun of my clothes. Make fun of my fat ass.
Stare, judge me, and say mean things when I pass.
I can take it. All of the names and things they say.
I'll get up again. It's just another day.

Hank is sitting with Mom at the kitchen table. I get a Maikel-sized bowl of cereal and go to the living room to join Tash watching music videos on MTV. Through the beat of the *Duran Duran* song, I overhear Mom telling Hank about her job.

"They don't like me at the prison. The other day, they made me stand in front of the other guards and turn around. Everyone was staring at me and judging me. They said, 'This is how you are not supposed to look.' Some of the guards call me 'Fat Ass.' Every day, my supervisor stares at my boobs. I started wearing t-shirts because the uniform shirts have gaps between the buttons, but t-shirts are against the dress code, and they don't like it. I see how the men look at me and gawk at the other women. It's as if they are undressing us in their minds. They don't look at our eyes, but right at these or this. I made a complaint and wrote up a guard for harassing me, so they put me on guard duty in the psych ward in retaliation. They also put me up in the guard towers where there's no bathroom. They're supposed to give me a bathroom break every two hours. No one ever comes. I started bringing a coffee can, so I don't have to hold it eight hours."

I turn the TV volume down on the television. Mom is now bawling. Tash and I go to the kitchen to give Mom a hug. None of us know what to say.

Mom asks Tash and me, "Give Hank and me some time. Go watch music videos."

She doesn't want us to fret. She's being humiliated by her coworkers, but because Mom needs the insurance and the money, she has to take the abuse and keep going. She starts talking again, and I listen intently over the music.

"One day, I went to the psych ward, and one of the prisoners says to me, 'How are your children Maikel and Natasha doing?' That freaked me out. The prisoner was upset at me because I kept writing him up for throwing his shit at me. That's why I keep a second uniform in my car."

Hank is speechless, but lets out, "Punk!"

"Someone told them my children's names. How can I protect my children? I just want to be left up in the tower. I don't want to work in the psych ward. They know I have phlebitis and can't stand long. In the psych ward I have to stand for eight hours, and it kills my legs. They're trying to get me to quit. At least in the tower I can sit and pee in my coffee can. They can kiss my 'Fat Ass!'"

Hank responds, "They're a bunch of assholes. If I see one of them, I'll take care of it. Gimme a name."

That is all Hank can do. He wants to protect Mom and us the only way he knows how, with his fists.

Mom moves on. "Did you hear about the attempted prisoner escape last week?"

"I heard some folks at *Mama Johnson's* talking about it. What happened?"

"I was on guard duty in Tower Four. I saw the lights come on at

Tower Five. I step outside the tower room to the balcony with my assault rifle and noticed a prisoner trying to escape. The guard in Tower Five hysterically yells, 'Stop or I'll shoot!' The prisoner gets untangled from the wire on the first fence and starts running toward the second fence. The yelling continues. 'This is your last warning! Stop or I'll shoot!' I hear her start to sob uncontrollably."

"BANG! BANG! BANG! Bullets are flying everywhere! The prisoner drops and covers his head. After her gun is out of ammunition, other guards tackle the prisoner, who was already on the ground, and drag him away. The next day, the prisoner tells the other guards and prisoners, 'That woman was crazy. She was laughing and looking forward to shooting me. I thought she was enjoying it, so I dropped to the ground.' Come to find out, the guard was having a nervous breakdown because she had to shoot someone. Apparently, she'd just been randomly shooting into the air. The prisoner thought she was delighted to take him out."

Hank opens another beer. "That's some crazy shit. Who was more freaked out?" Hank asks, "The guard or the prisoner?"

Mom talks more about the prison. "You know my friend Jane Brewer who works at the prison?"

Hank's thinking with his voice. "Jane. Jane. Oh, yeah. She lives over across the bridge. Didn't she die in an accident or something recently?"

Mom speaks softer. "Yes. She was in a car accident. They say the car accident didn't kill her."

I want to make sure I hear this story. Tash is absorbed with MTV. I move to the vent between the living room and kitchen to hear the conversation. I can barely see Hank's face through the screen.

Mom continues in a hushed tone, "She managed to get out of the car after it crashed. She crawled away and ended up drowning in a nearby mud puddle. The mud puddle was only two inches deep. I don't think she drowned by herself. I think someone did it to her."

Hank is soundless and twitchless.

Mom continues, "Did you know she had been suing the prison?" She continues before Hank can answer. "I'm going to do the same. Not for much. I think I'm going to sue them for $2,001 just to teach them a lesson for mistreating me and all the other women who work there."

Mom could be spiteful. The extra one dollar was a poke in the ribs.

After a swallow of her drink, Mom continues. "I'm scared, though. I think someone has been following me the last few nights when I drive home from work. I took the long way through Skipwith by Bluestone High School, and they followed me the whole way until I turned down Shiney Rock Road. I'm scared for Maikel and Natasha."

Mom takes a long drag from her cigarette. "I should just shut my mouth and work as much overtime as I can."

Hank says, "Punks!"

Hank had a way of saying "Punk" that would get the recipient, if they were there, all riled up and ready to start swinging. When he called a person that to their face, which I've witnessed twice, it was better than any other Southern insult. "Punk!" was a verbal spit in the face, a backhand, and a provoking finger poking hard in the chest all at the same time. He had mastered that word and used it against any who crossed him.

"They're a bunch of punks. If they touch you, they'll have a problem with me."

I crawl away, sit back on the couch, and pretend I didn't hear a thing.

The Breakout from the Escape-Proof Prison

Thursday, May 31, 1984 – Mom Protecting and Being Scared.

Mom is waiting in the shadows behind the front screen door as Tash and I hop off the school bus. I hear the phone ringing behind her as we step up onto the front porch.

"Come inside quickly! Don't pick up the phone! Do not check any messages! We are NOT at home!" Mom looks seriously at both of us. "There's a prison breakout. They want me to come in. Quick. Get in the house. Do NOT answer the phone!"

Ring. Ring. Ring, blares through the house.

We're frightened. South Piedmont Correctional Facility is famed as being escape-proof. All the prisoners there either have life sentences or are on death row. When Mom started this job, she told us there were murderers, rapists, and all manner of bad people there. I'm scared. At least one of prisoners knows my and Tasha's names.

Mom's friend from the prison, Elaine, stops by our house just before dark. Mom hurries her into the house. She shuts the front door quickly, and they move to the kitchen to talk. Mom doesn't want to stand by the door or be seen outside. All the curtains are now closed or have sheets covering the curtainless windows.

Elaine starts updating Mom on the prison breakout. "They say the Briley Brothers escaped with at least four others. They're calling up all the prison guards. Some of the guards were dropped off on the back roads, but they need more guards. I heard they don't have any more guns to hand out, so they're giving out billy clubs. I don't think much of being by myself with only a billy club. I tell you what. I'm not going in, and you shouldn't either. Those people at the prison don't give a damn about us. I don't trust them. Dolores, don't go in. Stay safe. I'd best get going. I'm staying out of sight."

Mom is clearly grateful that her friend had validated her instincts. Tash and I sit there with Mom. "I'm not going. You two have lost too much, and I'll be damned if you are going to lose me, too. I'm going to call in sick after my two days off. Just don't pick up the phone. Go downstairs and lock all the windows and doors. Move some furniture in front of the door that doesn't lock."

After securing our nonsecure basement, I head to my bedroom. From under my bed, I remove my Savage 410 Shotgun from its case and insert a slug. The walnut stock is polished, and the gun oiled. I leave it on top of my gun cover on my bed, loaded and ready. Mom, Tash, and I sit in our darkened home with the curtains closed and most of the lights off. Mom leaves to hide her car behind the house next to the maple tree. I have a question about our cousins that has been eating away at me, and this seems like as good as time as any to ask.

When Mom returns, I directly ask, "Mom. I've always known that Hank has that nervous twitch with his mouth and nose, but until lately, I never thought much about it. Or why his brother Travis is… mmm…different. Come to think of it, their sister Clarabelle is a little different too. Why is that?"

Mom takes a drink of her tea and lets us in on some dark family history.

"Son, the same year you were born, my sister, their mom Caroline, died. She married a mean old drunk who used to beat her and your three cousins. Hank had it particularly rough. I don't know if Hank got his twitch because of his dad or not, but I suspect that's why he's that way. After a while and when he was old enough, Hank started fighting back when his dad got drunk and mean-spirited. He tried to protect Travis and Clarabelle and his mom. Sometimes, Hank stayed with us at Granny's when his old man kicked him out after a fight. Growing up, we were all we had. We looked after each other. I suppose that's why he looks out for us now."

I always wondered why the Smithfield cousins were a little off. Twitching or funny talking, they were different. In the end, though, Hank is always on our side and Travis was always helping Granny on the farm.

For the next two weeks, Hank stops by almost every night to make sure we're doing okay, that Mom is okay. One or two at a time, all the prisoners are eventually caught. Some of them had made it as far as Pennsylvania. Though they never came after us, we didn't sleep too well and jumped whenever a door would creak, or the house made funny noises settling. We also started locking all our doors and windows.

When Mom finally goes back to work, she's reprimanded for not volunteering to stand guard by herself on a dark dirt backroad with only a billy club. Part of her punishment is to work more shifts in the psych ward. She stands through the pain, and she's grateful. She's alive, and we still have a mama.

Firecrackers and Shaving Crème

Sunday, July 1, 1984 – Fifteen Years Old.

Throughout most of June, we continue to fret about the prison outbreak. Even though all the prisoners have been caught, Clarksville has an uneasiness that still pulses through the community. Mom asks us nearly every day if we are doing okay.

Now that we're allowed to pick up the phone, we talk to Pop weekly. During the prison break, Pop had moved out of a relative's place to Ogden, Utah. He invites Tash and me to come visit during the summer. He seems to be doing well.

This summer is a little boring since David isn't living at Edgewood Estates anymore, but occasionally, I see him walking downtown. He'd done what he said he'd do. He ran away from home and the academy. I sometimes go to the barn with the Playboy centerfolds, but I don't see any signs that he's visited there recently.

Then one day out of the blue, Mom says, "I think it would be good for you to get away for part of the summer. You should go see your father."

Mom somehow scrapes together enough money for two airplane tickets. Airplane tickets are expensive, and Mom had to work a lot of overtime to pay for them. On our flight out, Tash and I are glued to the window looking at fields, mountains, cities, and clouds from 35,000 feet. When we arrive at the Salt Lake City Airport, Don, a relative we've never met before, picks us up. The only way we know he's there for us is his sign: *Wise*.

On the drive to Pop's place, I can't help but notice how devoid Utah is of trees, grass, and all types of eastern vegetation. The steep

Rocky Mountains are impressive, even in this desert. The Great Salt Lake to the west is so vast that I can't see the other side.

Excited, Tash asks, "How far are we going?"

"See that tallest mountain straight ahead? It's called Ben Lomond Peak. We'll be close to it."

I chime in, "That doesn't look far."

"Things out west are farther and bigger than you think. That peak is about forty miles away. The animals out here are bigger, too. You guys have those small white-tailed deer back east. If you hit one of them driving, it'll hit your grill. If you hit a mule deer out here, you'll need to duck. It might come through the windshield."

Don is right. We pass a couple mule deer on the side of Highway 89 heading north. They're noticeably bigger or, as we say in the South, "corn-fed." After smelling the foulness of the Great "Stink" Lake and driving for forty-five minutes more, we aren't too far from the base of the mountain. We pull up to a three-story brick building, Union Gardens Assisted Living. Pop stands in front of the building in the brilliant sunshine. Since he's blind, I suppose there's no need for sunglasses. However, his red forehead with a receding hairline could use a hat. We unload the car and give Pop a big bear hug as Don drives off.

"Hey, guys! How was your flight?"

"It was a little bumpy over the mountains. Everyone was freaking out about turbulence, but it was fun! We got nuts and ginger ale and didn't have to pay for them."

"Good. Good. Let's go around and meet everyone."

We push Pop into the dining hall where a bunch of elderly people are playing card games, standing around a piano, or watching TV.

One of them, a tall, slender old man in coveralls is watching us through coke bottle bifocals. With a thick British accent, he asks, "Is this Maikel and Natasha?" His accent is so heavy that I can barely understand our names.

Pop proudly speaks for us. "Yes. Guys, this is Ernie. He's the maintenance guy here."

After meeting a bunch of grandmas and grandpas, some of whom smelled funny, we stroll back to the front desk to meet the younger brunette receptionist. A few minutes later, a younger man makes his way through the front entrance double doors. I try to open the door for him, but instead I awkwardly get in his way.

"I've got it, man," he says.

I back off while he makes it through the second door.

He's confined to a streamlined burgundy wheelchair that appears to have racing wheels. He has a scraggly mullet and sparse facial hair. I can't decide if he looks like a burnt out 80s rock singer or Shaggy from *Scooby Doo*. I notice the sticker on his wheelchair, Quickie. I wonder if Quickie is a brand name or an invitation.

Shirtless, tanned, and skinny, he asks Pop, "Hey, Gary. Are these your kids?"

Proudly, Pop responds, "Yep. Maikel and Natasha, this is Rudy."

"Hey, Rudy," I say.

Rudy sticks out his right arm for me to shake. He uses his other hand to pry open his fingers on his shaking hand so he can grasp my hand properly.

"Gotta go! I have a date tonight." Rudy rolls away with his Quickie sticker.

With Tash leading the way, I push Pop to his apartment, which is located right next door to the dining hall. Being so close, Pop won't ever miss a meal.

Tash asks, "Pop. What's wrong with Rudy's hands? They don't open up all the way."

"Paralysis differs depending on where the spinal column is damaged. I'm a paraplegic. I have the use of my arms. He is a quadriplegic. Rudy is paralyzed from the neck down. He's got some mobility in his arms but has severely limited movement in his hands."

Only partially understanding, I respond, "Okey dokey."

By the time Pop is done showing us his room, we're hungry. We can hear the ruckus of chairs and tables sliding next door. It sounds like they're setting up for lunch time. When we go back into the dining hall, all the games are put away, and everything is set up for lunch.

Pop divulges, "They make lunch for us Monday through Friday. Today, it's Salisbury steak with mashed potatoes and gravy. My favorite!"

We wait for some of the older guests to get their food before we gather our stainless-steel trays. Ernie the maintenance man is serving at the counter. He gives me a wink and serves me an extra half steak. Apparently, he has more than one job.

About halfway through lunch, Rudy rolls in. "Hey, guys. My date cancelled on me. Maikel and Natasha, want to cruise in my car downtown after lunch?"

Tash asks, "Can we go, Pop?"

"Sure."

"Come by my place afterward." Rudy glides back to his apartment at the end of Pop's hallway. We gulp down our lunches and enthusiastically walk to Rudy's place.

Rudy has changed into a blue t-shirt. He brushes up his mullet again and throws his brush on the bed. "Let's roll."

We follow Rudy outside to the parking lot as he approaches a beautiful burgundy '68 Camaro with chrome Cragar wheels. This muscle car matches his wheelchair but is scratch-less and with no labels offering Quickies. My cousin Hank would like this car.

"Who's driving, Rudy? We aren't old enough yet," I venture, confused.

"I'm driving."

I don't question him, but I'm interested to know how this is going to work. Using a highly polished wooden board, Rudy slides from his Quickie to the front seat. I notice there's a customized lever on the right side of the steering column. It appears the lever could serve as a gas and brake pedal for hands.

"Hey man, take off the wheels and put my chair in the trunk, would ya?" Rudy directs me.

I pull off the rear wheels, fold the back down, and set the wheelchair in the trunk. When I get in the car, Rudy fires up the V-8. It isn't as deep-sounding as the over-cammed 454 cubic inch block of Hank's old Camaro, but the 350 still sounds strong. From the exhaust, I can smell it's carbureted and isn't running too rich either. Hank's car was a four-speed with a difficult-to-depress racing clutch, so I try to imagine how Rudy is going to perform this task. Then I notice his car is an automatic.

After his car warms up, Rudy puts in a cassette tape—Def Leppard's *Pyromania*. He turns up the volume and starts jamming. Soon, we drive down Main Street listening to *Rock of Ages* with the windows down and music blaring. The lower part of Rudy's mullet sways in the wind. I make my decision—he's an 80s rock singer like on MTV. Cruising down Main Street in Ogden, the stoplights go south as far as I can see on an exceptionally straight road. Roads back east aren't this straight. Rudy catches every light green.

"Rudy, how'd you do that? We didn't catch any red lights."

"You gotta go twenty-three miles per hour, and you'll catch them all green."

After rewinding and playing the songs *Pyromania* and *Rock of*

Ages a few more times, we cruise back toward Union Gardens. At the nearby main intersection of Five Points, I spy a firework stand.

"Rudy, that's a big firework stand. I bet they have stuff I've never seen before."

"Fireworks are here all through the month of July. Pioneer Days in late July is more popular in Utah than July Fourth. More fireworks go off then than on Independence Day. You'll see."

The next day I ask, "Pop. How do you reckon I can earn extra money here? I'd like to get some fireworks, but Mom only gave us twenty dollars each. I spent half that at *Taco Time* yesterday."

"You could wash windows. Some of the people here can't move that well. I have some vinegar and ammonia under the sink. You could mix up a solution. I'm sure Ernie would let you borrow his squeegee."

I mix up a solution and try it on Pop's windows which greatly benefits us more than him as he can't see. I talk to Ernie and have my first customer minutes later. Word gets around this small community faster than free donuts on the reception desk. Within three days, I have earned almost sixty dollars. And I'm only charging each person $5.00. The firework stand is within walking distance, and I quickly become their best customer. I spend some of the money on nostalgic fireworks I remember having as a younger lad. Blacksnakes, sparklers, and snappers are okay but get a little boring. I decide to invest in some bigger, better ones.

The field next to Union Gardens is bone dry and full of weeds and is the only nearby open space. I am warned by Pop not to start a fire. Although I long to, I can't purchase bottle rockets or Roman Candles. Some of the older folks have already complained about the noise of firecrackers going off across the street all hours of the night. I want to get some firecrackers and blow some things up, but I know the noise may get me in trouble. One day at the firework stand, I notice firecrackers that I've never seen before. They're significantly smaller and may not be as loud as the normal-sized ones. They should be big enough to fulfill my pyromania addiction on a micro scale, so I buy a large pack of the string-pulled firecrackers.

I stroll back to the Pop's apartment, opening the package on the way. Curious, I pull one. *Bang!* It's definitely not as powerful as normal-sized firecrackers and maybe only half as loud. I have one in hand as I walk into Pop's apartment. *Bang!*

Irritated, Pop hollers, "Dammit all to hell. Don't do that. You scared the shit out of me."

Tash and I make our pallets to sleep on Pop's living room floor. I come up with a plan and share it with Tash. Excited, we wait and giggle, but Tash and I snicker a little too loud.

Pop shouts, "Go to bed, you two!"

We quiet down and wait. Pop continues to listen to books on tape for about an hour before going to sleep. Our cue is Pop's snoring. Just as when he lived with us, his snores are deep and long. I grab my bag of remaining stringed-firecrackers and crawl on the floor to his room. Pop's hearing is even keener now that he's blind, so I have to be *quieter-than-a-mouse* quiet. He conveniently has his wheelchair closer to the bedroom door, so I don't have to sneak as far—less opportunity of getting caught. I tie three stringed firecrackers between his wheelchair spokes and frame and creep back out of his room. Pop never hears a thing. Tash and I wait for a while but eventually fall asleep. Sometime later in the night, *Bang!* Silence for a few moments. *Bang!* By the second bang, Tash and I are now fully awake. We bury our faces in our pillows so Pop can't hear us laughing.

Pop mutters to himself, "Dammit all to hell. I got a flat tire."

Knowing Pop can't see me, I sneak to the edge of his bedroom door to watch as his hands rub the circumference of each tire.

He mumbles, "Ummm. None of them are flat. I don't understand."

I sneak back. Pop starts rolling toward the end of his bed. He's trying to feel for anything on the floor, searching for anything he may have run over. I can see his forehead showing he's perplexed as to why his tires aren't blown and nothing is on the floor. By the time he's almost to the bathroom, the third one goes off. *Bang!* I can clearly see through the door his right hand go down beside his wheel. He feels the strings from the fireworks and instantly figures it out.

"You little shit! Hey! Get up! I know you can hear me. You little shit!"

Tash and I can no longer restrain ourselves. We laugh and laugh. After a well-deserved scolding, we reluctantly go back to sleep, anticipating being awakened by ice cold water.

The next day, Rudy goes for his daily wheelchair cruise. Wheelchair cruising for Rudy means no shirt and saying hi to every woman he passes on the sidewalks. If he's lucky, he gets a date. Sometimes I walk with him, but on this day, I decide not to join him. I wait for him to leave, and I go to his apartment. He always leaves his door unlocked. I open the door and unscrew the door's locking plate so that I can attach a string firecracker. I connect the other side of the firecracker to the inside door handle. Rudy usually returns around midafternoon, so I wait. I watch him roll up as I go hide. He gets to his door. *Bang!* I hear him mumble something. He knows I did it. He's mad. I jerk my head back into Pop's room just as Rudy whips his chair around. He pounds on Pop's door with a fierce knock.

"I know what you did. Not funny, man." Then he rolls away. After he goes into his apartment, I hear his door slam.

Rudy and I avoid each other for the next couple days. Pop gets after me for picking on Rudy and encourages me to go apologize to him. Shamefully, I remedy my firecracker tomfoolery with Rudy.

"I'm sorry, Rudy. I shouldn't have played that joke on you."

"It's okay, man. We're okay."

Rudy stretches out his hand and untangles his fingers to shake. We hang out in his apartment for a while and talk about cars and a hot girl he met on his daily stroll. When he lights up a joint, I walk back to Pop's place.

As soon as I walk in the door, Pop yells at me. "Maikel! I'm not going to tell you again! Stop leaving your acne cream beside my toothpaste! If you do it again, I won't give you a whippin', but I'll teach you a lesson."

The next morning, I do it again. Pop yells at me but I just laugh.

"Okay, we'll see how funny you think it is."

Sometimes when I walk by the receptionist's desk or in the dining hall, I'll grab a donut treat, but there are none today. It's a warm day. I walk into Pop's place and gulp two large glasses of water.

After the second glass, Pop says, "Hey, Booger. One of the ladies made us banana crème eclairs. I ate one already. They're delicious."

Since we're the closest to grandkids that some of these elderly people have, we're often recipients of homemade pies, cakes, and other baked items. Like my Granny, these folks like seeing our faces light up with sugary delights, and I have no problem obliging them.

Pop quickly calls Rudy.

It's such a hot day that a chilled banana crème eclair sounds good. Tash and I open the fridge and grab the biggest ones. We sit down at the kitchen table as Pop starts cheerfully whistling. There's extra crème on top of the eclairs, too. I can hardly restrain myself. Tash and I take a big bite simultaneously. Instantly I sense something's wrong.

I start coughing. There is no sweetness. There's only bitterness. Tash and I run to the sink. I spit it out and flush my mouth with water.

Rudy opens the door and rolls in. I turn to see Rudy laughing so hard at Tash and me that he has a hard time breathing.

"Pop. I think this dessert's bad."

Rudy can hardly restrain himself. His arms are waving with joy. I don't get it.

Pop is bellowing. "Ha! Ha! Ha! Ha! That's not regular crème. That's shaving cream! That'll teach ya to mess with a blind guy and a quadriplegic. I betcha didn't see that coming."

He's right. I didn't.

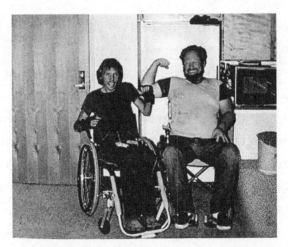

**Rudy and Pop, after they got me
back with shaving crème eclairs.**

Hospice Care (Day 12)

Sunday, March 4, 2007 – Cheech or Chong and Mom.

When you need a bit more, what do you do?
Grow a crop, for extra money to pursue.
Nervous breakdowns from a cruel, hard life.
Risking it all. Not a typical housewife.

Mom eyes haven't opened all morning. She's disconnecting from this world. I am, too. Rubbing her feet, massaging her hands, and brushing her hair is better for me when I can watch her enjoy it. Without her emotional response, I don't see much need for it.

Why bother? I think to myself.

Then I imagine myself in the future looking back to this moment: *How will I judge myself? Why do I do these things? Don't be so selfish. It can't be for me. I don't want to be like others, who have turned their back on my mama.*

I pick up the lotion and start rubbing Mom's face. She likes this, even though she doesn't express joy in it anymore. After several minutes, I stop. It's time to start clearing out Dusty's things. Dusty was Mom's second husband and left Mom on bad terms. He met someone on the internet while living with Mom. He chatted and talked with her for a couple months and then gave Mom a two-week notice that he was leaving her. After Dusty left her, Mom had a severe nervous breakdown and was hospitalized.

I first met Dusty in 1985. He reminded me of Cheech or Chong. Dusty was a hippy who never fully conformed to the 80s or any other era. He had slightly long dark hair, a mustache and tinted glasses that I could envision on Elton John. Sporting a little alcohol-induced belly, he always wore tie-dye or Beatles t-shirts. I don't think he even owned a tie or a suit. He fancied himself a Southern Virginian audiophile complete with high-end Pioneer and Acoustic Research equipment. When compact discs came out, Dusty stayed old-school and held onto his vinyl records. His Eagles, Bob Seger, and Beatles records were always hits on the back porch during Christmas and New Year's parties.

The back porch parties became legendary.
Dusty and Mama Wise.

Mom had held on to Dusty's records for years as a way to get back at him. Dusty had died a few years back, so we decide to give the records to his brother Randy, clearing out one more large pile.

I move back down to the basement again. The piles of Mom's belongings are finally dwindling. As I'm sweeping up years of accumulated dirt, I notice two wires going the length of the room. On the closet, there's a padlock installed but unlocked. Inside on the cold, gray concrete floor lay old quilts loosely folded.

When Tash comes down about one hour later, I ask, "Tash, what's this wire? Why's there a lock on the closet?"

"Oh, you don't know? I guess you wouldn't. This is where Mom and Dusty processed marijuana."

"WHAT?! Tash, are you serious?"

"Oh yeah. Dusty would hang up the plants all across the length of this room."

"Tash, this room is about thirty feet long!"

"Yep, and it was slap full of plants, too. Do you remember when you would come home on the weekends when you were in the Navy? How they always wanted you to call before you got here? That was so they could put everything in garbage bags and lock it up in that closet."

"Wow! I suspected that Dusty grew pot but didn't know he grew that much."

Tash gets serious. "Dusty was known for growing some of the best marijuana in all of Southern Virginia. It was really strong."

"Tash, is there anything else I should know that was hidden from me?"

"Well, do you remember when Mom had her nervous breakdown when Dusty left her? You know, the time she ended up in the psychiatric ward?"

"Yeah, I remember. The house was a disaster."

"Mom was so depressed that she stopped paying all her bills. Trash just piled up in corners. It was a mess. Since it looked like Mom was going to be in the hospital for a while, I started cleaning the whole house. When I went downstairs, I found garbage bags full of pot! I was freaking out. I didn't know what to do, so I loaded up my entire truck with the pot and took it to the dumpsters down the road. Maikel, I tell you, the entire bed of my truck was full! It must have been nearly ten yard-sized garbage bags of plants. I just wanted to get rid of it."

"Tash, I remember Dusty and Mom going for drives. Is that when they would check on the plants?"

"Yep. They grew it all over the county and had several fields. They had fields from Prestwould Plantation to Grassy Creek. Mom tried smoking it once but didn't like it. She said it made her head feel weird. They sold it to people all the way down to Florida."

"Do you remember those people who would show up? I don't remember their names. Mom would say, 'They left their clothes here' as she filled their entire trunks with garbage bags. Was that pot?"

"Yep."

Susan snorts, laughing.

I started thinking about the crops of pot I found in the woods by Edgewood not far from David's house. When I would come across a marijuana field, I would backtrack out the same way and say nothing. This also explained why sometimes I would run into Dusty walking in the woods at random places.

"Do you remember that crop the police found behind Betsy's house?" I ask.

"Yep. That was Dusty's and Mom's. Dusty was pissed off. He guessed that each plant was worth about a thousand dollars. The police took over a hundred plants. A hundred-thousand dollars just gone. Betsy knew whose it was, though. Not long afterward, neighbors would call Betsy on the phone to rile her. They'd disguise their voices and ask, 'Betsy, do you have any weed you could sell me? My glaucoma is flaring up.'"

Betsy would tell them, "You're asking the wrong person. It ain't mine, but I suspect I know whose it is."

"Betsy and I would laugh about it when I went over to her place for coffee some mornings. She liked all the attention, though. It was a source of gossip for months on Shiney Rock."

Susan is listening intently, getting a kick out of Mama Wise's shenanigans.

Susan chimes in, "Tash, why'd she do it?"

"Her pension from the prison wasn't enough. She needed a little more. She ran up a few bills with the doctor after her varicose-vein surgeries. Maikel, do you remember when you were in college and money was tight?"

"Of course, I do. The worst was about a ten-month period where I lived on about $450 a month. It just wasn't quite enough."

"Mom knew that. She'd try to send you extra money when she could."

"You mean to say that some of my tuition, books, food, and my mountain bike, was from Mom's weed sales?"

"Yep."

Susan is now rolling with laughter. She even snorts a couple more times.

As my mother is lying on her death bed, I discover that she sold weed to help support me during my college years. All of her ghosts are now showing their faces. Her grip holding those doors shut on the skeletons in her locked closet is loosening. I don't believe weed should be illegal. Alcohol is by far a worse drug—it paralyzed and blinded my dad. Alcohol led to the deaths and accidents of some of my high school friends. In the Navy, I saw many alcohol-fueled fights. The only problem I see with someone high on pot is that the refrigerator might be a little emptier or they may drive slower. Even so, the Southern Baptist conditioning had scared me from ever trying weed despite all those around me who did.

The basement closet is filled with memories. I look on the floor for any residual traces of Mom's and Dusty's pot. I can't believe Mom took such a risk dealing so much marijuana. However, I'm grateful for the extra pizzas she bought me in college. For months before the weed cash arrived, I had survived on potatoes, popcorn, and handouts from others. In the basement's huge weed closet, I glance at the hanging boxing gloves and think of my high school buddy Mike. I have some good memories with the gloves. These gloves were a source of entertainment but not a good thing to leave out when people started drinking. Pushed in the corner of the closet are three faded yellow poster boards and an old red apron with my nametag from the Winn-Dixie grocery store.

Dusty smoking a joint and drinking a beer while canoeing down the Dan River.

Pickin' Birdseed from the Cornfield

Saturday, March 8, 1986 – Seventeen Years Old. Twelfth Grade.

Keep your guard up. I ain't telling you again.
Even though we're boxing, I hope we'll stay friends.
I'm alone and jealous. All by myself.
Encouraging me. To put my self-pity on a shelf.

The phone rings around 8:00 A.M. and Mom yells, "Maikel. It's for you. It's Mike Thompson."

I pull myself out of bed and drag myself to the phone. "Hello."

"Hey, Maikel. You gotta work tonight at Winn-Dixie, too?"

"Yep," I say as my stomach grumbles, and I notice my pajama bottoms are too short.

"Would ya mind if I hang out with you, and go in with you later today? I still don't have a car, and I can't get a ride from my folks."

"Sure, Mike. Give me about an hour. I'll pick you up."

Although Mike and I only started hanging out together when I was fifteen, we'd gone to school together for most of our lives. Mike has short, curly, dirty blond hair. His square shoulders give him the appearance of someone who does a lot of push-ups. He's a touch shorter than the rest of us twelfth graders and likes using a tad too much cologne. If I look like a golden retriever, Mike is a muscular, wiry terrier. I drive to the nearby town of Finchley and take Mike back home with me.

"We still have a few hours before work. Whaddaya want to do?" I ask.

"I haven't seen your whole house. Show me the basement where your mom used to have parties before the back porch was fixed up."

We walk down the steep steps. I turn on the beer logo signs still hanging above the bar.

Mike sees the polished bar and perches on one of the barstools.

"Pop and Mom got this bar years ago from an old barn near Boydton. It was a long bar. Pop cut it in half. Half of the bar is here. The other half is on the back porch. You've seen that one during the Christmas party. Before we refinished the back porch, parties used to be down here in the basement."

Mike and I start spinning in circles on the barstools. We each can get up to five rotations on a single push if we pull our knees in.

"Maikel, what's that dangling on the post by the steps?"

"Those are old boxing gloves from Granny's."

"Cool. Let's try 'em out."

"These are so old. There's not much padding in them."

But Mike is already putting one of them on.

"Come on. Let's box."

"I don't know Mike. Have you boxed before?"

"Nope. Come on man, let's go. We've got these gloves."

"Okey dokey."

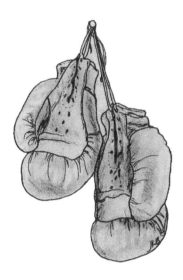

Old boxing gloves from the basement.
(Artist Judie Battle)

I shake out the gloves to ensure there aren't spiders in them and reluctantly yank on the other pair. We start gently tapping, hitting each other's arms and forearms.

"A friend of mine, Robbie Matthews, from Mom's newspaper job taught me how to box for about six months. Protect your face! Raise your guard!" I call.

Mike raises his hands, then lowers them after about ten seconds or so.

"Mike, raise your guard!"

The same thing happens again. He raises his hands and then promptly drops them again. *Bap!* I hit Mike straight in the face, and his head pops back. Mike gets a surge of adrenaline. He starts swinging violently. After about twenty swings, Mike slows down, completely out of breath.

"That hurt, motherfucker! You hit me in the head! Where the hell did that swing come from? You reached back and brought that swing from the cornfield."

"I told you to raise your guard."

"Let's go, Maikel! Let's go you Children-of-the-Corn-fucker!"

"Okay. Raise your guard." He drops hands yet again. I pretend to punch but stop short before making contact. "MIKE. RAISE YOUR GUARD!"

This time, Mike holds his hands up for fifteen seconds longer, but not long enough *Bap!* I hit him a little harder on the top of his nose.

Mike erupts again with another two dozen swings. Later, he says, "You cornfield swingin' fool! That's enough."

"When I was getting trained to box, I did the exact same thing, except my trainer hit me a lot harder when my guard dropped. He knocked me to the ground a couple of times before he took it easy on me."

"Damn, Maikel. Your punches really hurt."

"I didn't mean to hurt you. Let's put these gloves away. It's time to go to work anyway. I heard three grocery trucks are coming tonight. One broke down Tuesday, and they sent a third one tonight to make up for it."

We arrive at Winn-Dixie early. The manager, Mr. Cash, sees us waiting by the clock to punch our timecards.

"You boys can check in early. Truck is already here. There's a lot to unload."

I assume my post in the truck with Ebbie Day. Ebbie is a year older than me and fast. Every time we'd see Ebbie, we'd say his name like a song *Every Day* by Elvis Costello. He can pick up boxes and load them on the conveyor faster than two people can unload them. Mike and Wayne unload the boxes and place them on the carts in the back room that correspond to aisles in the front of the store. Since

Ebbie and I don't want to work too late, we pick up the pace and load the conveyor with sometimes up to three boxes at a time. Mike and Wayne are struggling to keep up.

Mr. Cash walks back to check on us. "Ebbie. Maikel. Go help them clear the conveyor."

All sweaty, Ebbie and I help Mike and Wayne unload the conveyor. Throughout the night, Mike and Wayne continuously get behind, and we repeat helping them catch up.

The last truck backs up to the dock, and I'm dog tired. I'm looking forward to this night being over. Ebbie opens the door, and we're grateful it isn't full front to back and floor to ceiling like the previous trucks had been. Ebbie and I start loading boxes again as fast as we can. The conveyor is filling up faster than normal. Wayne and Mike are nowhere in sight. I hear them laughing and notice orange objects flying through the air inside the back room.

"You boys had better stop messing around," a random voice calls out.

They are throwing cheese slices. I focus on my job and ignore their horseplay. Mr. Cash requests that Ebbie and I clear the overflowing conveyor again. He turns to walk in the back door right toward the flying orange cheese. *Smack!* A cheese slice hits him directly on his face. I turn toward the origin of the slice and see Mike's hand lowering from the throw.

"Punch out! Punch out now!" Mr. Cash demands.

Mike's head drops. He passes me solemnly. The rest of us are quiet and quickly get back to work. Our crew finishes right afterward at 9:00 P.M. When I walk out to my car, Mike is there waiting.

With creases in his brow, Mike asks, "Do you think I'm fired?"

"No. He's just mad. I wouldn't mess around when you come in next time. If I were you, I'd go in and apologize."

With his short terrier tail tucked between his legs, Mike says, "I'll be right back."

When he returns, Mike tells me, "He's going to be watching me, and I have to pay for the cheese."

"Could've been worse for you. You were lucky you weren't fired. You shouldn't have been throwing cheese slices at the 'Big Cheese'."

Mike and I chuckle.

As I drive back across town to Mike's house, I spot the Chief of Police, Fishtail Hogan, lurking at the beginning of the bridge. He's waiting for someone like my cousin Hank to speed by. As I drive across the bridge spanning Buggs Island Lake, my head droops with tiredness, and I abruptly raise it. I drop and raise my head several times.

Mike notices. "You pickin' birdseed?"

It takes me a moment before I can respond. "What?"

"You pickin' birdseed? I see your head bobbin' up and down like you're pickin' birdseed. Wake up, dude!"

I roar with laughter. I've never heard of *pickin' birdseed* to describe dozing off. I'm certainly awake now. *Pickin' birdseed* and *back from the cornfield*. Where does Mike come up with this stuff?

Newton's Third Law
For every action, there is an equal and opposite reaction.

Saturday, March 22, 1986 – Seventeen Years Old. Fighting Back.

Most of my life. I'd roll over and quit.
Stopped making effort. I hardly gave a shit.
I'm a timid mouse encouraged to fight.
Finally growing up. A bird takes flight.

It's Saturday night, and I'm at Hardee's drinking Southern sweet iced-tea. I think about some of the conversations I heard during school this week. Some of my friends talked about their after high school plans: *"I got into Virginia Tech," "I'm going to Old Dominion University,"* or *"I'm going to Danville Community College."* I'm not one of those lucky ones. My grades are horrible. In school, I did just enough to get by, and now I'm living with regret. I hadn't bothered to take the college entrance exams because I know we don't have enough money for college. Even if I did, I'm not smart enough to go. I don't know a single person in my entire family who ever finished college.

Mr. Cash told me to apply for the manager prep program at the Winn-Dixie grocery store. I'd work in the meat department for a year and the produce department for another year. Eventually, I would become an Assistant Manager. Then after a few years and a little attrition, I could become a manager at Winn-Dixie in Clarksville or, more likely, in another town.

I avoid my friend's questions about my future endeavors by getting them to talk about themselves. Most folks prefer to talk about themselves anyway. Any topic is good as long as I don't have to talk about my non-academic plans.

I return to my freshly-cleaned and waxed Honda Civic. I turn on the radio and change the channel to Clarksville's radio station. Tonight is *Song Request Night*. I like hearing someone's name I know over the radio. It's almost as if they're famous when the announcer says their name.

After a girl calls in dedicating a song to her love, a guy calls in. "Would you play that song from Wham, *I'm Your Man*? We'd like to dedicate this song to Maikel Wise from the guys who love you."

Excited, I think, *Wahoo! That's me!* Then I hear snickering in the background. The song starts to play, and it hits me! They are playing a "gay" joke on me. I'm embarrassed.

I drive straight home humiliated. Why would they do this to me? What did I ever do to them? I've never even dated anyone. I'm too nervous around girls, but I'm not gay. I make myself look in the mirror. "Why would anyone want to go out with me? I'm ugly with all of this acne and the gap between my teeth."

I go to bed early, lying there in self-pity until I eventually fall asleep.

Early the next day, Tash knocks on my door. She had heard what happened. "Cale, whatcha you gonna do?"

"I don't know, Tash. It really doesn't matter."

At breakfast, Tash tells Mom. I can see the pain in Mom's eyes. She's had this type of humiliation happen to her, too. Fully capable, she wants to give those boys a whipping, but she knows I have to resolve it. This is my fight.

"Son, you could call the radio station and do the same thing to them. Or you could make a sign out of a big sheet and hang it across the road. When they go to school, everyone will see it. Write something that will embarrass them."

I'm starting to feel less mopey.

"Well Mom, the problem with a sheet and rope is that I'd need a ladder. I'd want to put up a sign quickly and get out of there. The sign also needs to be high enough so that buses and trucks won't hit it."

"Wait! I have another idea for your signs. Gimme a minute." Mom races off and comes back with five bright yellow poster boards left over from last year's yard sale.

Encouraged, I ask, "Mom, Tash, what do you think it should say?"

I can see Tash's teeth grinding. I know she's brewing up something really evil. Something that couldn't be displayed in public, especially in the Bible Belt.

"I know. How about *Hunter Preston loves Raymond Lyman forever?* Add some hearts, too." Tash howls with laughter.

Tash is enjoying seeing my humiliation focus on revenge. "I'll help you hang them signs."

The three of us work at the kitchen table perfecting the five bold, insulting signs.

With the signs complete, my mind shifts to implementation. I think about where to place them, and say, "Let me scope things out on Monday. Then we can hang them early Tuesday morning."

When I arrive at school on Monday, groups of students look, point, and laugh at me. I feel my face flush red with embarrassment. I drop my gaze and walk past.

"We love you, Maikel," some of the guys say, mocking me as I walk past. My stomach turns, and I feel like I'm going to vomit.

I realize more people were apparently listening to the radio Saturday night than I thought. I ignore their comments and head straight to homeroom with my tail tucked between my legs. I put my head down on my desk, waiting for school to start. When I get to physics class, Raymond and Hunter mockingly laugh at me. They try to make light of the hurtful joke. I don't say a damn word to either of them. I just plot my revenge.

Bluestone High School has three main roads that the teachers and students use. One comes from Chase City, one comes from Boydton, and one comes from Clarksville. I know these roads well from helping Mom with newspaper deliveries. I choose the most visible telephone poles. If I only used three signs, EVERYONE would see at least one sign on their drive to school.

When Tuesday morning arrives and my alarm clock goes off an hour early, I'm already awake. The stapler is fully loaded and the posters are ready. I drive straight to my objective with my sister helping. We hang each sign, securing them with extra staples to ensure the wind doesn't blow them off. We finish quickly and get to school earlier than normal. I wait in my homeroom. The teacher and students start filtering in. A few people pop their heads in saying, "Good one, Maikel," And, "They deserve it."

Even with their support, I feel torn inside. *I don't like being hurtful to anyone, but those jerks started it.* My stomach churns all morning. I can't focus in any of my classes. My legs stiffen when I stand or walk. I reluctantly drag myself to physics class and sit on top of my table, waiting for class to start, for the inevitable confrontation. This is the only class Raymond, Hunter, and I are in together. I'm not looking forward to seeing either of them.

I watch as six-foot-plus Hunter walks in. He slams his books on a table and angrily heads straight at me.

"Your ass is mine!" he hollers.

Hunter grabs me by the shirt. He throws me off my table. I land on the floor. My shirt rips and is pulled partly above my head, entangling my arms. An uncontrollable rage overcomes me. Anger about being humiliated. Anger about not having enough courage to ask girls out. Anger about my whole life. I tear off the remnants of my thrift store shirt with my right hand. I grab Hunter by his authentic Izod shirt just below his neck with my left hand. And then I hit him as hard as I can. After several punches, Hunter turns his head sideways.

I yell, "I didn't say you can turn your head!"

He turns his head slightly back toward me. I keep punching. Harder.

People begin piling up at the door. They watch me unleash my rage.

Our small-frame physics teacher pushes the spectators aside and yells, "Stop! Stop! Stop!"

I let go of Hunter and push him away.

"Now you two stop it! Stop it! What happened?"

I hesitate. I find that my hands are shaking as the adrenaline pumps through my veins. My right hand is bleeding under my class ring. Blood trickles down Hunter's forehead. My face feels flushed. I quiver as I mumble a summary of the events that led to this fight.

"You two are some of my best students. Now apologize and go sit down."

We glare at each other. I grab my ripped shirt off the floor, put it on, and sit down. I'm embarrassed that the other students can now see the acne on my shoulders, back, and chest. I can't focus for the rest of the class. I glance at Raymond, who is sitting next to Hunter. He looks at me, furious. I think, *To hell with Hunter.* I'm mad at Raymond, but sad, too. Raymond was my friend.

After physics class, I walk to my locker to find Mike anxiously waiting.

"Maikel. I heard you gave him some. Everyone's talking. You gave him some. Did you bring it back from the cornfield?"

"Maybe. He should've kept his guard up."

Mike's tensing up. He's angry at Hunter, too. "Come on, man. Tell me how you Children-of-the-Corned-his-ass."

I can't help but laugh. I'm grateful I have a friend, but I'm still shaken up. Even though I don't feel like telling, Mike wants a story. He's encouraging me to embellish the fight. I give him what he wants.

"Mike, I shucked the hell out of his corn. I was shuckin' and his head was jivin'. He should've kept his guard up. I Jiffy popped his kernels. When he turned his head, I yelled, 'I didn't say you could turn your head.' I cornfielded his ass."

Mike is eating it up. I can see his teeth grind together, his fists tighten, and his anger swell. He's excited that I defended myself.

"You shucked and jived. You Jiffy popped his ass. Good job, buddy."

Mike turns around and walks off to his next class mumbling, "Shuckin' and jivin'. Shuckin' and jivin'." I'm sure the rest of the school will hear it soon, too.

The rest of the day is quiet until I see our principal, Mrs. Talbott, in the hallway.

"Maikel, come here please."

"Yes, ma'am."

"What happened to your shirt?"

I quickly lie. "Nothing. I was horseplaying in shop. We were just messing around."

"Really? I heard you and Hunter were in a fight. Go wait in my office."

I walk to the principal's office and wait. Shortly afterward, Raymond and Hunter show up. No words are spoken between us.

Mrs. Talbott walks in and says, "Sit down. Tell me what happened."

We tell our stories and provide halfhearted apologies to each other. Mrs. Talbott says, "Action will be taken."

I go home not knowing my fate.

Mom is waiting for me, and I tell her the events of the day. Though she had helped me make the signs, I don't know if she's okay with me getting into a fight. She sits down at the kitchen table, looks straight at me and asks, "Are you okay?"

"Yes, ma'am. You should see the other guy. I may get suspended, though."

"I don't give a damn about suspension. I'm proud of you, son. You stood up for yourself. Don't let anyone run over you."

"I thought you'd be mad."

"No, son. You need to fight back. Don't let folks run over you and take advantage of you. I remember when you were younger and those kids on the bus bullied you. I remember when they stole your lunch money. Do you remember?"

"Yep."

"I wanted you to fight back then. I knew you'd eventually find your way. For all my life, people have made fun of me and picked on me. They tell me I can't do this or can't do that. Fight back and never quit! I haven't and never will. Understand?"

"Yes, Mom."

Hospice Care (Day 12, Afternoon)

Sunday, March 4, 2007 – Visiting Lost Family and Friends.

Manicured grass. Weathered, plastic flowers.
A simple headstone doesn't really matter.
I see you lying there. A granite name tag above.
Remember our exploits? Doing what we love.

Tash and I have another decision to make. We don't know if we should bury Mom's ashes under a headstone or not. I told Mr. Lyon that we'll decide after visiting the cemetery. I don't want to go, but we are running out of time.

"Hey, Tash and Susan. How about we go to the cemetery? We can't put it off any longer."

I know Tash is dreading going there, too. We leave Mama Wise with our faithful friends Gladys and Betsy. Driving to this place forces me to face people long gone. For Mom, death is waiting, ready, and close. As we turn off Buffalo Road into the manicured graveyard, I have flashbacks of memories. We see the Yancey section and stop. I drag myself out of the car, and I see the cold granite headstones of Grandpa Jimmy Lou and Granny Ruby. Beside them are Mom's siblings: Caroline, Earl, and Loretta. I miss Aunt Loretta and Granny the most. We had so many good times together. I don't care for my Grandpa Jimmy Lou after finding out about him choking Granny and what he likely did to the man who worked for him. All of the family headstones lying in front of me are free of leaves. Unfaded, fresh plastic flowers are next to the graves from a recent visitor. I try to imagine Mom's headstone here with her family, just lying here with a granite marker that will slowly deteriorate and fade away too. She wasn't one to stay idle unless she was drinking tea and smoking a cigarette. Mom resting in a graveyard doesn't seem right to me.

I look around for Hank's marker, and don't see my cousin. "Tash, where's Hank?"

"Oh, he's at the end of the graveyard. We can walk there."

On our somber saunter to Hank, I see my childhood friend's headstone marked, "David Buchanan."

"Hey, Susan. See that grave? That was my friend growing up. Remember David?"

Susan grabs my hand. She knows I'm in pain. She knows I miss my friend. David and I did so much together. He was my best friend growing up. I'm not prepared for this.

My voice trembles with memories. "I first met David at the swings in elementary school. We would compete to see who could jump the farthest. He'd always win. As we got older, we'd do the same thing on bicycles, sleds, and motorcycles. I remember his pa, Mr. Buchanan, always pushing him to work. Back then, I think Mr. Buchanan had three jobs at one time: Mayor of Clarksville, technician at John H. Kerr Dam, and helping David's grandpa at a TV repair business. He expected the same from David: work, work, work. David went down a different path, though. He ran away and quit school. The last time I saw him was outside the Pizza Pub the year before I got out of the Navy. He asked to borrow some money. I only had thirty dollars but gave him a twenty-dollar bill. I knew he had a drinking problem and was going back inside for more beer. I was okay with that. He died the next year. I miss him."

Susan holds me. "It's okay. You're okay."

This was the first time I'd actually said goodbye to David. I feel sad and at the same time relieved. I'm letting go of something I've carried with me for many years. Susan cleans a few stray sticks and leaves from around David's headstone. She puts her hand on the headstone. Silent, she's silently praying for him in her own way.

Tash is already on the other side of the cemetery. Susan grabs my hand, and we continue our walk to my Cousin Hank's grave. I'm bawling before I even see where he is lain. David was close to my heart, but Hank was closer. I approach and see his picture on the gravestone. Hank's headstone has fresh plastic flowers, too. I abruptly turn around. I can't look at where he lies.

"It's okay. I know you miss him," Susan reassures me.

Tash starts tearing up, too. Hank was our foundation growing up on Shiney Rock Road. Like my friend David, many judged him because he was different. He wasn't the church-going type and drank several beers too many, too often. I think of him, my aunt, and Granny resting in this place.

"I suppose we could get a gravestone for Mom," I say, "but I have other plans for her ashes. I want to take her to places I go and spread them. Take her on adventures and let go of her a little at a time."

Tash responds, "Okay, Cale. We'll split her ashes after she dies. We can always get a gravestone later."

Significantly relieved that we have a plan for Mom's remains, we get back into the car and head home.

Gladys meets us at the door. "Hey, y'all. Did everything go okay?"

Susan replies, "Sho 'nuf." She's messing with Gladys, since Gladys recently told Susan, "You okay for a Yankee."

After Gladys leaves, we eat some Southern comfort food, Hardee's chicken. We need comforting.

Between bites, Tash says, "Hey, Cale. I forgot to tell you. I was going through my closet and found your old navy uniforms."

Susan excitedly says, "I'd sure like to see my man in his navy outfit. Go get 'em and put 'em on."

Winn-Dixie or Military?

Saturday, March 29, 1986 – Seventeen Years Old. Twelfth Grade.

Some folks know what they want to be at the age of five.
Others do just enough, simply to get by.
Some folks are late bloomers, taking a while to sprout.
Play it safe, or take a chance, and maybe strike out.

I'm grateful I don't have to work this morning. Saturday mornings at Winn-Dixie are busier than the chicken coop at feeding time. The shelves with bread, sugar, lard, and everything else to make Southern delights empty fast. Sometimes, I have to refill them twice in one morning. I try to keep up as I weave between all the shoppers. *"Excuse me, sir. Which aisle do I find the Crisco?" "Sugar, can you help me carry my groceries to my car?" "Maikel, please come to cash register six."* I didn't mind working but completing 50% of two dozen tasks conflicts with my self-diagnosed OCD. Normally, I don't have OCD-type issues, but certainly feel that way on Saturday mornings at Winn-Dixie. I need to stick to one task at a time.

On this beautiful stress-free spring morning away from Winn-Dixie, I walk outside and notice my stepdad Dusty's van has already left. He's probably golfing at *Kinderton Country Club*. From my own personal experience, golfing with Dusty means taking a shot of tequila after each hole lost. Win or lose, he'll be feeling good by the time he returns. Across the street, I see Sam walking to his workshop. Sam owns the second house next to his and has transformed it into a workshop. I haven't visited him in a while and decide to drop in. I've been wanting to ask him about his job.

Sam's workshop is cluttered with homemade lamps hanging on hooks, wires, and nails. A soldering gun, sheet metal, and tools fill every horizontal surface. The work bench has dozens of burn marks and splattered, solidified solder blobs.

"Wow, Sam! I knew you tinkered around, but this is significant."

"They call me the Tin Man. It keeps me busy, I suppose."

"These candle lamps are nice. What do you do with them all?"

"Gladys and I give them away as gifts. We need to give away more. I'm running out of room."

I came here on a mission and ask, "Sam, can I ask you about your job? What was it like being a hospital administrator? Did you have to go to college for it?"

"I went to college. It helped get me the job. It paid well. I had to deal with a lot of people problems, though. There was always something bothering someone. Why do you ask?"

"I don't know what I'm going to do after high school. I could get on the manager training program at Winn-Dixie. I could go into the military. I don't think my grades are good enough for college."

Sam's penetrating eyes look at me through his glasses. "Maikel, you could always go to a community college."

"I guess so. I don't believe anyone in my family has ever finished college. At least no one I know."

Just then, the power goes out in the entire room. Sam's soldering gun, fan, and lights cut off.

"What's going on, Sam? You pop a breaker?"

"Nope. Gladys shuts off the breaker when she wants something. I shouldn't have never shown her where that breaker was. I'd best go see what she wants. Here, Maikel. Take one of these lamps for your mama." He gives me a random lamp and heads off to attend Gladys.

Sam Newton's workshop across the street on Shiney Rock Road.
(Deborah Newton Photo)

I exit the still-dark workshop and wonder if Sam is currently flipping the breaker back on.

I see Dusty's van is back in the driveway. He's already assumed-the-position on the black leather Lazy Boy in the front room. His eyes are bloodshot, so I guess he lost quite a few holes during his golf outing. He has his Tar Heel t-shirt on and is holding a white and blue pompom on a stick ready to shake.

"Hey Dusty. What's going on?"

"Just gettin' ready for the Tar Heel's game. It's March Madness, and my boys are going to take it."

I'm completely uninterested in the Tar Heels or any other basketball game. Although men in this area love college basketball,

I never figured out why they're so obsessed. Like Mom says, "Men are obsessed with balls. Basketballs, footballs, or their own balls if nothing else is available."

"Dusty, can I ask you about the military? About the Navy?"

"Yep. Go ahead."

"Why did you choose the Navy?"

"I didn't want to go into the Army or Marines. I wanted to learn something more than firing a gun. I suppose they do other things, though. I heard it was hard to get promoted in the Air Force, and your skills are more specialized. I went into the Navy to learn about electronics. At the time, I could move up in rank faster and make more money, too. I had a family to support and a kid. After boot camp, it was just like any other job. All you have to do is show up and do what you're told. Then you can play. If you're lucky, you can travel a bit, too. It was the easiest job I ever had."

"What did you have to do to get in?"

"I had to take a test. I think it's called an ASVAB test. I don't remember what it stands for. Just take it and put in for what you want to do. That's real important. You gotta pick your job BEFORE you sign up. Remember that." Dusty emphasizes again, "BEFORE. Otherwise, they can stick you to painting ships or a shitty job." Tar Heel's game starts, and Dusty turns his head to the TV, shaking his pompoms.

This gives me a lot to ponder. The military does seem to be my best choice. I can learn more about electronics and possibly get to travel. I'm getting excited that I may have found something to do with my life.

Arriving at Bluestone High School on Monday morning, I visit the guidance counselor and ask her about joining the military.

"Maikel, regardless of which branch you join, you'll have to take the ASVAB test. We happen to have a test scheduled. Have you signed up?"

"No, ma'am."

"Here's the sign-up sheet. Take these instructions. Be there promptly at the start time."

Two weeks later, I take the test. I'm not sure how well I do. I go over and over some of the questions in my head. One question I think I missed: "If *do-floppies* are equal to *thing-ma-jigs*, and *thing-ma-jigs* are equal to *whatever*, then all *do-floppies* are *whatever*." Later in the week, results are finally in, and I'm called to the guidance counselor's office.

"Maikel, we got your score back. You did really well. There'll be recruiters here at the end of the week. You can talk to each one of them to decide which branch you want to join."

I take the summary of my results and find it's an 82 out of a 100. Barely a C grade by Bluestone High School standards, but good enough. As I'm walking out, I pass Mike Thompson walking in to get his results. Mike quickly puts his fist up pretending to box, and chants, "Guard up, shucking and jiving." I laugh and wait for him outside the office.

"How'd you do, Mike?"

"All right, I suppose. I'm gonna be in one of the Special Forces, maybe the Marines. Those Marines are bad-asses."

"My Uncle Jim was a Marine. He'd said things were crazy in Vietnam. He knew a lot of men who came back and weren't the same. I was thinking about the Navy. My stepdad says the schools are great."

"I'm not sure which one I'm going to join, Maikel. We can talk about it later this week. Gotta go."

I'm left staring at the Navy poster outside the counselor's door.

Cornrow Faux Paus

Friday, May 2, 1986 – Deciding my Future.

The presentation displays for the various U.S. Military are lined up in formation. All the representatives sit by their tables welcoming any who approach. Intimidated, I walk by without making eye contact. Looking out the corner of my eyes, I notice the Marine has a marksmanship metal just like Uncle Jim's. I remember playing with it with my G.I. Joe before getting scolded. I recall sitting with him in our basement after going to Vietnam. He must have witnessed some horrible things that haunted him. Every time I'd ask him about it, the response was always, "I don't want to talk about it."

In my morning classes, I think about the pros and cons of each branch. I eliminate the Coast Guard, Air Force, and Army. Gym class starts. I don't want to play basketball with the other students. I just sit on the bleachers thinking about joining the military.

"Maikel, come over here."

I look over to see Rita, Debra, Demetris, and Rhonda, girls from my class.

"Sit down in front of us."

"Why do you want me to sit down in front of you? Are you messin' with me?"

"No, silly. We are going to braid your hair."

I sit down, and Debra starts braiding cornrows into my hair.

"Well, it ain't quite long enough but I'll make it work. Your hair is so soft."

My face instantly flushes red. I'm not used to girls touching my hair. I look over at Demetris and think about the first time I'd seen cornrows in her hair on the school bus. I remember asking if it hurt. My head pulls back and forth as the cornrows start forming on the top of my head. The braids are so tight that it feels as if my hair is getting ripped out by the roots. By the end of class, I have a headful of aching cornrows. Oh yeah, it hurts.

At lunch time, I realize I need to make a decision. It's either the Navy or the Marines. I approach the Marine recruiter.

Proud and confident, he looks right at me. "Hello, sir. Are you interested in joining the Marines?"

"I don't know yet. I'm just looking."

The recruiter in his spiffy uniform hands me some information. I glance over it.

"What can you tell me about the schools? I hear the Navy schools are some of the best."

"Well, sir, we go to the same schools as the Navy."

As we're talking, my friend Mike Thompson walks up. Mike is more informed and asks questions while I listen. When I'm done listening to Mike, I move to the Navy recruiter. He reminds me of my stepdad Dusty. The Marine reminds me of sergeant on the *Gomer Pyle* TV show, someone who is wound up just a little too tight and should masturbate a little more often.

The sailor recruiter asks, "Are you interested in joining the Navy?"

"Maybe. What jobs do you have in the electronics fields?"

"Jobs are called *Rates* in the Navy." The Navy recruiter describes *Electronics Technician* and I'm immediately drawn to it. He seems less serious than the Marine guy. If the Marine guy was a wrinkleless tuxedo, then this Navy guy was shorts with flip-flops.

"Nice hair," he comments.

I move my hands to my head. I still have the cornrows. With

my face turning red again, I casually mention that the ladies in gym thought my hair needed braiding.

"Thanks, sir," I say.

The recruiter hands me his business card. I felt no pressure or tension. He has a *you can do whatever the hell you want* attitude.

I grab my lunch and sit down in the cafeteria. I read the Navy literature as I eat lunch. Mike sits down next to me.

"Those Marines are some bad motherfuckers." He starts quoting some of the posters. *"Be all you can be! Semper Fi! Get some!"*

"They sure are, Mike. Are you gonna join the Marines?"

"I don't know yet. The Navy SEALs are bad-asses, too."

"I think I'll join the branch with the best electronic schools. I'm leaning toward the Navy. My stepdad liked it and had a good time traveling."

"We don't have to choose now. We've still got some time. Gotta go."

Mike was always saying, "Gotta go." He was likely off to flirt with some girl.

After another week of thinking about it, I have to make a decision regarding what to do with my life. I decide to go into the Navy. After high school graduation, one by one, my friends go down their paths. By late June, I don't see most of them anymore. I've made my choice.

Goodbye Shiney Rock Road

Wednesday, June 25, 1986 – Seventeen Years Old.

Self-esteem low, but I have a good heart.
Strong foundation. Mom gave me a good start.
Still a mama's boy, but now on my own.
Leaving Shiney Rock. Leaving my home.
I have no idea which way the wind will blow.
Stay true to myself. To the things that I know.

Mom cries as she hugs me. "You'll be okay, son. I've taught you all I know. You'll be fine. I'm proud of you."

Dusty gives me a thumbs up as the bus leaves the parking lot. I'm off to the next stage of my life. After a really long ride, I arrive in North Chicago. Boot camp starts as soon as all of us green recruits offload from the Greyhound bus. We are being yelled at to hurry up. We are verbally scolded to expedite reloading onto a military transport to take us to the Great Lakes Naval Training Station. We pour out of the transport in a severe thunderstorm. It's dumping rain hard. We are corralled from the parking lot into a large room. For nearly an hour, a room full of zit-covered, hormone-filled teenagers fill out paperwork. When we're all done, the Chief Petty Officer says, "Okay boys, drop them. Take off your pants, strip down, and no playing with yourselves." All I can think of is the song *In the Navy* by The Village People. All eyes are looking forward, trying to avoid this awkward moment. Whew! Nothing happens. They're just making sure we're all males. We put our wet clothes back on and march to our barracks. It's 2:00 A.M. Exhausted, I lie down in a rack.

BANG!

I abruptly awake to an empty trash can hitting my rack. I look at my watch. It's only 4:30 A.M. How that can be? I just laid down.

"Get up! Your mama isn't here anymore. No one is here to change your diapers. Get the hell up! No talking."

I put on yesterday's rain-soaked cold clothes. One guy starts talking and a small two-by-four flies across the room. The chunk of wood hits the talker in the shin and the perpetrator drops to the floor. I look over and see a Chief Petty Officer with a Navy SEAL gold emblem flashing in the light.

In a calm tone, he says, "Quiet."

No one says another word as he moves us outside. All of us stand outside in another severe thunderstorm in a sorry formation. My clothes re-saturate as we get yelled at some more.

I think to myself, *What did I do?*

The Chief yells out, "One of you tried to kill himself last night with a safety razor. He didn't die. It's a good thing, too, because that would mean more paperwork for me. If you don't want to be here, I'll show you where the hole in the fence is. That way, I don't have to do any of the paperwork. Line up! Nuts-to-butts."

I'm really uncomfortable. Even with the cold downpour, I can hear and feel the warm breath of the nuts guy behind my butt. I don't like it. The others who moved out of formation because they didn't like it are now doing push-ups until exhaustion. I hold my ground, staying put.

KA-BOOM!

A crash of lightning strikes not even one Mississippi count away as we march to the cafeteria. We have five minutes to eat lunch before marching in even more rain to the uniform shop. After being fitted for our new uniforms, we put our wet clothes back on again, get our hair whacked off, and return to the barracks.

I think again, *What did I do? Am I going to have six years of this?* I just signed my life away and have to find a way for this to work.

Then I remember what Dusty told me. "Boot camp is just a mind game. Get through it, and the rest of your time will just be like a job."

I don't know when I'll ever see Shiney Rock Road again. The Chief was right about me though. I am a mama's boy. I'm still a mama's boy. It's time to find my own way and take care of things myself. At this moment, I realize that going back to Shiney Rock Road will never be the same.

Posing for Mom after Navy A School graduation.
I stand in the same spot where she would die
years later.

Hospice Care (Day 13)

Monday, March 5, 2007 – Collection of Pictures of Granny and Loretta. Inhaling Helium. Story of Granny and Loretta Dying.

Do Not Resuscitate. Do not try.
No CPR. Let her go. Watch her die.
Let her leave this place with all her grace.
Remember her love. Remember her face.

Mom's tracheal hole gurgles with phlegm. I feel like I'm betraying her for not easing her labored breathing. The nurse told us that this could happen.

I recall her saying, "It's likely Dolores will have fluid fill her lungs. I know this is hard for you to hear this, but you shouldn't remove this fluid. It's your choice, but you may prolong her pain."

Her body is fighting to live. Despite labored breathing, her stubbornness is finding a way to keep going. Sometimes the mucous fluid comes out and dribbles down her neck. I wash it off. I didn't imagine that she would drown in a dry bed when all of this started. Hank had died this way. Mesothelioma caused his lungs to fill with fluid.

Tash told me what had happened. "He was just lying there, and I could tell he couldn't breathe. I tried CPR, but they told me there was nothing I could have done. His lungs were full of fluid."

I glance up at the mantle. The DNR order taped there stares at me, reminding me of a harsh truth. I read it again. "STOP. Do Not Resuscitate. Patient's Name: Dolores Wise." When Mom's time is up, there will be no CPR. It's a blow of reality hitting me hard. Part of me wants her to die now so her pain will end, but I feel guilty for thinking it. I feel nauseated with guilt.

The house is empty in more ways than one. The treasure that filled this home was Mom. Removing all her possessions reminds me of taking away a piece of her at a time, bit-by-bit. I think, *What did I do?* I got rid of so many of her possessions. While the rest of the house is empty, this room is filled with love because Mom is in it. It won't be long now. Mom wakes up and moves her arms around. She's surrounded by flowers and balloons.

Tash asks, "What's wrong, Mom?"

Mom's hazy eyes move toward the balloons.

Concerned, Tash asks, "Mom, do you want me to move the balloons?"

Tash and I shuffle the closest balloons away. Mom seems happier that they're not so close anymore. We move the rest of the balloons to the other side of the room.

Some of the balloons are losing their helium and only hang a couple of feet off the ground. Tash, Susan, and I decide not to let the rest of the helium go to waste. We move to the kitchen so Mom can rest. Susan takes the smiley face balloon, unties the bottom, and inhales deeply.

In a squeaky high-pitched voice, she says, "All of these balloons are making me crazy."

Susan passes the balloon to Tash, and she inhales. In a squeaky voice, she says, "All I want to do is dance."

We are cracking up. It's a relief to laugh. It's my turn.

With my best helium-pitched tone, I say, "Well bless your heart. Would y'all like a bucket of chicken?" I start singing a Michael Jackson song and throw in some uncoordinated dance moves. We completely lose it, roaring with squeaky laughter. I notice Betsy is standing outside the screen door looking in.

"What y'all laughing at?"

"Come in, Betsy. Want some helium?" Susan asks in a high-pitched voice.

"I ain't into that. Y'all are crazy."

Susan inhales deeply and sings the Oscar Mayer theme song.

Betsy starts laughing so hard that she has to sit down.

**(L-R) Maikel, Gladys, Tash, and Betsy
with the helium-filled balloons.**

Tash says, "Betsy, this is more fun than the weed you were growing behind your place. Do you have any marijuana? My back is hurting."

Betsy rolls with laughter. "Y'all know it wasn't mine. Y'all having a good enough time without any weed. You'd better get working on them plans for your mom's funeral."

"Tash. We should collect some more pictures of Aunt Loretta and Granny. It would be nice to have them for the funeral."

"Okay, Cale. I saw some more pictures on the back porch."

Tash and I sort through a pile of pictures, finding photos of each of them. As I look at the picture of Granny, I remember when Granny passed away.

I explain my misty eyes to Susan. "I was in the Navy. I was going through a tough section in school and about one month from graduation. This school had about a sixty percent dropout rate, and there were only four of us left from the original class. Granny was in the hospital, and I asked Mom what I should do.

"Mom said that Granny would want me to finish school, to keep going. She was so proud of me. I knew Mom was right, but I still felt guilty for not going back home. I finished second in my class, but the last month was tough. I couldn't concentrate or remember anything. Granny passed away on July 2, 1987. I remember what Mom said to me when Granny died. 'It's okay, honey. You spent a lot of time with her all your life growing up. She loves you. Granny would want you to succeed. She enjoyed it when you came over and spent time with her. *Hee Haw*, potato rocks, and all.'"

Susan turns to my sister. "Where were you when Granny died?"

"I was in Utah finishing up high school. It's a long story."

There's silence, a clue not to discuss it further.

**Grandma Ruby Yancey with those
thick RC-Cola-bottle glasses.**

Susan asks, "When did Aunt Loretta pass away?"

Tash and I started talking at the same time.

"Go ahead, Cale."

"She passed away in 1990. I was still in the Navy, training to take the Navy SEAL entrance test to get into BUDS (SEAL Boot Camp). I changed my mind after Aunt Loretta died. Our ship was doing helicopter pilot certifications off the coast of Virginia when they notified me that Aunt Loretta passed away. I asked if I could go to her funeral."

"The commander refused and said, 'You are vital to remain here to keep our communication systems going. If she was a parent, sibling, or grandparent, it would be a different matter.'"

"That was it. I tried to explain how close she was too me. I left his office and said, 'Fuck you.' I did the remainder of my military service and got out. Aunt Loretta was important to me."

Susan asks, "Tash, what happened to Aunt Loretta again?"

"Yes. I'd like to hear it again, too. I'm not sure if I ever heard all of it."

Tash shares the story. "Aunt Loretta died of cancer. Like Mom, she started smoking when she was a teenager. After a double mastectomy, the doctors thought they'd gotten all her cancer. A few months later, they found cancer in her lungs. She started chemo and lost all her hair. After a few months, it spread to her brain, and lymph nodes. I was here in Clarksville when she called Mom. She said to Mom, 'Dolores, I'm dying. Can you come down here and help me? My sons won't help. They're avoiding me.'

"Mom immediately loaded up that beat up Dodge Colt and drove straight to Nashville that night. Mom said she knocked on the door just before bedtime. The door cracked open with the chain lock still secured. When she asked Gavin to let her in, he told her that she couldn't stay there. Gavin promptly shut the door and secured the other locks. Mom didn't know what to do, so she knocked on Loretta's neighbor's door.

"The neighbor knew Mom and let her in to use their phone. None of the neighbors thought much of Loretta's kids, especially Gavin. Mom said she kept calling Loretta, but Gavin just kept hanging up on her.

"The downstairs neighbor, Jane, heard what was going on. She'd tried to help, but she knew Loretta's sons, if around, wouldn't let her. Jane warned Mom about Dale, the eldest, that he'd come and go and was into drugs pretty bad. Jane didn't think much of the youngest, either. She let Mom stay in her extra room.

"When Mom told me this, she said she teared up and could only say, 'Thank you.'

"The next day when Gavin left for work, Mom used the neighbor's emergency key to get into Loretta's townhome. Mom went to Loretta's room and held her sister. Loretta had lost all her hair. She was lying in bed with pee-soaked sheets because she couldn't get out of bed to use the bathroom. Mom told me that Loretta didn't care about the wet sheets, but she was hungry. Loretta told her, 'Gavin left and didn't give me anything to eat.'"

I interrupt. "Tash, I'll bet Mom was ready to give him a spanking. I can see her jaw clenching and saying, 'You little shit. Go pick your switch.'"

Tash continues, "Mom fed her and brought her some special painkillers that Loretta had hid in her underwear so Dale couldn't find them if he visited. Mom said that Loretta had wet herself and the joints she hid a couple of times, but Mom just dried them out. Loretta didn't hold back on the marijuana, either. She said she smoked at least a half a dozen joints each day. Then Loretta had a big favor to ask. Loretta had broken her vibrator."

Susan snorts.

"She asked Mom to take it back and get her another one. Mom did exactly that and came back just before Gavin returned. Mom told the sex shop clerk that it had been broken out of the package, so he gave her a new one."

"Tash, this was just like when Mom returned our shoes to Leggett's when we were kids. 'Those shoes or the vibrator were defective.'"

Susan, Tash, and I laugh out loud.

"Mom discretely puts the new unbroken vibrator in a discrete, easy-to-reach place for her sister before her youngest nephew walks in the door. Mom said, 'Now look here, you spoiled little brat. I'm going to take care of my sister. You don't want me to stay here, fine! But I'm going to take care of my sister. You'd better open that damn door when I knock. If you don't, I'll call Health and Human Services. Got it?! Don't piss me off!'

"Gavin got mad and slammed the door on his way out. She was mad that he'd abandoned his own mother. He could at least bring food and water. On the second day, Loretta asked Mom for another vibrator. She broke a second one in less than a day. Mom returned the 'unused item' and got a replacement.

"After a few days, Loretta perked up. Before Mom left her sister to come back home, she laid into Gavin and told him to man up. Over phone conversations, I could tell she was a nervous wreck. Not three days had passed, and she got another call from her sister.

"Sometimes when Mom and I have a few drinks, she tells me what Loretta told her. 'Dolores, I call and call, and my children won't come.'

"Mom was super angry. I was, too. Before leaving Clarksville again, she called Loretta's neighbor. Mom asked Loretta's neighbors if they could take care of Loretta before she got there. Mom got to Nashville late at night again. Gavin left early before she got there, knowing the potential wrath of Mom.

"Mom said that the first thing Loretta asked for was water to drink. Her son had ignored her when she called for him. Loretta wasn't doing well, so Mom called the doctor. He said to bring her to the hospital. Mom packed up things for Loretta, including hiding her still functioning vibrator number three and a resupply of rolled paper pain medication. She left a note for Gavin on the kitchen table.

When they got to the hospital, the hospital staff carted Loretta off to do some tests. Mom waited in the smoking room.

"Eventually, the doctors told Mom that Loretta's cancer had spread aggressively. She only had a few days left and could stay in the hospital to die. Mom decided this was best and stayed with her. When Loretta woke, Mom didn't sugarcoat it and told her sister she only had few days left.

"Mom called Loretta's neighbors and updated them. When Loretta's neighbors went upstairs to tell Gavin, he wouldn't open the door. The neighbors slipped a paper under the door for Gavin with the address and room number of the hospital. They asked if they could get Mom's clothes and take them to the hospital. Gavin initially ignored them. After a few more calls, Gavin placed Mom's luggage just outside the door and locked the door again.

"The next morning, Loretta's neighbors came by with flowers, cards, and Mom's clothes. They updated Mom on what happened. Loretta woke up hoping her sons were there. The neighbors let her know they'd given Gavin the address and phone number of the hospital.

"Maikel, Mom said she lost it when Loretta asked her neighbors to beg her children to see her before she died. A couple more days passed, and Loretta's sons never showed up. Mom said that even with morphine, Loretta was suffering. Gavin and Dale never called back or came to the hospital.

"Loretta asked Mom why they were abandoning her and wouldn't see her. Loretta shifted her abandonment to anger. A switch flipped. She decided to change her will and immediately tried to remove their inheritance and change her life insurance policy.

"Mom wrote down Loretta's wishes and had her sign it. They tried to get ahold of the lawyer to make the changes. Loretta and

Mom waited for a return call for a few hours. Mom said that she was holding Loretta's hand when a steady tone indicated that Loretta's heart had stopped. Loretta had died."

"I never knew the whole story," I say softly.

Susan chimes in. "Sounds like your cousins are assholes."

"Yep. Tash and I knew that Gavin was a spoiled brat, and that Dale was an addict, but when Loretta died and they abandoned her, I think the term 'assholes' is appropriate. I told myself then when I heard this story that I wouldn't be like them. I want to be by Mom's side when she dies."

Loretta captured the hearts of all who came her way.
She had a light about her with the words she would say.
Contagious energy that she graciously passed on to others.
When her light went out, her fire kept going, in all of those who loved her.

Aunt Loretta.

Hospice Care (Day 14)

Tuesday, March 6, 2007 – Mom Dies.

The last exhale. Then, there is life again.
Torture for the living. Causing so much pain.
Spitting at Death, her will I can't deny.
Finally gone. The angel closes her eyes.

Before sunrise, Susan comes into my bedroom. She's been taking the night shifts because Tash and I are exhausted.

"I'm sorry. I think Mama Wise is close."

I hear her waking up Tash up in the other bedroom.

Susan already has coffee brewing and a piece of buttered toast for each of us. I can't eat. I don't think I can swallow anything at the moment. Mom's tracheal hole is filled to the rim with respiratory fluid. Her breathing is labored. Tash is on her left side. I'm on her right side. We are here and by her side. Death is, too.

We watch her breathing deteriorate. I'm torn and am fighting with myself inside. If I could just remove a little fluid, it would be easier for her to breathe. The sun is rising, and a ray of light highlights her face. Mom takes one more breath and then nothing. Tash and I are holding her hands. Susan rests a hand on her forehead. Death. Nothing.

Then her chest rises and falls again. Not death. Bubbles are expanding and popping from her throat. Life is finding a way to hang on. Torture for the living. Then nothing once more. We wait. Is it done?

A few moments later, Mom's chest rises, then falls. She's fighting.

Her body is fighting to live. A blur of time goes by, and Mom takes a breath. How long will this last? I don't know if I can take this wait in between each breath. The time between breaths is now an eternity. Once more, nothing. We wait the longest five minutes. Her lips turn a pale blue. The heat drains from her forehead. Nothing.

We don't know if she'll breathe again. We wait, hoping. For life? For death? Nothing. After ten more minutes of crying and holding her hands. We know. She's gone. Goodbye Mom.

Susan calls the funeral home as Tash and I cut a lock of Mom's hair. We hide in the kitchen when they arrive. I can't bear to witness watching them put her lifeless body in a bag or on the cart. I can't see her strong arms dangle lifeless. I want my last memory to be holding her hand and seeing her fight to the end.

The funeral van drives away slowly. I manage to walk back to the front room where Mom wanted to die. The bed is now empty. There is no more Mom. She's gone. I granted her wish to die at home but never knew how painful it would be. On the birdfeeder I placed outside her window, a cardinal looks at me. I try to make it into a symbolic moment. A sign of her saying goodbye. A sign from a friend coming back to visit. I don't know if it's anything more than a hungry bird. It doesn't really matter. I take it as her leaving as the cardinal flies away.

I open the front screen door and knock over the flower arrangement that the funeral home placed on Mom's front porch. "Damn it!" I set the giant mass of lilies upright and go back inside to the kitchen where Tash and Susan are drinking coffee with red eyes.

"They put the flowers on our front porch. Tash, quick. Help me put them on Betsy's porch before she wakes up."

It's not long before Gladys, Sam, and Betsy come over. One of them knocks over the now-mangled lilies.

"Maikel and Natasha. You are just like your Mama. You are your mother's children. We're going to miss her."

We hug. We laugh. We cry. Gladys, Sam, and Betsy leave.

A few minutes later, *Knock, knock, knock.*

Tom is standing there. "Goddammit! Goddammit!"

"I know Tom. Come here, buddy."

Tom completely breaks down. He sobs on my shoulder. I hold him as tears stream down both our faces. He loved Mom, and now one of his best friends is gone. Someone who loved him, Tourette's and all.

After a few moments, which seems like an eternity, I tell Tom when Mom's funeral will be and offer him a ride with us. After another hug, he leaves.

I close the door. I don't want to see or talk with anyone else. Not now. Not today. We sit at the kitchen table quietly consuming coffee.

Teary-eyed, Tash says to me, "Look at that tumbleweed over the kitchen table."

Susan interjects, "I remember when we got that for her. We were driving and it was windy. Suddenly, a tumbleweed whips across the road. Then another and another. Maikel said, 'That's what I'll get her for Christmas. A tumbleweed. She's always wanted one.'"

Tash, a little less teary, says, "You suck, Maikel. I got her expensive 600-thread-count sheets that Christmas. And you mail her a damn weed. When she got it, she hung it here and put lights and Christmas decorations on it. It hasn't come down since. It just stares back at me every morning when I drink coffee."

We want to laugh, but nothing resides but profound sadness. It's funny how something so small could make Mom so happy. Of all the presents I got her over the years, I think the tumbleweed was the best.

**Mom and me under her Christmas tumbleweed
a few months before she died.**

Planting New Seeds

Friday, March 9, 2007

We affect others more than they think.
A smile. A handshake. Even a wink.
Every action. Everything that we do.
Can change a person, like someone she knew.

Tash and I sort through more photos to display at the funeral.

"Here's one, Tash. Remember this?"

She giggles. "That's Chocolate Mouse."

"This was when you and Mom came to Boulder to visit Susan and me. Do you remember when we woke up that morning? There was chocolate on the fridge door handles and chocolate on the countertop. There were chocolate footprints from the kitchen, through the living room, and to her bedroom. We knocked and opened the door. Mom was lying there in bed with a smile and a chocolate ring around her mouth."

"Yeah, Cale. We told her there was a Chocolate Mouse in the house. When we got home to Clarksville, she told me she ate ice cream to ease the pain in her throat and mouth. Mom had that fungus growing in her throat before the doctors figured out it was cancer. She was hurtin' and didn't want you to know. Sometimes she put her false teeth in the freezer, too. One time she lost them for two weeks until she needed ice cream again."

"I remember."

There's a photo of Mom standing by the five-foot twig of the silverleaf maple. A picture of her sitting on the front porch with kids who attended her Jack-and-Jill Daycare. A picture of her standing in a creek in Occoneechee State Park. I look at the picture with Mom standing by my cousin Hank. I hope they are together now laughing and causing mischief. There's a picture of Mom with Granny at Christmas. So many memories. We solemnly drive to the funeral home.

Unlike traditional funerals in Southern Virginia, Tash and I choose not to have a viewing. For us, a still body feels like a continuance of the suffering. Susan, Tash, and I tape the photo memories of Mom on posters in the middle of the flowers from our community. I look at the empty seats and think, *Will any come?* I look at the funeral card. I open it and start tearing up. Mrs. Lyon chose a fitting poem.

Remember When

Remember the fields both green and gold.
Remember the crooked creeks and how they fold.
Remember the Band-Aids after you played.
Remember the innocence as childhood fades.

Remember my love and things I would say.
Remember me long after, after I pass away.
Remember those who stumble, finding their way.
Remember to be kind with the words that you say.

Remember to keep trying. Don't ever give up.
Remember you'll fail. Simply stand back up.
Remember the birthdays and give what you can.
Remember to stand tall. I taught you all that I am.

Remember the porch and the storms some days.
Remember the life after, when dust washes away.
Remember, I'll be waiting. You'll see me again one day.
Remember to live. Like it could be your very last day.

Dolores Yancey Wise

In Loving Memory
Dolores Yancey Wise

Born
October 14, 1947

Died
March 6, 2007

Memorial Services
6PM Friday, March 9, 2007
Watkins Cooper Lyon Funeral Chapel

Officiant
Reverend Jane Lyon
Reverend Greg Randall

Scattering
Oakhurst Cemetery

Survivors
Daughter
Natasha Wise
Son and Daughter-In-Law
Maikel and Susan Wise

Arrangements By
Watkins Cooper Lynn Funeral Home

Mom's Funeral Card

It's time. The door opens. Relatives, friends, and people I don't even know pour into the funeral chapel. Soon, the chairs are completely filled. It's standing room only along the back wall. I can't believe it. I didn't know the undying breath of influence nor the quantity of love she'd had on now our two-stoplight town until that moment.

Reverend Lyon steps up front. She holds a precious branch with new growth leaves from the silverleaf maple tree Mom planted behind our home. She begins speaking. "See this branch of leaves? Look how it's spread. Look around you. Look at all the seedlings and leaves in this room."

This is too much for me to gaze upon. I love that tree and deeply miss the woman who'd planted it. It is sacred.

"Maikel told me he didn't know if anyone would show up. He thought Dolores may have burnt too many bridges. That she was too eccentric. There aren't enough seats in this room for the love this town has for Mama Wise."

She bows her head for an opening prayer. Next, she pulls out the poem I wrote for Mom years ago for her birthday. Mrs. Lyon reads:

She Waits For a Friend

A morning sun brings the heat from below.
A maple rustles with new life that it knows.
A woman peers through the glass with no sound.
Speechless is she; in hiding but soon found.

She hears me not and I look so I can see.
There is nothing there but simply a tree.
The tree bears strength as roots always deepen.
So much like the woman, with eyes that have spoken.

I hear a sigh as she turns toward me.
A smile comes forth. I then ask this of thee.
What caught your eye through that **pain** of glass?
Was it the tree? Or was it times past?

I get a reply. They are not from words.
Emanating from her soul, reaching from within her.
Telling of a time that went to extremes.
Tired some days, but always replying jubilee.

Generously she asks, "What do you need?"
I reply, "Nothing. Just a hug if you please."
Leaving the room, I say goodbye again.
To a woman I love, my mother, my friend.

She reads a Bible verse. I think she said from the Book of John, but I immediately forget. I'm in another place in my mind. Once she finished reading, we bow our heads in a final prayer. After a few moments of quietness after she says, "Let's go outside and share some memories and say our goodbyes."

We form a circle and Reverend Lyon asks, "Does anyone have anything to share?"

I can't muster a word. Susan tightly grips my hand. There are a few moments of stillness until my high school English teacher, Nancy Talley, steps forward.

"Maikel was in my 12th grade English class. I also taught his mother Dolores. As a matter of fact, I've taught most of you here. Dolores was kind person, and she will be missed."

Nancy steps back, and one-by-one, others come forward. "Dolores babysat me," and "Dolores helped me." There are so many seeds. Mom had planted all these seeds that have turned into a field of daisies.

Though I can't speak, I say in my heart, "Goodbye, Mom. Goodbye One-Beer Daisy." Folks line up and give us final hugs as they leave.

Outside, a lady approaches us. "Maikel and Natasha, you don't know me, but I knew your mother."

With red-stained eyes, we look at her as she continues, "Your Mom was a kind woman. Years ago, somehow, she found out I was a single Mom. We didn't have much, and I don't know how she knew. Every year on Easter, she'd leave an Easter basket for me and my son. She'd sneak off and never say a word. Sometimes I'd catch a glimpse of her out our window as she walked away. Your Mom always gave my son a generous basket of treats. She'd always included an envelope with several hundred dollars. She gave us extra money after I lost my job at the Burlington Factory. She'll never know how much that helped us. She didn't ask for anything. I'll miss her."

I don't know what to say as my eyes water again.

She leaves as a handful of others come up to us. These folks want to personally share their stories about Mom. "Your Mom used to babysit us," "She gave us," and "She fed us." I can't believe it. Mom's love and generosity rippled through the community. She gave when she'd hardly had enough for herself. I didn't realize how much until now. A big smile paints my face.

Inquisitively, Susan asks, "What are you smiling at?"

"I wonder how much of her weed money helped these folks."

Tash, Susan, and I erupt in laughter. Laughing at her mischievousness is a great way to finish her funeral. It's what she would have wanted.

On the drive home, we pass by the places where Mom, Tash, and I spent our lives. The places where we bought food off the reduced table. The places where we got haircuts, dinners, clothes, and ice cream. Each place has a story and a memory. Each place was sacred.

(L) Demetris, my friend. (M) Nancy Talley, Bluestone High School
teacher and me. Mrs. Talley taught us all.

Epilogue

1,584 Unread Emails

Monday, March 19, 2007

I return to work and find *Post-its*, red-lined documents, and other engineering items to review on my desk. There are piles of product documents and test specifications. I open my lab notebook to read my notes, trying to remember what I was working on before I left. My perspective of life and priorities has changed. None of this seems important to me. I reluctantly check my emails: 1,584 unread emails.

Unenthusiastically, I think, *Yay. Job security.*

I've been away from work for over two weeks, and I begin the tedious process of catching up. Many items and requests have already been resolved. I ignore some low priority tasks. My friend Jeff stops by to chat and check on me. Recognizing I'm distraught, he encourages me to take my time. Eventually, all my coworkers dribble into the office. It's business as usual. My project was being refined during my absence. It's supposedly finished, ready for my final approval and qualification. I enter the lab to assess and determine my priorities. I'm still scattered and unfocused. Even so, in short order, I find numerous software issues and work with the software engineers to get them resolved. I'm also supposed to train another engineer how to qualify these temperamental beasts.

Two weeks later, the tester, a coworker, and I are shipped to China. After getting my work visa in Hong Kong to enter China, I'm escorted to the factory to begin the time-consuming process of factory qualification. Sergio, my trainee, takes notes and questions everything. When Day One is complete, we ride a bus back to the hotel, eat dinner, and analyze data in the lounge while drinking a couple of beers.

After almost an hour of analysis, I say to him, "Dammit, I found another software bug." I'm going to have to wait for the programmers to fix the issue and then start Day One qualification all over again. I'm more annoyed than normal at the programmer for his repeated lack of thoroughness, but I try to stay upbeat for my trainee. The next morning, after installing the new software, I start the qualification process again. My foggy mind drifts to a dark, sad place, and I have an overwhelming desire to not be here. I drag myself to the office feeling an intense pain building. My chest tightens. I can't breathe. I'm having a heart attack.

Sergio looks at me. "Señor, you don't look so good."

The pain and pressure deep in my chest hurts so much that I have to take shallow breaths.

"Sergio, I'm going to lie down on the floor for a few minutes."

Despite the dusty tiled floor, the coolness feels soothing. I'm still not recovering.

In short breaths, I say, "Sergio, you'd…better…call…an ambulance."

A short time later, some of the factory staff and two young medics rush in. The two teenage-looking medics take my blood pressure. It's 185 over 130. I'm coherent enough to know I'm in trouble.

I don't want to die here. Not now, and not without Susan. Am I going to die right after Mom?

"Maikel, we're taking you to a hospital in Hong Kong."

After two hours of transporting by a van shuttle, a boat ride, and a taxi, I arrive at the Hong Kong Hospital. If I had died, rigor mortis would have surely set in by then. Stress tests, X-rays, an EKG, and blood analysis reveal nothing. The only anomaly is high blood pressure. While I'm under observation the next day, the weather woman on the English-speaking Hong Kong channel announces that two typhoons are heading toward us.

Ah great! Here comes a different kind of storm.

As the typhoons approach, a coworker comes to my hospital room. Initially, he asks how I'm doing but quickly shifts focus, asking how to proceed with work questions. Several minutes into our discussion, Susan calls. I inform her of my test results and assure her I'm okay.

"I hear someone there. Is there someone in the room with you?"

"Yes. It's Stephen. He just has a few questions."

"It better not be work-related!"

She insists that she speaks to Stephen. Susan tears into him. Stephen mutters, "Okay...yes...I see," and sheepishly hands the phone to me before leaving. He doesn't return. After another day, the rains dissipate from the first typhoon, and I fly back home before the second typhoon hits. I have an unknown health issue. My engineering brain tries to figure out what happened, but I can't come up with a solution. I just want to be home.

Two days later, I arrive at work back in Colorado and do something I've never done before. I put my feet up on my desk as I numbly stare out of the window at the Flatiron Mountains. Pop, who disowned me, died last July. Mom just died. I'm having chest pains. All I want to do is go someplace outside and sit by a tree. I don't know what the future will bring, but I know I don't want to be here. I'm simply surviving. I'm empty.

What else can go wrong?

I leave work early, go home, and walk until sunset.

Control, Alt, Delete...Rebooting

Thursday, September 27, 2007

Months have gone by since my heart issue in Hong Kong. I'm simply existing. I don't feel joy in my life anymore. To escape my grief, I consume myself with work. I remember an acquaintance once saying, "The graveyard is full of dedicated employees." I feel as if I'm slowly dying. I put in my resignation two weeks later.

Susan and I decide we need to take a year off to reset our lives. We decide to buy an RV, which turns out to be a bigger decision than we originally anticipated. There are too many options. We want an RV that is roomy yet is still small enough to get us into most campsites, especially national parks. A fifth wheel feels too gluttonous, since the truck required to pull it would either be horrible on gas or a stinky diesel. A Class A rig would be too large to fit into the places we want to go. A Class C or Class B RV would work, but we would have to maintain two engines, since we would need a tow vehicle. Two vehicles would also be more expensive, and insurance would cost more. We like the Airstreams, though they're pricey. For weeks, I read RV forums, RV magazines, and talk to other RV folks.

Consistently, RVers tell us, "Whatever you get, the RV will probably be too small. You'll want to get rid of it and get a bigger one."

Susan and I are the opposite of the norm. Over the years, we camped for weeks with her VW beetle and a tent. For a new RV, our only real requirements are a bed, a bathroom, and shower. Sick of me talking about RVs, Susan just nods, waiting for me to sort it out.

I narrow my decision to an RV travel trailer, but I'm not sure about size or type.

We decide to take a three-week trip to Utah. During our excursion, I ask RVers about their rigs: reliability, generators, repairs, and endless questions.

On our trip, we visit our friends Scott and Brook. We visit my Uncle Jim and his wife. We explore Zion and Bryce National Parks. Our final stop is at Capitol Reef. We set up our old backpacking tent across from two extravagantly large RVs and go out for a long hike down a slot canyon. After six hours, we return dusty and dirty with smiles on our faces. We cook dinner on a small green propane Coleman stove that Mom bought us as a wedding gift years ago. I feel alive again.

After we finish eating and cleaning up, Susan and I sit down to watch the sunset over the historic apple orchard. The red rocks light up, making the valley glow. I wonder if this is an alpenglow of the desert that I've read about but have never experienced.

I look at Susan. "Today was a good day. It's the simple things that are important."

On our drive home the next morning, Susan says, "I have something to tell you. I have a lump in my breast. It's been there for a few weeks. It aches."

I'm scared. My mind goes to a dark place. I've seen what cancer did to Aunt Loretta and Mom. The last year and a half was hell. It feels like another harsh hickory stick of life knocking me to the ground.

"Make me a promise. Please go to the doctor immediately when we get back."

"I will."

Three Titties Are Better Than Two

Monday, October 22, 2007

When we get back, Susan visits her doctor. When she comes home, she lets me know he is sending a tissue sample out for a biopsy. We can't jump to any conclusions, but the nurse practitioner thinks she could have cancer. I can feel something isn't right. We have to wait for the biopsy results.

"Whatever happens, we'll deal with it and hit the road. Okay?"

In a voice of denial, she says, "We'll know soon. Let's go look at some more RVs."

We lean toward buying an Airstream. The others we consider seem cheaply built. We simply can't make up our minds.

I think about our wedding and what our friend Scott said, "We have your back. I've got your back." Those words seem more appropriate now than ever. I'm scared. Susan and I are heading into the unknown.

I look at Susan. "I have your back."

We drive back home to wait several days for the results.

Now with the RV itch, Susan says, "Let's go look at the Airstreams again."

We get in the truck to drive down to Denver for a second look, but before we hit the city of Golden, Susan's cell phone rings.

"Hello. This is Susan Wise. Hold, please. Maikel, pull over."

By her tone and directness, I know how serious this is.

"It's positive? Yes, ma'am. I'll set up an appointment."

Susan hangs up her cell phone as she turns to me.

"Maikel, I have breast cancer. It's a rare form, but they think they caught it early."

Susan's eyes water and contagiously make mine water, too. I don't know what else to do but hold her. Pop's dead. Mom's dead. I have heart issues. Now my wife could die. I am so afraid for her.

"Susan, what do you want to do?"

"Fuck it. We're buying the Airstream and travel for a year."

We buy a smaller twenty-foot Airstream and start making our plans.

The following week, Susan's right breast is removed. The cancer, only stage 0 with the lymph nodes negative, has not metastasized. When Susan comes out of surgery, still groggy from her anesthesia, she asks, "Maikel, would you tell the doctors that I want a third boob? Like in the movie *Total Recall*. One for each of your hands and one for your mouth. Better yet, I want a Camelback bladder installed where my boob used to be. That way, I don't need a backpack."

This is new material for the nurses. We all laugh. I tell her I don't know about the Camelback, but the third boob sounds like a great idea. When the anesthesia finally wears off, she becomes more coherent and is mortified by what she said.

She reassures me, "This cancer is an inconvenience. Let's get ready to go."

Inconvenient or not, I'm scared. I've waited for someone like Susan for years. I don't want to lose her. I convince myself that Susan is fine, that she won't die. I try not to think about the past.

I avoid saying, "What else can go wrong?"

One-sided Susan keeps planning our trip and all the things we want to see. That keeps us focused. We want to see it all. We don't know what may happen tomorrow.

Not All Who Wander Are Lost

Saturday, December 29, 2007

Life is too precious. So many things to do, to see.
We don't know when time is up, when that time will be.
We hike the forest's floors and canyon's rims.
Once lost, we find what's important again.
Tethered to adventure, on few things we depend.
We're growing old together. Together, as friends.

In late December, we finally hit the road on our new RV adventure after more inconveniences. Susan and I squeeze out between two Colorado winter storms on icy roads. For several months, we travel to Arizona, New Mexico, Utah, Wyoming, Idaho, and Montana. We're slowly healing as we drift from park to park. Every sunrise, sunset, flower, bird, and rock feels precious. We hike, and we deal with the follow-up cancer surgeries that reconstruct my wife's breast.

While exploring Montana, Susan says, "Let's go to Two Medicine Campground in Glacier National Park."

When we arrive, we find a beautiful glacial lake surrounded by mountains. Of all the wonders on our journey, this is our place and our peace. In this magical valley, we feel as if we're finally beginning to heal from all the death, cancer, and loneliness. We discover that this place, sacred to the Blackfeet, is a place of healing for them, as well.

One morning, Susan remarks, "I need this. Two Medicine is healing me."

She's right. Two Medicine is good medicine for our souls. For nearly seven months, we had gone from place to place searching for something, as if we were trying to squeeze it all in before we died.

One day while there, we join Ranger Pat Hagan on a hike to Dawson's Pass. We pass scraggly goats, chirping pikas, and alpine flowers. Once we're at our destination, we find a nice flat rock and sit with an upslope breeze in our faces. This is a place where I can spread more of my mother's ashes. I've already released her ashes at places we've visited earlier in the year. I'm at peace as calmness caresses my soul. I remember my friend, David Buchanan, who died in 1992. I think about Pop disowning me and the choices he made. I think about Hank's shenanigans with Hogan. I think about sitting with Granny on the front porch drinking Southern sweet iced-tea. Some of my friends are alive but not living. Some have died.

Months before, I sealed Mom in a couple of Ziploc bags and wrote with a Sharpie: *Mama Wise's Ashes*. Mom probably would have preferred to be in a bread bag like she used to put on our feet before venturing out in the snow. A Ziploc bag will have to do. Sometimes Susan finds her ashes in the glovebox, the side door of the truck, or deep in my backpack.

Susan often says, "Even now, your mama keeps showing up."

In this sacred moment, Susan smiles as I pull out another stash of Mom's ashes from my backpack to sprinkle a few of them on the colorful lichen-covered rocks beside us.

"There ya go, Mom. Now you can enjoy this, too."

Susan puts her hand on my shoulder. We've been through a lot together. We were beside each other the whole way.

I look at Susan. "I place her where she can't go. Places she could never go or see when she was alive. I don't think she could have made it up that pass. That's why I keep her in my backpack."

I gaze at the beauty that surrounds me—the red-algae snow on the mountains, the blue-iced glaciers, and the oxbow river below. At that moment, I realize Mom gave me one of the greatest gifts of all. Life was tough growing up, but we had a rich life. We had it better than most. I always worried about what we didn't have. We didn't have a paved driveway, but we had trails through the woods. We didn't have a swimming pool, but we had a Slip n' Slide with extra plastic. We didn't have stuffed lobster, but we had hobo chili. It took Mom dying before I could figure things out.

I can hear her, what she would say. "I didn't fall off the turnip truck."

That wasn't true. Mom fell off the turnip truck all the time. But each time, she got up, dusted herself off, hopped back on, and kept going down the road.

**Two Medicine. Looking toward
Dawson's Pass where Mom's ashes lie.**

Maikel L. Wise

Letting Go of One-Beer Daisy

I lay her ashes at random places,
Random places where kindness and love lives.

I lay her ashes at the feet of a Bristlecone Pine,
So she can nourish a tree that is as stubborn as she.

I lay her ashes at the Grand Canyon,
So she can watch the light and shadows and slow, changing time.

I lay her ashes at the top of the Tetons,
So all who pass can look up to her.

I lay her ashes at Two Medicine,
So she can be there to help others who go there to heal, too.

I lay her ashes at Virginia places,
Spots where memory and love merge.

I lay her ashes by her mother's side,
So they can swing on the porch and relax right after supper time.

I lay her ashes by her sister Loretta,
So she can hold her sister once again.

I lay her ashes by Pop,
So she can nag him after his second beer.

One-Beer Daisy

I lay her ashes by my friend David,
So she can tell him, after all these years, he's still missed and loved.

I lay her ashes by my cousin Hank,
Because he was always our foundation growing up.

I lay her ashes by the silverleaf maple,
Because that is where it all began.

I hope you laughed, I hope you cried. I hope you remembered your childhood. If you enjoyed this book, please leave a review at Amazon / Goodreads and pass the book to someone who you know would appreciate it.

Big Hugs,

It Takes a Village

I'm grateful for all my friends and family who helped me with my book. For hours, days, weeks, and months, they offered suggestions and help edit. I'm grateful to you all: Susan Wise, Natasha Wise, Daphne Turner, John Houle, Neal Wedum, Pat Hagan, Deborah Newton, Rita Goode, Maggie May Rappleyea, Mary Rappleyea, Jamie Schumaker, Demetris Harris, Jay Waldo, Judie Battle, Janet Ross, Richard Faucett, Debra Kastner, Ryan Forsythe, and so many more.

Kris Webb. You get your own paragraph. I can't thank you enough for teaching me how to become a better writer and express my thoughts. There were days where I didn't like what you had to say, but I value your honesty. I appreciate your patience and generosity. I've learned that I have a lifetime to keep learning how to write. You are a beautiful Sonoran Desert Rose.

Olga Vynnychenko. I wanted to hire a book cover designer from Ukraine to support Ukrainians during the war. I appreciate your help and patience with me in this process. I love the book cover! I recall the one night you apologized for not getting back to me because the city turned off the electricity. The next day I saw your city was bombed. This broke my heart. You said, "Things have changed since February 24th, and life goes on in the front." That shows the spirit of the Ukrainian people. Be safe and thank you.

About the Author

Raised in Clarksville, Virginia, Maikel L. Wise now travels with his wife in a small Airstream currently located somewhere in the U.S. After high school, Maikel served in the United States Navy and then attended Weber State University, where he received his B.S. in Electrical Engineering Technology. Maikel loves to hike, cycle, bird, and saunter in national parks or any remote wilderness. He and his love, Susan, are exploring together and she still laughs at his jokes after 20 years.

This is the end. The book is over. Go! Live!

Maikel at South Teton Peak.
A place where Mom's ashes lie.

Copyright © 2023 by Maikel L. Wise

Made in the USA
Monee, IL
14 April 2024

56596102R00229